The Church of
Evangelical Council

Studies on the Bible and same-sex relationships since 2003

Martin Davie

GILEAD
B O O K S
PUBLISHING

Gilead Books Publishing

Corner Farm

West Knapton

Malton

North Yorkshire

YO17 8JB UK

www.GileadBooksPublishing.com

First published in Great Britain, March 2015

2 4 6 8 10 9 7 5 3 1

Copyright ©CEEC 2015

British Library Cataloguing-in-Publication Data:

A catalogue record for this book is available from the British Library.

Full Report: **ISBN: 978-0-9926713-8-9**

Summary: **ISBN: 978-0-9926713-9-6**

All rights reserved.

No part of this publication may be reproduced, stored in a retrieval system or transmitted in any form or by any means, electronic, mechanical, photocopying, recording or otherwise, without the prior permission of the publisher.

Unless otherwise stated scripture quotations are from the Revised Standard Version, copyright © 1946, 1952, and 1971 National Council of the Churches of Christ in the United States of America. Used by permission. All rights reserved.

Scripture quotations marked (NIV) are from The Holy Bible, New International Version®, NIV® Copyright ©1973, 1978, 1984, 2011 Biblica, Inc.® Used by permission. All rights reserved worldwide.

Scripture quotations marked (NRSV) are from the New Revised Standard Version Bible, copyright ©1989 the Division of Christian Education of the National Council of the Churches of Christ in the United States of America. Used by permission. All rights reserved.

Scripture quotations marked (ESV) are from the ESV® Bible (The Holy Bible, English Standard Version®), copyright © 2001 by Crossway, a publishing ministry of Good News Publishers. Used by permission. All rights reserved.

The publisher makes every effort to ensure that the papers used in our books are made from trees that have been legally sourced from well-managed and credibly certified forests by using a printer awarded FSC & PEFC chain of custody certification.

Cover design: Nathan Ward

Contents

Preface

I am grateful to the Church of England Evangelical Council for their invitation to write this report.

I am also grateful to Andrew Goddard for working with me on the report, for Evelyn Cornell for helping me to obtain books through Oak Hill Library, to Roland Chia, Sean Doherty, Beulah Herbert, Amos Oei, John Nolland and David Wenham for their helpful comments on the draft text and to Chris Hayes for all his work in publishing the report.

All remaining errors in the text are the author's responsibility.

This report is dedicated to the memory of Michael Scott-Joynt (1943-2014), bishop and theologian, who worked tirelessly to ensure that the Church of England remained faithful to the teaching of Scripture on the issue of human sexuality.

Martin Davie

Chapter 1

Introduction

The current debate about same-sex relationships in the Church of England and the wider Christian Church is a debate about a number of different issues:

- There is a debate about what Christian discipleship means for those who experience same-sex attraction or who are in a same-sex relationship;
- There is a debate about how the Church and individual Christians should minister to those in that situation;
- There is a debate about who it is right for Church to marry or ordain.
- There is a debate about whether, and if so how, the Church can live with differences over these issues;

Underlying all these issues, however, there is a debate about the teaching of Scripture and is this last debate which is the subject of this report.

In 2003 *Some Issues in Human Sexuality* stated in paragraph 4.4.34-35:

> The various suggestions for revising the traditional view of the biblical material have not succeeded in changing the consensus of scholarly opinion about the meaning of the key passages in Leviticus and the New Testament. At the moment, the traditional understanding of these passages remains the most convincing one in the minds of most biblical scholars.
>
> Unless this situation changes, it is difficult to see that an appeal to a revisionist interpretation of the passages in question provides an adequate basis for a Church that takes the scholarly reading of Scripture seriously to alter either its traditional teaching about homosexuality or its traditional practice,

however much it might seem desirable to do so on the basis of the pastoral considerations noted earlier.[1]

By contrast, in 2013 paragraph 312 of the *Report of the House of Bishops Working Group on Human Sexuality* (the Pilling Report) declared: 'In the face of conflicting scholarship, as well as conflicting beliefs, we believe that the Church should be cautious about attempting to pronounce definitively on the implications of Scripture for homosexual people.'[2]

The question which is explored in this report produced on behalf of the Church of England Evangelical Council is whether a survey of studies of the biblical material relating to same-sex sexual activity produced since 2003 justifies the shift from the confidence in the biblical basis of the Church's traditional teaching shown in the first quotation to the caution expressed in the second.

No one can deny the existence of conflicting scholarship or conflicting beliefs about how to understand and apply the Bible in relation to the issue of homosexuality. It is a simple matter of fact that scholars hold different views and people hold different beliefs about this matter. However, the mere fact of the existence of conflicting scholarship and conflicting beliefs would not in itself justify the Church being cautious about declaring the implications of the teaching of Scripture for homosexual people and their behaviour. This is because there are three possible scenarios:

- It could be the case that the existence of conflict shows that the teaching of Scripture on this matter is inherently unclear and that therefore caution is required.
- It could be that case that the scholarly debate about the teaching of Scripture on this matter is currently inconclusive and that for this reason caution would be sensible.

---

[1] *Some Issues in Human Sexuality*, London: CHP, 2003, pp.157-158.
[2] *Report of the House of Bishops Working Group on Sexuality*, London: CHP, 2013, p.91.

- It could be the case that the teaching of Scripture is clear and that the conflict is due to the fact that the people on one side of the conflict have simply failed to interpret Scripture properly. In this last case caution would not be justified. The Church should declare the clear teaching of Scripture.

The issue that needs to be addressed, therefore, is which of these three possible scenarios is correct. Is Scripture itself unclear? Is the current scholarly debate about the teaching of Scripture inconclusive? Is the teaching of Scripture clear and the conflict due to faulty interpretation by one side in the conflict?

In order to answer this question, this report looks at material from both sides of the current debate in the Church about same-sex relationships produced since 2003 with the aim of seeing (a) whether a survey of this material still allows us to say that Scripture gives us clear teaching about homosexuality and (b) what this teaching is. The report also looks at the prior question of the nature of the Bible and its proper use in the debate about sexuality, again looking at material from both sides of the debate.

For the sake of convenience, it refers to those writings and texts which challenge the Church's traditional teaching in this area, either in whole or in part, as 'revisionist' and those which support it as 'traditionalist.' What is meant by the Church's traditional teaching is the belief that Scripture regards the existence of same-sex sexual attraction as a result of humanity's alienation from God and that it explicitly and implicitly prohibits both gay and lesbian same-sex sexual relationships.

The use of these terms, which have been employed by those on both sides of the debate about sexuality[3], is intended to be purely descriptive rather than to imply any judgement about the value of the material. There is currently no agreement about the best terminology to use when describing the two sides in the sexuality debate. Terms that have

---

[3] See, for example, James Brownson, *Bible, Gender, Sexuality*, Grand Rapids/Cambridge: Eerdmans 2013 and Ian Paul, *Same Sex Unions – The Key Biblical Texts*, Cambridge: 2014.

been suggested include 'change affirmers' for those this reports calls revisionists, 'revisers' and 'conservers', 'liberals' and 'conservatives,' or simply 'Side A' and 'Side B.' Nothing in this report hangs on the use of the specific terms 'revisionist' and 'traditionalist' and readers should feel free to substitute any alternative term should they wish to do so.

The distinguished Australian New Testament scholar Professor William Loader, who has written extensively on the biblical material relating of sexuality, takes a revisionist approach, arguing that the Church should accept same-sex relationships. However, his writings on the biblical text often come down in favour of the traditional interpretation of the text, which is why some of his work is included under the heading of 'traditionalist approaches.'

The selection of writers and texts surveyed in this report has been intended to be as comprehensive as possible within the limitations of the report's size. The criteria for selection has been that the choice of writers and texts should enable the reader to get an accurate sense of the discussion about the interpretation of Scripture in relation to same-sex relationships that has taken place in this country and elsewhere since 2003.

Some of the writings surveyed are academic while others are more popular and no attempt has been made to distinguish between the two. Some of the most influential writing about the Bible and same-sex relationships at the moment is in non-academic publications and what matters for the purpose of this report is not the academic status of a piece of work, but whether it says things about the Bible that illuminate what the current debate is about.

Some of the writings surveyed were written to contribute directly to the discussion. Others, however, are commentaries on, or academic studies of, the key biblical texts, which were not written to contribute to the discussion, but nevertheless form part of it because of what they have to say about these texts.

There are a number of writings which have contributed to the current debate about sexuality in the Church which have not been included in this survey. Examples include Professor Richard Burridge's book on New Testament ethics, *Imitating Jesus*,[4] Professor Sarah Coakley's essay *God, Sexuality and the Self* [5] or Wesley Hill's autobiographical 'reflections on Christian faithfulness and homosexuality,' *Washed and Waiting*.[6] The reason they have not been included is not because they are not important pieces of work, but because they do not address, or do not address in any detail, the specific questions of how we should handle the Bible in relation to the debate about sexuality or how we should interpret the biblical texts that relate to the issue of same-sex relationships.

The structure of the report is to set out the revisionist approach in Part 1 then to look at the traditionalist response in Part 2 and finally to evaluate the two in Part 3.

Parts 1 and 2 mirror each other, with each part looking first at the issue of the nature of the Bible and its use in the debate about human sexuality, then going on to look at the key biblical texts (Genesis 1-3, Genesis 19 and Judges 19, Leviticus 18:22 and 20:13, Deuteronomy 23:17-18, Romans 1:26-27, 1 Corinthians 6:9-11 and 1 Timothy 1:10 and Jude 7), then looking at the teaching and practice of Jesus, and finally considering whether there are any examples of gay and lesbian relationships that are viewed positively in Scripture. The reason why the revisionist material is considered first is that a lot of the time traditionalist writers are responding to revisionist proposals and so it makes the discussion easier to understand if we begin by looking at these proposals.

The report contains a very large amount of direct quotation from the writers surveyed. The reason for this is to enable these writers to speak for themselves as far as possible and to separate exposition from

---

[4] Richard A Burridge, *Imitating Jesus*, Grand Rapids: Eerdmans, 2007.
[5] Sarah Coakley, *God, Sexuality and the Self*, Cambridge: CUP, 2013.
[6] Wesley Hill, *Washed and Waiting*, Grand Rapids, Zondervan, 2010.

evaluation. It is hoped that those on both sides of the discussion will feel that their views have been accurately represented whatever they think of the final evaluation in Part 3. The extensive quotations also mean that those readers who do not have access to libraries can be confident that they are getting the discussion as far as possible at first hand.

Part 1
Revisionist Approaches

Chapter 2

The nature of the Bible and its use in the debate about human sexuality (I)

Since 2003 revisionist scholars have taken a variety of different approaches to the question of the nature and interpretation of the Bible and how the Bible should be used in the debate about human sexuality. Some have taken a quite conservative approach, others have been fairly radical, and there has been a spectrum in between. The examples below have been chosen as representatives of this variety. They are listed in order of publication.

> **Dan Via (2003) - The Bible is an existential rather than an *a priori* authority.**

The American New Testament scholar Professor Dan Via prefaces his substantive discussion of the biblical material in his published debate with Robert Gagnon, *Homosexuality and the Bible – Two Views*[7], with an explanation of his view of the authority of the Bible and how we should approach its interpretation.

On the authority of the Bible he declares:

> I take the Bible to be the highest authority for Christians in theological and ethical matters, although I recognize also the legitimacy of tradition, reason, and experience. Authority does not mean perfection or inerrancy or complete consistency. The authoritative norm is the one you finally listen to in a situation of competing norms. (p.2)

He then goes on to contrast two views of the nature of biblical authority, the *a priori* and the experiential or existential, of which he favours the latter:

---

[7] Dan O Via and Robert Gagnon, *Homosexuality and the Bible – Two Views*, Minneapolis: Fortress Press, 2003.

There are two basic views of biblical authority. (1) The *a priori* view says that the Bible is authoritative in all of its parts and is so *prior to* interpretation. Since this affirmation of total authority is made before one interprets the Bible – it is assumed before one interprets particular texts – the person who makes such an avowal must do so on the basis of someone else's opinion – a parent, pastor or teacher's. The affirmation is not made on the ground of one's own experience. (2) The experiential or existential view says that the Bible is authoritative only in those parts that are existentially engaging and compelling – that give grounding and meaning to existence. This avowal can be made only after and in the light of one's own interpretation. At the same time it should be recognized that the Christian tradition and community are a part of the individual's location... I take the latter view. (p.2)

On the interpretation of the Bible, Via notes that the interpretation of a text 'is always governed by its context' and that this context is two-fold, consisting of 'the literary and historical/cultural context' of the text itself and 'the religious, intellectual and cultural context' of the interpreter. (p.2) As a result, he says, there is no 'completely objective interpretation.' We always approach the Bible from 'some -limited- point of view.' (pp.2-3)

As he sees it, the Church's recognition of the existence of an authoritative biblical canon provides:

> ...a rich and diverse – sometimes contradictory – context in which to try to understand individual texts. Since texts mean different things in different contexts, texts do not necessarily *mean* what they *say*. Context may positively extend the meaning of a text and provide a multiplicity of applications. (p.3)

In addition 'some larger aspect of the canonical context may simply disagree with a particular text.' This raises the question:

Does the content of a particular text agree with and do justice to the larger context of the biblical book in which it is found or the context of Scripture as a whole? Pursuing this question may lead to the conclusion that some texts are simply disqualified by the whole meaning of the gospel. (p.3)

Finally, Via argues that we also have to take into account our own cultural context and this means asking 'how does the unambiguous condemnation of homosexual acts in certain biblical texts accord with what social science has taught us and with the contemporary experience of gay and lesbian Christians?' (p.3)

> **Christopher Rowland (2005) – The Bible should not be read as a law code**

Professor Christopher Rowland contends in his 2005 essay 'The letter killeth, but the Spirit giveth life'[8] that the examples of St Paul shows us that Christianity has never been a 'religion of the book':

However comforting appeal to precedent or a written text might be, there is in Christianity's own foundation texts the story of a movement which, when it came to the crunch, was prepared to sit loose to ancestral custom and to prefer patterns of life which seemed to be in conformity with something fundamental to the Christ they experienced. Thanks to Paul, Christianity has never been a religion that used the Bible as if it were a law code. In his second letter to the Corinthians, Paul writes: 'the letter kills, the Spirit gives life.' By this he means that engaging with Scripture is to try to get at what the Bible might point to about conformity to Christ rather than be preoccupied with what its literal demands are. Paul pioneered an approach to the Bible of his own day (what Christians would now call the Old Testament), therefore, which should also apply

[8] Christopher Rowland, 'The letter killeth, but the Spirit giveth life,' in Nicholas Coulton (ed), *The Bible, the Church and Homosexuality*, London: DLT, 2005, p.29

to those of us who now look back on his words preserved in the Scripture which we now call the New Testament. We should not be concentrating on the letter of Paul's words, but trying to get at the underlying point of his words, to discern how they might help us, at a different time and place, to be imitators of Christ. That is what Paul's words suggest: not to be slavish followers of his words. (p.29)

The application of this for the debate about human sexuality is that:

> Basing one's attitude towards gay and lesbian people merely on two verses from Romans and 1 Corinthians runs the risk of ending up treating the Bible as a law code. Instead we need to be aware that Christ, who is alive and active in the world, may be calling men and women to new adventures in the life of faith. This will depend not on the letter of the text, but on using the Bible as part of the complex way of discerning what the divine Spirit is now saying to the churches. The appeal to 'what the Bible says' is what Paul so emphatically opposes, for he would point us to what a loving God is doing in transforming and enabling lives in the present through the Spirit. (pp.29-30)

As Rowland sees it, the era of Paul and the early Church 'was a time of experiment as to what it meant to be God's people.' This means its example may be 'particularly apposite' for us today:

> Like Paul and his communities, the simple appeal to Scripture and tradition may have to be questioned as we seek to discern the call of the divine Word, who bids us recognise that the gifts of God are at work in gay and lesbian Christians, and in their loving, committed relationships, as in heterosexual relationships. Furthermore, the God who called Paul to explore new patterns of relationship is at work in committed same-sex relationships, and this tells us something of the love of the divine Spirit who seeks to guide us into all truth, which is the goal we seek. Meanwhile, we see in a glass darkly (1 Corinthians

15

13:12) and in conformity with Christ practise love one towards another, as together, we seek to follow Jesus Christ who is the truth and who will reveal that truth when we stand before him on the Last Day. (p.34)

> **Ronald Long (2006) – There needs to be a critical reassessment of what the Bible says about same-sex relationships.**

In his introduction to the *Queer Bible Commentary*, [9] first published in 2006, Professor Ronald Long writes that it might come as a surprise that the Church as the repository of 'the faith once delivered to the saints' might change its mind on moral matters 'it has done so throughout history' as is demonstrated by the issues of usury, once forbidden but now accepted, and slavery, once accepted, but now 'universally recognized as both unscriptural and immoral.' (p.1)

He then notes that such changes of mind have required a re-assessment of the biblical material:

> ....to the extent Christian bodies take the bible as the 'Word of God' – although in classical Christian theology, Jesus is the Word, and the Bible the 'Word' in but a secondary and derivative sense – each time the Church has changed its mind regarding specific moral prejudices (here I am using the term literally in the sense of 'pre-judgement') has required a revision and re-evaluation of its scriptural heritage. It has had to ask, 'Does the Bible really say what we have taken it to say?' 'What are the grounds for saying what it does?' and finally 'What authority does textual accuracy or biblical moral reasoning have for the Church in the matter at hand?' (p.2)

As he sees it, a similar process of re-assessment now needs to take place over the issue of same-sex relationships:

---

[9] Deryn Guest, Robert E Goss, Mona West, Thomas Bodache (eds), *The Queer Bible Commentary*, London: SCM, 2006.

In our own day, movements for the moral equivalence of homosexual and heterosexual love – that which I take to be the issue in GLBT rights and liberation – have caused fault lines to appear not only in society at large, but among, as well as within, denominations as well. The 'traditionalist' - even those who do not really care much about what the Bible might say one way or another on other matters – protests 'The Bible says it's a sin.' Only close critical attention to the biblical witness, it grounds and authority can disabuse the traditionalist of his or her biblically based homophobic presumption. Contemporary rhetoric notwithstanding, the theme of homosexual sex is really not very prevalent. While some episodes or passages, like the story concerning the exposure of Noah's nakedness to his son Ham (Gen 9:18-29) and others, would need to be employed in framing a complete biblical view of sex, the traditionalist who would hold that homosexuality is invariably sinful normally has recourse to three passages: a twice repeated Levitical proscription (Lev 18:22; 20:13); the story of Sodom and Gomorrah (Gen 19) and the first chapter of Paul's letter to the Romans. And it is these texts which are chiefly in need of revision and evaluation in the light of the moral status of homosexual love in our day. (p.2)

> ## Dale Martin (2006) – We need to challenge a fundamentalist appeal to Scripture.

In his essay 'Arsenokoitês and Malakos – Meanings and Consequences' in his 2006 collection *Sex and the Single Savior*,[10] Professor Dale Martin questions the 'fundamentalist' appeal to 'what the Bible says' as the basis for Christian ethics. At the end of this essay he declares:

My goal is not to deny that Paul condemned homosexual acts but to highlight the ideological contexts in which such

---

[10] Dale Martin, *Sex and the Single Savior*, Louisville: Westminster John Knox Press, 2006.

discussions have taken place. My goal is to dispute appeals to 'what the Bible says' as a foundation for Christian ethical arguments. It really is time to cut the Gordian knot of fundamentalism. And do not be fooled: any arguments that tries to defend its ethical position by an appeal to 'what the Bible says' without explicitly acknowledging the agency and contingency of the interpreter is fundamentalism, whether it comes from a right wing Southern Baptist or a moderate Presbyterian. We must simply stop giving that kind of argument any credibility. Furthermore, we will not find the answers merely be becoming better historians or exegetes. The test for whether an interpretation is Christian or not does not hang on whether it is historically accurate or exegetically nuanced. The touchstone is not the historically reconstructed meaning in the past, nor is it the fancifully imagined, modernly constructed intentions of the biblical writers. Nor can any responsible Christian – after the revolutionary changes in Christian thought in the past twenty years, much less in the past three hundred – maintain that Christian interpretations are those conforming to Christian tradition. The traditions, all of them, have changed too much and are far too open to cynical manipulation to be taken as foundations for gauging the ethical value of a reading of Scripture. (p.49)

Martin holds that we need to learn to embrace our contingency and work within the context set for us by our participation in Christian discourse:

The only recourse in our radical contingency is to accept our contingency and look for guidance within the discourse that we occupy and that forms our very selves. The best place to find criteria for talking about ethics and interpretation will be in Christian discourse itself which includes Scripture and tradition but not in a 'foundational' sense. Nor do I mean that Christian discourse can itself furnish a stable base on which to secure

18

ethical positions; it is merely the context in which these traditions are formed and discussed. Conscious of this precarious contingency, and looking for guiding lights within the discourse, I take my stand with a quotation from an impeccably traditional witness, Augustine, who wrote, 'Whoever, therefore, thinks that he understands the divine Scriptures or any part of them so that it does not build the double love of God and of our neighbor does not understand it at all' (Christian Doctrine 1.35.40).

By this light, any interpretation of Scripture that hurts people, oppresses people, or destroys people cannot be the right interpretation, no matter how traditional, historical or exegetically respectable. There can be no debate about the fact that the church's stand on homosexuality has caused oppression, loneliness, self-hatred, violence, sickness and suicide for millions of people. If the church wishes to continue with its traditional interpretation it must demonstrate, not just claim that it is more loving to condemn homosexuality than to affirm homosexuals. (pp. 49-50)

Maggi Dawn (2007) – We need to learn to live with uncertainty over the interpretation of Scripture.

Dr Maggi Dawn states in her 2007 essay 'Whose text is it anyway?' [11] that the Bible is:

> ...a collection of books, written, edited, copied and translated by human beings to record the history of salvation and to bear witness to Christ. It is also a book that, by virtue of its witness, becomes a text through which the living God continues to speak to us. And that speaking also takes account of the reader of the text – the reader's historical and cultural context; the scientific

[11] Maggi Dawn, 'Whose text is it anyway?' in Duncan Dormor and Jeremy Morris (eds), *An acceptable sacrifice? Homosexuality and the Church*, London: SPCK, 2007.

world-view of the time. What we are able to perceive of God through our reading is made possible through the inspiration of God both through writing and reading; it is also constrained by the limits of human knowledge and imagination. (p.19)

She then goes on to argue that in the case of the current conflict in the Church over homosexuality 'the art of biblical interpretation offers us nothing if we employ it as trickery with words to reinforce one point of view over another.' (p.19) However it does offer us a way forward:

> .... if we accept that the Bible may not answer the specific question we are asking, or it may not give us only one answer, or it may give us only a provisional and partial answer. Living with uncertainty and unclosed arguments is one of the hardest calls within Christianity. So often we want to close the deal, and settle the issue, and make things safe and certain. But that is not the way of the Spirit. (p. 19)

As she sees it, we need to accept that there is 'no interpretative method, nor combination of methods, that will unerringly elicit 'right answers' from the scriptures.' This is not because there is no truth:

> ...but because Christianity itself is not a matter of ascertaining a pure and certain set of beliefs, but of engaging with a living God. What I have proposed here is not a slippery slope theory that allows scripture to mean two opposing things at the same time. Rather, it is a call for enough humility to defend the interpretation you believe to be right, while still acknowledging that it may yet prove to be wrong. In so doing, it is possible to remain confident that whatever the eventual outcome, there is sufficient time and space within God's universe to see any errors corrected; and sufficient grace in the heart of God to live with error. The question is, is there sufficient grace in the Church of God to wait for God's ways to be revealed? Will we be able to hold on to the patient counsel and wisdom of Gamaliel?

Or must we insist on a clear and pragmatic answer, no matter what the cost? (pp.20-21)

In her view, the approach to Scripture that she is proposing offers us a higher rather than a lower view of the Bible:

> Holding different interpretations in tension, living with ambiguity of meaning, and searching for the right balance between continuity and discontinuity, do not leave us with a compromised view of Scripture, but one that is, in the end, a higher view than one that insists on one, clear and unambiguous meaning. Why? Because this is a view, not of the Bible as a flat impersonal book of rules, but a collection of texts that connect us to a living God. With all its frustrations and difficulties, this is a view of scripture – and a walk of faith – that is a much higher calling than mere obedience to the letter. (p.21)

Adrian Thatcher (2008) – Seven principles for peaceful and faithful Bible reading.

As its subtitle explains, Professor Adrian Thatcher's 2008 book *The Savage Text* [12] is concerned with 'the use and abuse of the Bible'. In this book Thatcher is critical of the way in which the 2003 House of Bishops report *Some Issues in Human Sexuality* holds that the Bible is both 'a witness to the grace of God' and 'a guide to Christian discipleship.' As he sees it, *Some Issues* is:

> ... right to emphasize the status of the Bible as a witness to Christ. But the guidebook view is incompatible with it because it endorses the supposition that Christians should follow the Bible, instead of following the One to whom the Bible is a witness. If we already have a guidebook to tell us how to handle our sex lives, why do we need Jesus Christ as well? Is God in Christ our guide, or is the Bible our guide? It is a serious matter to confuse a witness to the truth with the One who is the Truth

---

[12] Adrian Thatcher, *The Savage Text*, Chichester: Wiley Blackwell, 2008.

(John 14:6). John the Baptist was mistakenly confused with the Messiah, a rival, in fact, to Jesus himself (e.g. Matthew 11:1-19). The Gospel writers all needed to put clear, deep water between Jesus and John. And the Church of the present needs to put a similar distance between the One who reveals God and the writings that witness to that unrepeatable and unsurpassable revelation. (p.27)

After criticising the way in which the Bible has, in his view, been misused in relation to a range of ethical issues (including homosexuality), Professor Thatcher ends his book by suggesting a set of seven principles 'which will help to promote peaceable and faithful Bible reading and avoid the textual savagery that has disfigured the preaching of the Gospel past and present.' (153)

The first principle is 'read the Bible to learn of God's Word.' In line with his criticism of *Some Issues* noted above, what he means by 'God's Word' is 'God's self-communication in Christ to which the Bible bears witness.' (p.153)

The second principle is 'expect moral and spiritual development in the Bible.' The point here is that the Bible 'is always surpassing itself, and this is evidence for the growing spiritual illumination of its authors, reversing and cancelling the limited wisdom of earlier generations.' Professor Thatcher follows Professor Keith Ward in calling this process of development the 'sublation' of earlier texts and quotes him with approval as saying 'The Bible is filled with sublations, which means that many biblical passages, taken in their straightforward sense, must now be accounted false.' (pp.156-7)

The third principle is 'read the Old Testament through the New Testament.' This principle avoids saying that the Old Testament in its entirety is sublated by the New but 'allows priority to be given to the New, as the fulfilment of the Old.' (p.158)

The fourth principle is 'read the Bible through the Rule.' This means that 'The Bible should be interpreted through the 'rule of faith' or through the principal creeds of the Church.' 'The Bible must be read through the Church's understanding of it and that understanding is theological and creedal.' (pp.160-61) n

The fifth principle is 'make the Love Commandments the guide to ethical practice.' According to Professor Thatcher:

> The Love Commandments of Jesus are Christian ethical teaching and practice. The outworking of these is the fulfilment of the law (Matthew 22:40) and the ethical practice of the Church needs continuous revision in the light of them. These commands are the 'guide' to the treatment of the other and to negotiating difference. (p.162)

The sixth principle 'is treat the Bible as Primary Tradition.' Rather than distinguishing absolutely between the Bible and Tradition as some Protestants have done we should think instead in terms of giving the Bible primacy within Tradition:

> All new Christians affirm their continuity with the apostles and the early Church. They acknowledge that Jesus is Lord, the Son of God. They belong to some or other branch of Christ's 'Church,' which derives its identity from him, and from its relation to other branches of the same tree. This Church, being originally Jewish, accepted the Jewish scriptures, and in order to proclaim its faith that the Messiah had come produced Gospels which, as *Dei Verbum* insists, 'among all the Scriptures…have a special pre-eminence.' The Letters of the New Testament testify to God's coming in Christ and provide much evidence also of how the early churches responded to that unique event. The history of that response did not close at the end of the first century, and remains open today. It is not necessary to draw a firm line between the Bible and tradition. That is why it may be appropriate to think of the Bible, and especially the New Testament, as Primary Tradition and the extra-canonical and post-canonical sources as Secondary Tradition. (pp. 164-165)

The seventh principle is 'let the Spirit show us Jesus.' As Professor Thatcher sees it:

> Since the Spirit in Christian faith is a Person of God, Christians are licensed to say that the Spirit 'speaks' to them, and 'speaks' in a way that the Bible, which is not a person, does not and cannot. (p.166)

However, the fact that the Spirit has freedom 'to show us Christ through the Bible (as well as in many other ways' means that we do not need:

> ...a complex bibliology, an elevation of the Word to a divine or quasi-divine status, in order to hear what the Spirit is saying. Indeed, as soon as the Bible begins to 'speak' by and for itself, the voice of the Spirit falls silent. (p.166)

Jack Rogers (2009) – Seven more guidelines for biblical interpretation.

The American Presbyterian theologian Professor Jack Rogers also offers seven 'guidelines for biblical interpretation' in his 2009 study *Jesus, the Bible and Homosexuality* [13] which he thinks should be applied to the debate about same-sex relationships. These guidelines, based on the confessional statements of the Reformed tradition such as the *Westminster Confession* and the *Second Helvetic Confession,* are:

1. Recognize that Jesus Christ, the Redeemer, is the center of Scripture. The redemptive activity of God is central to the entire Scripture. The Old Testament themes of the covenant and the messiah testify to this activity. In the center of the New Testament is Jesus Christ: the Word made flesh, the fulfilment of Israel's messianic hope, and the promise of the kingdom. It is to Christ that the church witnesses. When interpreting Scripture, keeping Christ in the center aids in

---

[13] Jack Rogers, *Jesus, the Bible and Homosexuality*, 2ed, Louisville: Westminster John Knox Press, 2009.

evaluating the significance of the problems and controversies that always persist in the vigorous, historical life of the church.

2. Let the focus be on the plain text of Scripture, to the grammatical and historical context, rather than to allegory or subjective fantasy.

3. Depend on the guidance of the Holy Spirit in interpreting and applying God's message.

4. Be guided by the doctrinal consensus of the church, which is the rule of faith.

5. Let all interpretations be in accord with the rule of love, the twofold command to love God and love our neighbor.

6. Remember that interpretation of the Bible requires earnest study in order to establish the best text and to interpret the influence of the historical and cultural context in which the divine message has come.

7. Seek to interpret a particular passage of the Bible in light of all the Bible. (p.65)

Rogers also argues that the application of these guidelines supports the acceptance of same-sex relationships by the Church. Three examples will illustrate this.

On guideline 2 he comments that reading the Bible according to its 'plain text' leads us to ask:

...whether biblical statements that condemn idolatrous and immoral sexual activity can appropriately be applied to the sexual relationships of contemporary Christian gay and lesbian people who are neither idolatrous nor immoral. Is it right to take verses that condemn the worship of other gods and use them against Christian people who are worshipping the one true God who Jesus called us to worship? (p.57)

On guideline 3 he writes that, as in the historical examples of changes in Christian attitudes to Gentiles, obedience to kings, slavery and the subordination of women:

> It seems that the Holy Spirit is once again working to change our church – making us restless, challenging us to give up our culturally conditioned prejudices against people of homosexual orientation. As we come to know faithful, obedient Christian disciples whose sexual orientation is different from that of the heterosexual majority, we discover that they have been blessed by the Holy Spirit even as heterosexual people have been. Under the guidance of the Holy Spirit, a change in our attitudes and actions can be a faithful response to God's leading. (pp.58-59)

On guideline 7 he suggests that setting the controversy about homosexuality in the context of the whole teaching of Scripture will ease divisions on the subject.

> When we recognize that all of us, of whatever sexual orientation, are created by God, that we are all fallen sinners, and that we can all be redeemed by the life, death and resurrection of Jesus Christ, homosexuality will no longer be a divisive issue. Peace and progress will again characterize the church when we stop making exceptions to our fundamental principles and we restore the full rights of membership to all our members. (p.64)

The last sentence refers to a decision by the Presbyterian Church USA that those in same-sex partnerships should not be eligible for appointment as ministers in the same way as other members of the church.

Tobias Haller (2009) – We need to sift the Bible in the light of our experience.

Tobias Haller declares in his 2009 study *Reasonable and Holy – Engaging Same-Sexuality* [14] that the revelation given to the Church in Scripture consists of a 'rich collection of various documents composed at different times, to different ends and for different hearers.' (p.82) This being the case, the faithful in each generation have to find ways of using 'the tools at our disposal to find our way to discern the applicability of the many, and sometimes difficult to reconcile, commandments with which Scripture presents us.' (p.84) As a result there is necessarily a 'sifting process' by which 'any given culture or society or church, even while embracing the Bible as a whole, also separates out portions of it based on various modes of division or distinction. This process can be conscious and reasonable, but it can also happen under the influence of culture and external events.'(p.84)

According to Haller we have to engage in this sifting process in regard to what the Bible has to say about sexuality, separating out those parts which are applicable to our situation and those which are not. As he sees it, a key part of this process is making use of experience which has 'a limiting function even over the fundamental authority of Scripture.' When we learn some new reality, he says, such as the revolution of the earth round the sun:

> ...we can choose to ignore that experience and the new knowledge that it brings us, and turn back to Scripture and say. 'No, the sun goes round the earth, as it says in the Psalms' (19:5-6). Or we can accept that the Scripture is limited in its description of the real world – in part because the Scripture itself is limited by the experience of those who recorded it – and from time to time we have to readjust our appreciation of Scripture and realize its limitations when describing the natural world. This is true even in some areas of morality.

---

[14] Tobias Haller, *Reasonable and Holy*, New York: Seabury Books, 2009.

Our experience leads us to see that some things Scripture approved in the cultures and worlds of its composition can be found to be morally wrong at a later time and in a different world – like slavery or polygamy. We can also find that things condemned in Scripture might come to be accepted as morally neutral or even as good – like lending money at interest, which Ezekiel (18:13) said was an abomination, but which Adam Smith said was essential to the wealth of nations.(p.52)

> **Deidre J Good, Willis J Jenkins, Cynthia B Kitteridge and Eugene F Rogers (2011) – We learn to read the Bible rightly through our engagement in mission.**

In a 'theological colloquy' on 'same-sex relationships and the nature of marriage' published in the winter 2011 edition of the *Anglican Theological Review* those presenting 'A Theology of Marriage including Same-Sex Couples: A view from the Liberals'[15] (Professor Deidre J Good, Professor Willis J Jenkins, Professor Cynthia B Kitteridge and Professor Eugene F Rogers) write that the Church learns to read Scripture rightly as it engages in mission:

The church learns to interpret Scripture by being the body of Christ. It learns the truth of Scripture by living from marriage to its Bridegroom, therefore not from self-sufficiency but from self-donation to another. That means that the church reads Scripture not in purity but from mission, a mission that must leave the church changed. The church takes part in the mission of the Trinity when she goes out from the Father in the person of the Son and in the community of the Spirit. She evangelizes others and herself by going out of herself and receiving into herself those who are different, as the Son and the Spirit do in their missions. (p.59)

---

[15] 'A Theology of Marriage including Same-Sex Couples: A view from the Liberals,' *Anglican Theological Review*, Vol 93, No 1, Winter 2011, p59.

As the Church engages in mission in this way, they argue, the Spirit may change the way that the Church interprets Scripture by producing both learning and repentance:

> Reading with the Spirit may change Scripture's interpretation. If it does it can only be because the Spirit changes the interpreter. The Spirit must change the interpreter, if it is to lead us into 'all the truth' (John 16:13). The Spirit must change the interpreter because we learn over time. After the fall, the Spirit must also change the interpreter because we are sinners. Without growth in wisdom that the Spirit directs, immature readers will inevitably read Scripture in ignorance. Without repentance, Christians will inevitably read Scripture 'in ways that support their own sinful beliefs and practices.' Both learning and repentance are therefore necessary but neither is sufficient. Repentance without hope would be despair, and learning without love is sterile. Rather, 'recognition of sinfulness must lead into the practices of forgiveness, repentance and reconciliation.' These are the practices that take us out of our fascination with ourselves, our sin, and into community with one another. The Spirit of love must issue in love.' (pp.59-60)

They also argue in response to the arguments about Scripture put forward by those on the 'traditionalist' side, that liberals read Scripture in ways that can challenge the perspectives of the biblical authors because they read it as part of an expanded group of readers:

> We also read with an expanded community of readers, including many whom the church has not previously recognized and some whom the biblical texts do not address as subjects. In the authorial perspective of some biblical texts, women, slaves, Gentiles, and sexual minorities are subordinated as persons and silenced as mutual interpreters of God's revelation. The expanded readership of the Christian church now questions these attitudes and the social presuppositions on which they were based. We read scriptural texts about marriage in a

culture and a world of ideas where the model of the authority of husband over wife, master over slave, and parent over child has been substantially revised in the direction of egalitarianism, mutuality and democracy. We welcome this development as positive and related to Christian social witness. (p. 104)

> # K Renato Lings (2013) – We need a proper linguistic analysis of the biblical texts in order to correct a misleading tradition of interpretation shaped by post-biblical asceticism and misogyny.

In his 2013 study on homosexuality and the Bible, *Love lost in translation*, [16] the Danish Quaker biblical scholar Dr K Renato Lings argues that the presence of a 'long church tradition' has distorted the way in which we approach what the Bible has to say about sexuality:

> Two thousand years of theological reflection have created a pre-established bias, which affects modern readers of biblical passages dealing with sexual issues. Many church fathers took inspiration from certain dualist aspects of Greek philosophy, particularly Neo-Platonism with its emphasis on concepts such as intellect, soul, nature and salvation... A very large part of what today's Roman Catholic and Protestant theologians have to say on eroticism derives from theological treatises written by sexually chaste and/or celibate male clergy, often middle aged or elderly and given to misogyny... the magnitude of this historical legacy is such that no Christians today can declare themselves free from prejudice when it comes to interpreting biblical reflections of human sexuality. (pp.XXX-XXXI)

According to Lings, the result of this historical legacy is that scholars on the opposing sides of the debate about human sexuality generally agree about how the biblical texts relating to homosexuality should be

---

[16] K Renato Lings, *Love Lost in Translation*, Trafford Publishing, 2013.

interpreted. Where they differ are in the conclusions they derive from them:

> When dealing with the fierce controversy over the Bible and homosexuality, which has rocked the entire Christian world for several decades, it is intriguing to note that no great differences are found in terms of exegesis. Leviticus 18:22 is an example of a text to which most debaters seem to apply the same analytical methodology... Discrepancies among scholars arise in the hermeneutical conclusions they derive from these texts. Without excessively simplifying the panorama, two opposed theological schools may be said to exist. One school argues that the Bible condemns unequivocally any expression of a homoerotic nature. For this reason, it is deemed crucial that believers should reject this phenomenon in all its manifestations including recent lesbian and gay civil rights movements...At the other extreme of the spectrum, one finds debaters who suggest that scriptural statements on this issue echo specific social and cultural contexts of the ancient world, which do not apply to people today. According to the latter approach, it is legitimate to disregard the biblical prohibitions and emphasize the inclusive message proclaimed by the Christian gospel.(p. XXXI)

As Lings sees it, 'something essential' is missing on both sides of the debate that explains why the debate has got nowhere. The missing element is proper linguistic analysis of the texts that are being debated:

> ...few detailed academic analyses have been carried out of the literary and semantic aspects of the most controversial texts. This raises questions about the credibility of traditional exegesis. In order to find a way out of the current theological deadlock, I propose to introduce a different methodology, bypassing medieval tradition. Specifically the pronounced ascetic and misogynistic preoccupations of the post-biblical era should be sidelined. There is an urgent need to take a fresh look

31

at the texts based on their literary contexts and original languages in order to appreciate their literary, cultural and theological richness. (p.XXXII)

> **David P Gushee (2014) – We need to avoid assuming that our reading of the Bible is identical with 'God's own truth.'**

In his 2014 work *Changing our Mind*[17] Professor David Gushee notes that Christians have come to 'fundamentally different conclusions' about what the Bible has to say about a myriad of theological and moral issues.

He further notes that 'with each one of these issues, it is easy to find relevant contemporaneous literature labelling the various sides as 'the biblical position' and the opposing side as unbiblical. However, he then goes on to say that the most interesting interpreters of the Bible are those that resist the temptation to do this:

> The most interesting interlocutors in any contemporary Christian moral or theological debate are those aware that these oft-bloody historic interpretive backgrounds fill the Christian landscape. These wise souls are therefore aware *that the texts of Scripture on the one hand, and the interpretive process, on the other, are not the same thing.* They recognize that Christians fiercely committed to Christ, Scripture and truth, frequently do differ. They acknowledge that anyone's interpretation of a text or an issue at any given moment may turn out to be quite wrong. They understand that humility and charity are called for when engaging in theological and moral argument. The least interesting debaters are those who seem to have learned nothing from our own conflicted history, and who therefore repeat that history over and over again in their certainty *that*

---

[17] David P Gushee, *Changing Our Mind*, Canton: Read the Spirit Books, 2014.

their reading of a text is 'God's own truth.' (pp. 51-52 italics in the original)

He also declares that 'while theological and moral inquiry rely on excellent biblical exegesis and interpretation, *broader processes of analysis and discernment, in loving Christian community, integrating heart and head, are required to understand not just what a text once meant, but what it means for the believing Church today.'* (p.53 italics in the original)

Chapter 3

The interpretation of the key biblical passages (I)

Genesis 1-3

Revisionist writers have reinterpreted the first three chapters of Genesis in a number of different ways. However, there are four themes that emerge from their writings:

- The belief held by some revisionists that Genesis teaches that humanity was originally andgroynous and that this has consequences for our thinking about sexuality;
- A challenge to the belief that the Genesis teaches complementarity between men and women;
- A challenge to the belief that Genesis only supports traditional views of marriage and family life;
- The belief that Genesis 3 calls into question traditional views of sexuality.

Genesis teaches that humanity was originally androgynous

> **Michael Carden – the idea that the first human being was androgynous answers the questions raised by Genesis 1:26-27.**

In *The Queer Bible Commentary* Dr Michael Carden argues that the account of the creation of humanity in God's image and likeness in Genesis 1:26-27 raises a number of questions:

> Does God have a body and, if so, is it male or female or both? Given that human beings are commanded to be fruitful and multiply, 'Does God have genitals and, if so, of what sex?'...Other questions arise. Does Genesis mandate a two-gender only system? What of people who are neither male nor female?

Finally, is reproductive sexuality the only mandated sexuality in Genesis? (p.26)

As he sees it, an answer to these questions is provided by the idea that the first human being was androgynous:

An answer given in Jewish tradition and found also in some Christian accounts (including Origen) is that the first human was an androgynous being that would subsequently be separated by the deity. Jewish Kabbalah understands that Genesis 1 is a textual representation of the Kabbalistic Tree of Life, the map of the ten emanations/Sefiroth of the divine that give rise to creation. The seven days of creation are understood as representing the seven lower Sefiroth of the Tree. The Tree is equally a map of the divine, a map of creation and a representation of the Primal Human. The Tree consists of a male, female and intermediate column. While each Sefirah will present as female or male, it contains both aspects, the one overshadowed by the other. While being androgynous, the Tree of Life also embraces sexuality. Sexuality is not only part of the creative process of the Tree but also the way of restoring the primal union lost in the process of differentiation that is creation. The androgynous ambiguity of the Tree combined with the idealized erotic quest for union that underpins the understanding of the relationships of the Sefiroth means that, while ostensibly 'heterosexual,' the divine sexuality does not match the hierarchical subordinating sexuality of ancient (and modern) patriarchies. Consequently, I would argue that the Kabbalistic accounts do not necessarily warrant compulsory heterosexuality but instead provide a space for a more polymorphous and egalitarian sexuality. The Kabbalistic Tree suggests that the androgyne is the model for each and every human, that male and female represent a fluid continuum in each individual that must be brought into harmony. (pp. 26-27)

35

Carden further argues that the second creation account in Genesis 2 also points to the idea of a primal androgyny. He suggests that the story of the creation of the first woman in Genesis 2:23-24 echoes:

> Aristophanes' tale in Plato's *Symposium* according to which humans were originally dyads of three sexes – male, female and hermaphrodite. Because they were becoming too threatening, the gods took action and bisected them. From that point on, humans quest to find their other half, to reconstitute that lost primal unity of male, female and hermaphrodite so that each pairing can become one flesh. Similarly, in Jewish tradition, the human couple of Genesis 2 was understood to originally have been two sides or faces of the one being, which the deity finally separated to form women and men. Perhaps the author of this second account has deliberately eliminated the male and female dyads, leaving only the hermaphrodite in an attempt to eliminate the homoerotic. If so the attempt fails because the hermaphrodite inhabits the intermediate realm of the ancient gender hierarchy. To become one flesh, a husband must give up his gender privilege and with his wife descend to the intermediate level, neither male nor female. (p.28)

Renato Lings – Genesis 1 and 2 describe the first human being as being originally sexually undifferentiated.

In *Lost in Translation* Lings likewise holds that the creation narratives describe an originally sexually undifferentiated human being. He writes that Genesis 1:26-27:

> ...suggests considerable ambivalence by describing the *adam* as both male *and* female. At first readers are told that God created 'him' or 'it' (singular) only to learn immediately that 'male and female he created *them*' (plural or dual number). The presence of the pronoun *them* intimates that this *adam* has a dual nature from the start. Stated differently, several factors indicate that this new individual is characterized by lack of gender

differentiation. In all probability the phenomenon might be described using terms such as bisexuality, hermaphroditism, or intersex condition. (p.25)

As he sees it, this originally undifferentiated being or 'groundling (his preferred translation for '*adam*') is divided in two in Genesis 2:21.

One side keeps the name *adam*, which gradually evolves into the proper name Adam, while the part that was removed is shaped into an independent woman. In this manner, two separate sexes emerge. Allowing each half or side of the groundling to become the other's companion, the operation resolves the problem of human loneliness stated in 2.18. (pp.35-36)

Lings' overall conclusion is that the language used in the opening chapters of Genesis:

...sheds no direct light on the subject of homoeroticism in the Bible. Indirectly, however, Genesis 2.18-20 presents the idea of freedom of choice granted by the Creator to human beings for us to seek life companions capable of bringing us joy and happiness. To a major degree, the creation story focuses on the mysteries of gender and the awakening of sexual impulses in preparation for adult life. The narrative implies the existence of bisexuality or intersex condition in *ha-adam*, the first 'groundling' created. The popular tendency to quote this part of Genesis as an argument against intimate same-sex relationships has not taken into account the literary complexity of Genesis 1.26-27 and 2.21-22. (pp. 41-42)

> **Meg Warner – Genesis 2:24 is about recapturing the unity of the original androgynous earth creature. It is also about Israelite men choosing to marry foreign wives in a way that parallels the situation of gay and lesbian people today.**

The idea that gender differentiation was a second and subsequent divine act following on from God's original creation of humanity is also found in Dr Meg Warner's essay 'Set in tradition and history: Genesis 2:24 and the marriage debate.' [18] Warner argues that what is described in Genesis 2:24 is 'a compulsion within males and females to be re-unified – to re-capture the unification known in the earth creature (*adam*) prior to God's introduction of gender through the creation of woman (*ishshah*) from the rib of man (*ish*). 'Therefore a man abandons/forsakes his father and mother and clings to his woman and they become one flesh.' (p.14)

As Warner sees it, however, the focus of Genesis 2:24 in its original historical context is not about gender, but about ethnicity. What was normal in Israelite society was for people to marry within their own ethnic group and the language of a man leaving his father and mother to cleave to his wife challenges this by describing why Israelite young men choose to marry foreign wives:

> Genesis 2:24 suggests that in marrying outside their own ethnic group, Israelite men step outside the accepted order, at least as that is understood in the eyes of their parents. The implication is that the attraction between men and women is so strong that men are compelled to flout their obligation to honour their parents for the sake of marriage to a companion of their choice. (p.14)

In Warner's view there is a parallel between Israelite men choosing to marry foreign wives and the situation of lesbian and gay people today:

---

[18] Meg Warner, 'Set in tradition and history: Genesis 2:24 and the marriage debate' in Alan H Cadwallader (ed), *Pieces of Ease and Grace*, Adelaide: ATF Theology, 2013, p. 14.

Like the Israelite men contemplated by Gen 2:24, today's lesbian and gay women and men choose partners (often) against the established preferences of parents, society and religious communities. Those established preferences are grounded (often) upon an understanding of God's will for humanity as expressed in scripture. As we have seen, the books of the Old Testament contain provisions that expressly prohibit Israelites from marrying foreigners and from lying 'with a man as with a woman' (Lev 18:22; 20:13).

Gen 2:24 doesn't say that Israelite parents are misguided in their preference for Israelite partners for their children. Certainly, the scriptural prohibitions of marriages between Israelites and foreigners are relatively unambiguous. But Gen 2:24 does say that a choice of marriage partner, even if apparently contrary to parental wishes and scriptural injunctions, may nevertheless be the natural consequence of God's actions in creation.

For lesbian and gay women and men, then, Gen 2:24 need not be feared as scripture that excludes and discriminates. It is not a definition of marriage, to the exclusion of all other definitions. On the contrary, a better understanding of Gen 2:24 is a scripture that observes a plurality of models of love and marriage and that recognises in each a genuine expression of God's creative work. (p.14)

> **James Brownson – Robert Gagnon is wrong to suggest that Genesis teaches that the original *adam* was sexually undifferentiated.**

However, not all revisionist writers accept that Genesis teaches that humanity was originally androgynous. For example, in his book *Bible, Gender, Sexuality*[19], Professor James Brownson criticises the view of the prominent traditionalist scholar Robert Gagnon that it is only a sexual

---

[19] James Brownson, *Bible, Gender, Sexuality*, Grand Rapids/Cambridge: Eerdmans 2013, pp.27-28.

relationship between a man and a woman that can achieve the wholeness of the original undivided *adam*.

Brownson notes that both the idea that the original *adam* was sexually undifferentiated and the idea that it was a binary being contradict the biblical text:

> If the original *'adam* is a single sexually undifferentiated or androgynous being, than Gagnon cannot account for the plural 'male and female he created *them*' in Genesis 1:27. But if one gives weight to Genesis 1:27 and postulates that the original *'adam' is* binary with two centers of consciousness (but not two distinct bodies), then one cannot account for the statement in 2:18, 'it is not good for the *'adam* to be alone,' since two distinct centers of consciousness can scarcely be said to be 'alone.' (pp.27-28)

Furthermore, Genesis 2:23 'she shall be called Woman, because she was taken out of Man' assumes:

> ...that the first human (*'adam*) is already male (*ish*) before the woman is taken from his side. The same perspective on this verse is also reflected in 1 Corinthians 11:8, which also speaks of woman being made 'from man' in explicitly gendered terms. (p.28)

Genesis does not teach the complementarity of men and women

> James Brownson – Genesis 1 and 2 emphasise the similarity rather than the complementarity between men and women and Genesis 2:24 is about a kinship bond rather than physical complementarity.

Brownson also argues in *Bible, Gender, Sexuality* that Gagnon is wrong to say that the creation narratives in Genesis 1 and 2 emphasise gender complementarity, the idea that men and women have innate characteristics which are different but complementary.

> The focus on Genesis 2 is not on the complementarity of male and female but on the similarity of male and female.
>
> The fact that male and female are created in the divine image (Genesis 1:27) is intended to convey the value, dominion and relationality that is *shared* by both men and women, but not the idea that the complementarity of the genders is somehow necessary to fully express or embody the divine image.
>
> The one flesh union spoken of in Genesis 2:24 connotes not physical complementarity but a kinship bond. (pp.37-38)

Because Genesis 'does not teach a normative from of gender complementarity, based on the biological differences between male and female' it follows, says Brownson, that 'this form of moral logic cannot be assumed as the basis for the negative treatment of same-sex relationships in biblical texts.' (p.38) Furthermore, while it is clear that that the Bible assumes that a 'one flesh union' only takes place between a man and a women 'there is nothing inherent in biblical usage that would necessarily exclude committed gay or lesbian unions from consideration as one flesh unions, when the essential characteristics of one-flesh unions as kinship bonds are clearly held in view.' (p.109)

> **Tobias Haller – Genesis 2 stresses the likeness of men and women rather than the difference between them and the members of same-sex couple are different from each other.**

Haller also stresses that Genesis emphasises the likeness rather than the complementarity of men and women. He writes in *Reasonable and Holy* that:

> Genesis 1 (with its emphasis on procreation) partakes of the archaic and anatomical distinction of the sexes. The words for *male* and *female* – *zakar* and *neqebah* – derive, the etymologists

41

speculate, from the concepts 'worth mentioning' or 'pointed' and 'has a hole in it.' Genesis 2 moves towards a more unified view of *man* and *woman* as taken from man (*ish* from *ishah*). Even though this represents a folk etymology (and a folk biology) the emphasis is Genesis 2 is not on the *distinction* of the sexes but on the *likeness* of the man and the woman. It is their similarity, not their difference, that is important. While Genesis 1 emphasizes the likeness of the couple *to God*, Genesis 2 highlights the likeness of the couple *to each other*. (pp.46-47)

According to Haller, in Genesis 2:

> ...the man and the woman form a *pair*, they are *mates*; and it is clear that both of these words apply to two things *like* each other as much as to two things *unlike* each other, and in Genesis 2, the emphasis is on the *likeness*. In this sense, far from being complementary, the man and the woman are like the two blades of a *pair* of scissors – which work together *only* because they are the same as each other. (p.47)

Haller's conclusion is that it seems clear:

> ...that not only is there not true complementarity between the sexes, but that the relationship of the sexes, apart from procreation, is not based solely on the differences that exist, but at least as much as the similarities. (p. 47)

In response to the argument that there is insufficient difference in the case of a same-sex couple he notes that:

> ...*all* people are different from each other. Thus two men or two women supplement each other in bringing to their relationship something that makes that relationship greater than the mere sum of parts. People will sometimes quote what they think is a smart remark in saying 'God made Adam and Eve, not Adam and Steve.' But in fact God did create Adam, Eve, and Steve too- and each James, Tom, Suzie and Jan – and *all* the men and women

who each have come to be through God's grace – each and every one of us; and it is in how we treat each other that we find ourselves realizing God's intent for each and all of us. (pp.47-48)

Matthew Vines – Genesis 2 is about the similarity rather than the difference between Adam and Eve.

Matthew Vines in his book *God and the Gay Christian*[20] also argues that Genesis 2 is concerned with the similarity rather than the difference between men and women:

> ...what's remarkable about Genesis 2 is that, despite the need for procreation, the text doesn't focus on the gender differences between Adam and Eve, Rather it focuses on their *similarity* as human beings.
>
> When God declared Adam's aloneness 'not good,' he first brought every bird and wild animal to Adam. Among them however, 'no suitable helper was found' (Genesis 2:20). Animals could offer Adam some companionship, but that wasn't enough. God was looking for someone more *similar* to Adam than the animals were, someone with whom Adam could form a 'one-flesh' bond. That had to be another human being.
>
> Adam commented only on the qualities that he and Eve shared 'Bone of my bones and flesh of my flesh,' he said, 'She shall be called 'woman' for she was taken out of men' (Genesis 2:23). Adam and Eve were right for each other, not because they were different, but because they were alike. (p.46)

---

[20] Matthew Vines, *God and the Gay Christian*, New York, Convergent Books, 2014.

> **C Norman Kraus – the image of God is to be found in the social-spiritual human community and not in the sexual pairing between a man and a woman. It is the character of sexual activity not the sexual orientation of the partners that determines whether it participates in the image of God.**

Another writer who questions gender complementarity is Professor C Norman Kraus in his book *On being human – sexual orientation and the image of God.*[21]

He contends that if Genesis 1:26-27 teaches us that the image of God is found in a sexual pairing between a man and a woman then what it is telling us is that 'heterosexually oriented individuals are in the image, and same-sex oriented are not – or at least are a marred or perverted image.' (p.54) However, this idea raises a number of questions:

> For example, do celibate males or females, whether by choice of circumstance, only partially bear that image? And where do the developmentally impaired belong in the picture? What about 'eunuchs' and others of uncertain gender identity who in the ancient world were called 'effeminate' and considered defective humans? (p.54)

In Kraus' view we can set such questions aside once we understand that 'the primary referent of the image metaphor is the social-spiritual human community, which in the New Testament is referred to as the new humanity, and not the individual mammalian creatures named Adam and Eve.'(p.54) As he sees it, those who insist that 'the literal first male-female pair present the only legitimate moral possibility for human coupling' have overlooked this crucial distinction.

In the creation stories, he says, the image of God 'includes physical sexual relationships,' but it is not 'defined by gender complementarity.' Instead, it is the image of God:

---

[21] C Norman Kraus, *On being human*, Eugene Oregon: Cascade Books, 2011.

...which conditions the moral-personal character of physical sexual relations of whatever orientation. The essential moral-personal character and significance of the erotic physical relation (sex) is conditioned by its personal spiritual character and not by its gender complementarity. This implies further that the morality of physical erotic intimacies is not properly evaluated by the orientation of the partners but by the moral quality of such physical relationships. In so far as physical sexual intimacy reflects and furthers human *shalom*, it participates in the image of God. In so far as it is abusive and destructive of human *shalom*, it is a desecration of the image of God. This is equally true of all sexual activity. (pp.54-55)

Adrian Thatcher – being in the image of God does not require being in a sexed body and having fixed desires for the opposite sex.

Thatcher is also critical of linking the image of God to male-female relationships. Criticising the claim made in *Some Issues in Human Sexuality* that Genesis teaches that 'both men and women need each other in order to find their fulfilment as human beings' he writes in *The Savage Text*:

> So now we know. Genesis 1 is about human fulfilment through compulsory heterosexuality. Despite the testimony of historical theology that the image of God is to be understood as something spiritual, the opponents of same-sex couples now discern something quite different: it is about having a sexed body with fixed opposite-sex desires. Suppose we wanted to believe this? Wouldn't we need to insert a further, missing premise into the argument, i.e., that the text offers simple universal truths that admit of no, absolutely no, exceptions? From 'male and female created he them,' and from 'Be fruitful and multiply,' it is assumed that all males will always desire only females, and conversely; that no one might desire both and they will all have children. But the procreative purpose...is not thwarted if a few,

or even some, people of either sex use sex for other reasons than procreation. Most heterosexual couples do this almost every time they have sex. The very existence of men and women who don't fit this convenient pattern should be enough to indicate that the traditional understanding of these texts requires exceptions (and celibate people are a further exception). In any case reproduction is something that species do. But for species to reproduce successfully it is not necessary for every member of the species to be at it. (pp.30-31)

Genesis cannot be seen to support only traditional views of marriage and family life.

> **Keith Sharpe – there are three reasons why the creation narratives do not support a conservative view of marriage and the family.**

In his book *The Gay Gospels*[22] Dr Keith Sharpe suggests that there are a range of reasons why the creation narratives in *Genesis* fail to support a conservative view of marriage and family life.

The first reason is the evidence of the rest of the Bible:

> The Bible stories that follow on from Genesis offer a rich tapestry of diverse family structures and relationships between and within the sexes. We read, for example, of polygamy, serial monogamy, wife-swapping, concubines, male-male relationships, female-female relationships, rape, child abuse, incest and all manner of weird and wonderful sexual conduct, most of it simply taken for granted without a hint of condemnation from God. And of course the one thing we do not read about is the domestic nuclear bliss of hubby and the missus and their adorable two children and pets. (p.30)

---

[22] Ken Sharpe, *The Gay Gospels*, Washington and Winchester, O Books, 2011.

The second reason is that that the 'one flesh' union referred to in Genesis 2:24 simply means a new kinship group rather than sexual unity between husband and wife:

> ...the concept of 'one flesh' does not necessarily mean husband and wife copulating but rather implies the creation of a new kinship group, a new unity within society. This is the meaning of it 'not being good for man to be alone.' Humans are sociable beings and need to be involved in structures of relationship in order to thrive. (p.30)

The third reason is that there are a large number of people who do not fit the conservative model. In particular he draws attention to the estimate that up to two percent of the population have an intersex condition and are therefore neither clearly male nor female:

> Two percent of the population means that literally millions of human beings across the world were not created male and female and yet are still God's children. The existence of this group clearly shows up the absurdly simplistic nature of the evangelical assumption that there is a universal rigid distinction between male and female. The reality is that maleness and femaleness are on a continuum. We may be mostly male or mostly female but we are never exclusively one or the other. (p.31)

Andrew Mein – Genesis 2 is not about marriage and does not require sexual relationships to be between men and women.

Dr Andrew Mein argues in his essay 'Threat and Promise: The Old Testament and Sexuality'[23] that Genesis 2 is not about marriage, and that it does not require that sexual relationships should only take place between men and women.

On the first point he writes:

---

[23] Andrew Mein, 'Threat and Promise: The Old Testament and Sexuality,' in Dormer and Morris, *An Acceptable Sacrifice.*

Genesis 2 seems to me to be much more interested in explaining sexual difference and sexual desire than social institutions. The problem that God sets out to solve at the outset is one of solitude: 'it is not good for the men to be alone' (2:18). The animals, although interesting to name, do not stir the heart and loins. But when God creates woman, a second human being, he creates the possibility of real, passionate relationship. The man responds with joy and delight: 'Now at last...Bone of my bones! Flesh of my flesh! (2.23). The emphasis is on relationship, on our need for the other, and not on either children or legal customs. (p.28)

On the second point he follows Gareth Moore's 'creative interpretation' of Genesis 2 which holds that God respects Adam's judgment about who is a suitable partner for him. This shows, he says:

...that it is God's will for each of us to find the partner we delight in, and God will be prepared to respect our choice: 'Because God is at the service of the delight of Adam, the representative human being, then we must also suppose that he is also at the service of men whose heart is gladdened by a man and a woman who delights in a woman.' (p.29)[24]

William Johnson – Genesis 2:18 authorises the Church to bless same-sex unions.

Professor William Johnson argues in his book *A Time to Embrace*[25] that God's declaration in Genesis 2:18 that it is not good for the man to be alone authorises the Church to bless not just heterosexual marriages, but also same-sex unions. It is, he says:

...of great theological importance that God is the one who created the human desire for otherness. It is also important that

---

[24] Mein is quoting Gareth Moore, *A Question of Truth*, New York: Continuum, 2003, p.143.
[25] William Stacy Johnson, *A Time to Embrace – Same-Gender Relationships in Religion, Law and Politics*, Grand Rapids/Cambridge: Eerdmans, 2006.

in the biblical narrative God responds to this human desire by providing a companion who is suitable. For gays and lesbians, a suitable companion is one whose sexual orientation matches their own. Does this, then, give the church permission to bless gay and lesbian unions? I believe that it does. I have argued that marriage is not a fixed order of creation but an order of redemption. We encourage people to unite in marriage, not on the merits of who the people already are, but with expectations of who we hope they will become. Marriage is a means of transformation and grace; when it is, the couple's mutual desire and devotion are meant to reflect God's own desire for us and devotion to be our God. There is every reason to believe that, by the grace of God, gay and lesbian couples are just as capable as heterosexual couples of modelling a desire and devotion worth consecrating. (p.153)

> **David Gushee –Genesis 1 and 2 is now bring read in a way that finds a space for gay and lesbian couples.**

Gushee notes in *Changing our Mind* that there is an increasing trend towards reading Genesis 1-2 in a way that finds space for gay and lesbian relationships:

> The fact that it is a man and a woman, and only a man and a woman, referenced in the discussions of sex and marriage in Genesis 1-2 and the fact that only a man and a woman have been able to procreate (until reproductive technology came along) – has been pivotal in shaping traditional Christian opinion on the LGBT issue. Christian tradition has taken these texts as prescriptive for all times and all peoples pertaining to the design and purpose of sex, marriage and family life. That has excluded those who are unable to fulfil that prescription due to their sexual orientation. But increasingly today it is noted that core practices referred to in Genesis 1-2, including mutual care for children, helper-partner companionship (Genesis 2:18) and

total self-giving can and do occur among covenanted gay and lesbian couples. (p.83)

Genesis 3 calls into question traditional views of human sexuality.

> **David Gushee –sexuality in a Genesis 3 world is best handled through a 'covenantal-marital ethic' which could also include gay and lesbian couples.**

Gushee further argues that we need a theology of sexuality that draws not just on the creation accounts in Genesis 1-2, but also on the account of the fall in Genesis 3:

> My suggestion here is simply this: Traditionalists appeal to Genesis 1-2; God made them male and female and male for female, and so everyone needs to conform to this pattern or live as a celibate. But they rarely mention Genesis 3, which (most Christians have said) tells the story of the beginnings of human sin, with the disordering consequences that are so painfully described in Genesis 4 through Revelation.
>
> If we live in a Genesis 3 world, and not a Genesis 1-2, this undoubtedly means that everyone's sexuality is sinful, broken and disordered, just like everything else about us. Nobody has Genesis 1-2 sexuality. To paraphrase former defense secretary Donald Rumsfeld (surprised you there didn't I?), *we go into adult life with the sexuality we have, not the sexuality we might want or wish to have.* No adult is a sexual innocent. Our task, if we are Christians, is to attempt to order the sexuality we have in as responsible a manner as we can. We can't get back to Genesis 1-2, a primal sinless world. But we can do the best we can with the Genesis 3 sexuality we have. (pp.97-98 italics in the original)

His proposal for the best way to handle our Genesis 3 sexuality is that we should re-affirm the traditional Christian 'covenantal-marital ethic' that 'bans all non-marital sex, infidelity, abandonment and divorce (with rare exceptions), making celibacy the only alternative to marriage.' (p.103) However, he also suggests that we should recognise that this is an ethic that can include gay and lesbian couples:

> In exploring the LGBT issue here, I have never asked whether the disciplined covenantal-marital standard in Christian sexual ethics should be weakened to 'affirm' whatever casual, exploitative, experimental, out-of-control, drunk, hookup, polyamorous, sex-while-dating, or follow-your-heart sexual practices are bouncing around American culture, mainly among heterosexuals.
>
> I am instead asking whether devout gay and lesbian Christians might be able to participate in the covenantal-marital ethical sexual standard – one person, for life, faithful and exclusive, in a loving nonexploitative, noncoercive, reciprocal relationship, that is the highest expression of biblical sexual ethics – which, in fact, a goodly number are already doing. I can't find a compelling reason to say no anymore. (p. 106)

Deryn Guest – Genesis 3:16 can be read as subverting the idea of heterosexual norm.

Finally, Dr Deryn Guest argues in her book on lesbian biblical hermeneutics *When Deborah met Jael* [26] that while Genesis 1-3 has been the foundation for a Jewish and Christian world view in which heterosexuality is seen as normative, nevertheless, 'the key verses that prescribe gender complementarity and the ordering of male-female relations have their queer elements that disrupt the heterocentric rhetoric.' (p.149) Thus a lesbian reading of God's declaration in Genesis 3:16 that Eve's desire will be for her husband will note, 'not without

---

[26] Deryn Guest, *When Deborah met Jael,* London: SCM, 2005, p.149.

humour,' that this declaration forms part of the punishments and curses meted out after the fall and also that it can be read as an example of pressure on women to conform to a heterosexual norm that they might not naturally choose for themselves:

> Why does the male object of Eve's desire need to be so clearly and unambiguously stipulated? Could it be that it is because there is so little to be gained by complying with the sex-gender system that women might justifiably walk away from it? (p.150)

Read in this way, the text itself subverts the idea that a heterosexual norm is necessarily the best option for women.

Genesis 19 and Judges 19

The story of the judgment of God on Sodom in Genesis 19 and the similar account of what happens to the Levite and his concubine at Gibeah in Judges 19 have been seen within both the Jewish and Christian traditions as evidence of the sinful nature of homosexual practice. Revisionist writers have challenged this view of these texts in a variety of ways.

Some revisionist writers have argued that the texts are not about same sex sexual desire, but is instead about the threat of sexual violence involving homophobia, xenophobia, inhospitality, rape and the violation of male honour. Others have argued that the story of Sodom is not about sex at all, but about lack of care for the vulnerable and the oppressed. Still others have seen the story of Sodom as being about the threat of violence against angels, or have highlighted its 'mythic' quality, or have emphasised the morally problematic nature of the way in which women are treated in both the Sodom and the Gibeah stories by being offered up in the place of the angels or the Levite.

Homophobia and Xenophobia

> **Michael Carden – the story of Sodom is about homophobia and xenophobia rather than same-sex desire.**

In his commentary on the stories in Genesis 19 and Judges 19 in the *Queer Bible Commentary* Carden argues that the stories are not about same sex desire but about homophobia and xenophobia.

> The misogynist order prevailing in Sodom and Gomorrah is also shown by the story to rely on homophobic violence. The threatened rape of the angels is an attempt to inscribe outsiders as not real men and therefore queer. But in attempting to inscribe the outsider as queer the Sodomites are also trying to inscribe the queer as outsider. By doing so they are effectively declaring that they are all straight in the Sodom state. Similarly in the Judges account, the men of Gibeah accept the concubine because she belongs to the Levite. Raping her carries the same significance as raping him The Judges account has the added import that the attack on the Levite and the concubine represents a breach of ethnic solidarity. The men of Gibeah are treating fellow Israelites as foreigners (resulting in the civil war of Judges 20-21). Thus, rather than reading the attempted rape of the angels (or the Levite) as an instance of homosexual violence, I believe it should be more accurately read as an instance of homophobic and xenophobic violence. (p.38)[27]

Inhospitality

> **Stephen Greenberg – the story of Sodom is about xenophobic violence rather than sexual desire.**

---

[27] *The Queer Bible Commentary* p.38. Michael Carden gives a more detailed account of his understanding of the Sodom story in his book *Sodomy – A History of a Christian Biblical Myth* , London: Equinox, 2004.

Reflecting a Jewish tradition which has seen the primary sin of Sodom as one of inhospitality, Rabbi Stephen Greenberg also sees xenophobic violence rather than sexual desire as the key to understanding the Sodom story. In his book *Wrestling with God and Men – Homosexuality in the Jewish Tradition* [28] he writes that:

> In order to read this story as a story of inhospitality one must think about homosexuality in terms very different from our own. We associate men who engage in anal intercourse with a certain set of erotic desires. But there is nothing in the story about sexual desire. The story is about a city that wants to discourage brotherly care when it comes to outsiders. Newcomers with wealth, like Lot, may be admitted. But transient strangers are not welcomed, and the poor are utterly shunned. Outsiders who have availed themselves of the city's shelter unlawfully and those members of the community who have broken the rules of membership by welcoming such strangers are threatened with rape, not as a sexual act, but as a means of brutal humiliation and punishment. That is what the Sodomites mean when, after Lot refuses to hand over his guests, they say, 'The one who came as a stranger is going to tell us what is right and wrong!'

Jay Michaelson – Judges 19 and Genesis 19 are about violence towards strangers rather than homosexuality.

Dr Jay Michaelson argues in his 2011 book *God vs. Gay?* [29] that chapters 18 and 19 of Genesis are both concerned with issues of hospitality and that the story of Sodom needs to be read in this light.

> These chapters of Genesis are about variations of hospitality: Abraham and Lot's generosity, the wickedness of Sodom and Abraham's fear of the king of Gerar. The male Sodomites'

---

[28] Stephen Greenberg, *Wrestling with God and Men*, Madison: University of Wisconsin Press, 2004.

[29] Jay Michaelson, *God vs. Gay?*, Boston: Beacon Press, 2011, pp.68-69.

interest in men is incidental: if they were raging homosexuals, Lot would not offer his daughters in return. Homosexual rape is the way they violate hospitality – not the essence of their transgression. Reading the story of Sodom as being about homosexuality is like reading the story of an axe murderer as being about an axe. (pp.68-69)

According to Michaelson, the 'literary echo' of the Sodom story in Judges 19 makes this point even more clear.

As in the story of Sodom, the Levite is threatened by a Benjaminite mob that wants to 'know him.' His host offers his own daughter, the mob refuses, and finally the Levite hands over his concubine to the mob, who rapes and 'abuse[s] her' all night long (Judg 19:25). This horrible story, which concludes with the Levite dismembering the concubine, is meant to tell of the degradation of Israel prior to the institution of the monarchy. But in mirroring the story of Sodom, it also tells us that it is not the gender of the angels or the Levite that matters to the mob; it is the use of sexual violence to degrade and humiliate. The Benjaminites are neither 'gay' nor 'straight,' and neither are the Sodomites. Both are predators, humiliators, dehumanizers. (p.69)

> **Keith Sharpe – Genesis 19 is not about sex, but about reward and punishment for hospitality and inhospitality.**

In *The Gay Gospels* Sharpe also stresses that that stories of Sodom and Gibeah are about inhospitality. He writes concerning the story of Sodom:

This is not a story about sex at all. Still less is it a story about the wickedness of same sex love. This is a story about reward and punishment. Contrary to what so many Christians claim, it is not a story about the virtue of heterosexuality and the vice of homosexuality. It is about the virtue of Abraham and Lot's kind of hospitality and the vice of the sodomite's brutal inhospitality.

The former is rewarded, the latter is punished. It would make no sense to say that Abraham and Lot are rewarded for being hospitable but the Sodomite townsmen are punished for being homosexual. It would undermine the whole point of the story. And yet this is what most mainstream Christian churches have taught. Abraham's future son and Lot's safe passage ensure their continuity and future, as Sodom and Gomorrah disappear under fire and brimstone, because they show great hospitality to strangers. The two cities of Sodom and Gomorrah are completely destroyed, because of their flagrant inhospitality. (pp.8-9)

In similar fashion, he states that in the story of Gibeah:

> The offence of the Gibean townsmen has nothing to do with homosexuality or heterosexuality. Just like the sin of the Sodomites, they indulged in gross inhospitality, and for it they were robbed of any hope of posterity. The lesson is the same and is crystal clear. (p.12)

Rape and the violation of male honour

> James Brownson – Genesis 19 and Judges 19 are about homosexual rape as an affront to male honour.

In *Bible, Gender, Sexuality* Brownson contends that both Genesis 19 and Judges 19 are concerned with sexual violence and the affront to male honour caused by rape by another man.

> The Bible narration presents both stories as evidence of extreme degradation and corruption, Both stories regard a man being raped by other men as an expression of violence and extreme degradation; both assume that the rape of female members of the household would be preferable to the rape of male visitors, which underscores the deep violation of male

honor that is assumed in both stories to be attached to the rape of a male by another male. (p.268)

The fact that this is what these stories are about means, he says, that they are of limited value for Christian thinking about same-sex relationships.

> All Christians today will agree that sexual violence is a profound violation of human dignity. All Christians can also agree, I hope, that these stories reflect a limited moral perspective: that is, they assume that the rape of a female is less offensive than the rape of a male. Christians may also agree that these two stories can help illuminate the antipathy shown elsewhere in the Bible to sexual relations between men, given the fact that these two stories associate this behaviour with humiliation, violence, and inhospitality towards strangers – expressed in its most extreme form. But precisely because of this extremity, Christians should also recognize that these stories are of no more value in assessing lifelong, loving, committed same-sex relationships than heterosexual rape can be used to morally evaluate loving heterosexual relationships. The failure to distinguish between consensual, committed and loving sexual relationships and violent, coercive relationships represents a serious case of moral myopia. (p.268)

Matthew Vines – the stories of Sodom and Gibeah are about gang rape.

Vines also contends in *God and the Gay Christian* that the basic issue in the stories of Sodom and Gibeah is 'gang rape, not sexual attraction' (p.65). He writes:

> The men of Sodom demanded that Lot bring out his guests so that the men could have sex with them. But this was not an expression of sexual desire. It was a threatened gang rape. In the ancient world, for a man to be raped was considered the ultimate degradation. As we saw in chapter 2, men seeking to

shame a conquered foe would often rape him in order to complete his humiliation. Aggression and dominance were the motives in these situations, not sexual attraction. (p.65)

According to Vines this reading of the Sodom story is confirmed by the parallel story of Gibeah in which the Levite's concubine is raped and concerning which the Levite declares in Judges 20:5 'during the night the men of Gibeah came after me and surrounded the house, intending to kill me.' Vines comments:

> The men had demanded sex, but the Levite knew they were not motivated by sexual desire. The men of Gibeah wanted to gang rape and murder him.

> The men of Sodom were blinded by angels before they could break down Lot's door but the events of Judges 19 give us a clear picture of their intentions. They were not expressing sexual interest in Lot's guests. They were seeking to rape, and possibly kill, his guests as a show of hostility and dominance. (p.66)

> **David Gushee – the best parallel to the stories of Sodom and Gibeah is gang rape during wartime or in prison.**

Gushee likewise argues in *Changing Our Mind* that the stories of Sodom and Gibeah are about gang rape. He notes that in the biblical tradition Sodom become a symbol of human wickedness. However, he says:

> ....never once in these intra-biblical references to Sodom is their evil described as same-sex interest or behaviour. In Isaiah 1:9-23, a host of sins are named bit mainly related to abuses of public justice. In Jeremiah 23:14 it's adultery, lying and unwillingness to repent. Ezekiel 16:49 describes their sins as pride, excess food, prosperous ease and lack of care for the poor. In Amos and Zephaniah the issues are pride, mocking and oppressing the poor. Inter-testamental works of Sirach (16:8), 3 Maccabees (2:5) and Wisdom (19:15) still talk about Sodom and

Gomorrah, and still don't connect their sin to sexuality at all. (pp. 61-62)

However, he thinks when read on its own terms the nearest comparison to the Sodom and Gomorrah story is to gang rape in wartime or in prison:

> The most illuminating comparison to the Sodom and Gomorrah story is to wartime or prison rape. Think about how one of the first images that comes to mind when thinking about prisons is the fear of getting raped there.
>
> The men of Sodom want gang rape. They are more interested in men than in Lot's daughters because in a patriarchal society men held greater worth and thus their violation was viewed as a greater offense than violating a woman. I would also suggest that the men wanted to dominate, humiliate and harm the male visitors precisely by *treating them like defenceless women*. In sexist social systems the most outrageous thing you can do to a man is to treat him like a woman. The Sodom story is about the attempted gang rape of men, because they are strangers, because they are vulnerable, and because they are a juicy target for humiliation and violence. It is about a town that had sunk to the level of the most depraved battlefield or prison.
>
> Genesis 19 and Judges 19 are narratives with huge implications for the ethics of war, prison, gender, violence and rape. But they have nothing to do with the morality of loving, covenantal, same-sex relationships. (pp. 62-63)

Questioning the sexual element in the Sodom story

Renato Lings – the Sodom story is not about sex, but about the treatment of the vulnerable and the oppressed.

All the revisionist readings we have looked at so far, assume that there is a sexual component in the Sodom story. However, *In Love lost in Translation* Lings questions this He contends that the word Hebrew *yada* translated into English as 'know' does not have a sexual meaning in Genesis 19:5. Consequently his reading of the Sodom story is as follows:

> Lot the foreigner and his family are the victims of the sin of Sodom. Lot's life contrasts with that of his uncle Abraham. While the latter is blessed in many different ways, Lot's life deteriorates from the moment he decides to settle near Sodom. He is likely to have married a local woman. Two daughters are born to him and no sons. Despite his efforts, he never becomes fully integrated. While offering hospitality to two visiting strangers, conflicts of interest erupt between Lot and the city. The locals want the travellers to be handed over for interrogation, but he refuses to comply and proposes a compromise. As a vulnerable immigrant, he is aware that he must offer a token of his loyalty. If the men of the city will allow him to perform his hosting duties, he is prepared to give his children as a pledge. While such a deal is unheard of in modern times, it reflects cultural patterns of antiquity, particularly the exposed situation of women, children, and poor people, of which the H[ebrew] B[ible] provides numerous examples. (p.440)

Seen in this light, the purpose of the story is not to provide teaching about same-sex sexual activity, but simply to challenge Israelites about 'the ways in which they themselves treat the socially vulnerable and oppressed.' (p.441)

> **Meg Warner – Genesis 19 and other Old Testament texts do not suggest that the sin of Sodom had anything to do with homosexuality. Judges 19 may touch on sex between males, but is a troubling story and difficult to interpret.**

In her essay 'Were the Sodomites really Sodomites?'[30] Meg Warner also suggests that there is nothing in the text of Genesis 19 itself that suggests that the sin of the men of Sodom had anything to do with homosexuality and that this idea is also absent from other Old Testament texts that refer to Sodom such as Isaiah 1:10, 3:9, Jeremiah 23:14 and Ezekiel 16:49. Nevertheless, she argues that the way that *yada* ('know') is used in the story in Judges 19 means we cannot rule out a sexual element in that story:

> It would be wrong to insist that Judges 19 is a narrative that does not touch on the subject of sex between males, and any interpretation of the story needs to consider the impact of prevailing attitudes towards sexual activity (of whatever nature) between males if it is to deal adequately with the issues of power and sexuality that are unquestionably present. (p.8)

However, in her view this does not mean that Judges 19 compels us to take up a particular view about homosexuality:

> The story is troubling on many levels and notoriously difficult to interpret. It offers no explicit interpretation or identification of its own themes. Although issues of sexuality are certainly present, there is no unequivocal or even readily apparent 'moral' message and the final result is that it is no more appropriate to regard Judges 19 as a proof text about the sinfulness of homosexuality than is the case with Genesis 19. (p.8)

---

[30] Meg Warner, 'Were the Sodomites really Sodomites?', in Nigel Wright (ed), *Five Uneasy Pieces – Essays on Scripture and Sexuality*, Adelaide, ATF Press, 2012.

The threat of violence against angels

Steve Schuh – the Bible identifies the visitors to Sodom as angels and so in the Bible the story of Sodom is about violence against angels.

Dr Steve Schuh declares in his article 'Challenging conventional wisdom – How a conservative reading of the biblical references to homosexuality fails to support their traditional interpretation' that the consistent witness of the Bible from Genesis 19:1 onwards is that 'the visitors are identified as angels, not human males,' citing Genesis 18:2, 19:1, Jude 5-10, 2 Peter 2:4-12, Hebrews 13:2 and Matthew 10:11-16 in support of this view. The relevance of the Matthew passage is that Jesus' disciples are 'sent like the angels as God's messengers.' (p.3)

On this basis he then argues that:

> *Biblically speaking....the significance of the Sodom story lies in the mob's apparent threat of violence against angels.* That the major theme in the story's re-telling in the Christian era became homosexuality – rather than assault against angels, violent gang rape, the abuse of women, inhospitality, or xenophobia – tells us a great deal about the cultures that inherited the Sodom story but nothing about the biblical account itself.
>
> Contrary to conventional wisdom then, the Bible does not support the traditional association because of homosexual acts, threatened or otherwise, nor does it even hint that the men of Sodom were motivated by a desire for sex with other men, as opposed to sex with angels, or simply violence. (p.3 italics in the original)

The mythic quality of the Sodom story and the problematic morality of the Sodom and Gibeah Stories.

> **Alan Falconer, J Mary Henderson and Marjory A MacLean – the story of Sodom has a mythic quality and both it and the story of Gibeah have a troubling underlying morality.**

In their presentation of the 'revisionist case' in the report of the Church of Scotland's Theological Commission on Same-Sex Relationships and the Ministry, [31] Professor Alan Falconer, Dr J Mary Henderson and Dr Marjory MacLean also state that 'it is by no means clear that the 'Sin of Sodom', which made it a byword for depravity in future generations was primarily to do with homosexual practice.' (p.1/66) They note that 'some commentators have suggested that the offence which so outraged Lot (and his anonymous Gibean counterpart) was the demand that he should betray his guests by handing them over to the mob – a breach of the sacred duty of hospitality.' (p. 1/66)

They further claim that 'even if, as seems likely, sexual immorality in all its many forms was part of the lawlessness and depravity which caused God, in the story, to decide on Sodom's destruction, there is much in the tale to point to its mythic quality.' They concede that 'to identify a literary genre does not, of course, detract from the moral usefulness of the story,' but they say it should 'caution against any over-literal interpretation.'(p.1/67)

Finally they observe that the 'most disturbing aspect' both of the story of Sodom and the parallel story in Judges 19 is their underlying morality:

> ...which allows young women to be offered to a violent mob intent on rape, with no hint of consideration on the story teller's part. This alone, quite apart from other considerations, makes it

---

[31] *The Church of Scotland's Theological Commission on Same-Sex Relationships and the Ministry,* APS Group Scotland, 2013.

impossible to read these ancient tales as a guide to modern sexual morality. (p.1/67)

> **Adrian Thatcher – we need to ask hard moral questions about the morality of the Sodom story.**

Thatcher also highlights the moral problems raised by the Sodom story. He writes in *The Savage Text*:

> Our sense of the holiness of scripture should not inhibit the asking of hard moral questions about it. Bluntly here is a father who, in order to protect a couple of supernatural visitors from gang-rape, is prepared to hand over his daughters to be gang-raped instead. Nowhere in the narrative are this hasty proposal or his authority to make it criticized...Surely a story which casually records a father's betrayal of his daughters to a testosterone-crazed and murderous rabble cannot be used with much conviction by readers claiming high moral ground over same-sex relations? (p.21)

Leviticus 18:22, 20:13

Leviticus 18:22 and 20:13 have traditionally seen as providing an absolute prohibition on all forms of homosexual activity that are still binding on people today. Revisionist writers have challenged this view of these verses in three ways.

First, they have argued the verses only prohibit specific forms of male homosexual activity. The forms that have been suggested are male homosexual incest, anal penetration, ritual homosexual prostitution, or male homosexual activity that takes place among the people of Israel and within the land of Israel. No other forms of homosexual activity, is it said, are forbidden by Leviticus.

Secondly, they have argued that the Levitical prohibitions rest on assumptions derived from a particular historical context about ritual uncleanness, the importance of procreation, concepts of honour and shame, the need to avoid idolatry, male superiority over women and the need for Israel to maintain its distinctiveness from the indigenous inhabitants of the land of Canaan. As Christians in a different historical concepts we do not, or should not, share these assumptions and this means that that the prohibitions can no longer be regarded as authoritative for Christians today.

Thirdly, they have argued that it would be inconsistent to insist that the prohibitions against homosexuality remain in force while the other commandments in Leviticus are not seen as binding and the command to execute those guilty of homosexual activity is ignored.

Leviticus only prohibits specific forms of homosexual activity

a. The prohibition of incest.

> **David Tabb Stewart – Levitivus 18:22 only prohibits sex between two related men.**

In *The Queer Bible Commentary* Professor David Tabb Stewart argues that the repeated use of the term 'uncover nakedness' in Leviticus 18 is a reference back to the story of Ham and Noah in Genesis 9:21-22 and shows that what the chapter is concerned with is prohibiting incest. This means that Leviticus 18:22 is an 'incest rule' that 'extends the incest prohibition to all the male relatives of the same degree of relation as those forbidden women in 18:6-18.' (p.98) In other words, just as a man cannot have sex with women to whom he is related, so also he cannot have sex with men with whom he has the same sort of family relationship.

His overall conclusion is that:

> Leviticus 18:22 and 20:13 forbid male-on-male incest within certain degrees of relation. This abhorrent behaviour is one among a number including all the sexual crimes of Leviticus 18.

(Thus, a straight man sleeping with his lawfully wedded and menstruating wife is also an abomination.) These 'texts of terror' are not a general prohibition against all homosexual relations. One must turn to the pages of the history of interpretation to find that. The residuum, homosexual relations between two women and between two unrelated men, is subject to the purity rules covering leaking bodies – washing, laundering, avoiding blood associated with reproduction, and avoiding sancta [holy things] while polluted. (p.99)

b. The prohibition of anal penetration

> **Stephen Greenberg – the Torah only prohibits anal penetration, but no other forms of homosexual activity. What Leviticus is addressing is men who use other men in order to asset their own power and mastery.**

Greenberg takes a different view of what is prohibited. In *Wrestling with God and Men* he argues that the prohibition of a man lying 'with a male as with a woman' is a very specific prohibition of anal penetration. He writes:

> ...we have a law prohibiting a man from sexually penetrating (or being penetrated by) another man anally. This interpretation results in a number of surprising conclusions. First, there are a variety of ways that men can pleasure each other sexually. If the prohibition is defined by anal penetration, then a whole array of sexual engagement between two men, ranging from kissing onward would not be formally prohibited. Second, the centrality of the penetrating party in Leviticus portrays a very different set of cultural prohibitions than have been normative in other societies. Third, homosexuality, that is, same-sex emotional and physical desire, is not prohibited in scripture. Actions are prohibited, not psychological states or sexual desires. Fourth,

there is an enormous omission in the text: the Torah does not prohibit lesbian relationships. (p.85)

Greenberg goes on to argue that the rationale for the prohibition of anal penetration is to outlaw the kind of sexual activity:

...that is designed to effect the power and mastery of the penetrator. Sex for the conquest, for shoring up the ego, for self-aggrandizement, or worse, for the perverse pleasure of demeaning another man is prohibited. This is an abomination. (p.206)

It follows that:

Heterosexual men who use other men for sexual release would be committing an abomination. Where the ultimate motive is love and intimacy, sex would be permissible; where the motive is sexual predation it would not be. People who cannot find intimacy, companionship and love with a person of the opposite sex would simply not be the ones addressed by the verse. (p.260)

> **Jay Michaelson – Leviticus 18:22 prohibits anal sex because of its link with Canaanite idolatry.**

Michaelson, who is also a Jewish scholar, agrees with Greenberg that what is forbidden by the word *tishkav* ('lie') in Leviticus 18:22 is anal penetration. He writes in *God vs. Gay?* that recognising this 'allows us to bless same-sex unions while maintaining a strict interpretation of Leviticus 18:22. We only need to read the verse according to its plain meaning that *tishkav* means anal sex – only that.'(p.61)

Michaelson further argues that the word *toevah* ('abomination') links the prohibition of male anal sex to Canaanite cultic practices. He notes that Leviticus 18:

...describes several sexual sins, then mentions Molech worship (a form of Canaanite idolatrous practice), then says specifically that male anal sex is *toevah*, then describes the whole list of sins as *toevot* [abominations] that the Canaanites performed. Now, imagine if a similar structure were used today. Imagine if someone said to you, 'Don't Kill, Don't Steal, and Don't Eat the Cheese – It is Spoiled.' The first two instructions have no conditions; they are universal prohibitions. The third one, though, provides a reason for the ban, implying that when the cheese isn't spoiled, the ban would not apply. Likewise here. Leviticus says very clearly: no incest, no idolatry, no male anal sex because it is *toevah*. It is almost as if Leviticus is going out of its way to specify that male anal sex is prohibited because it is a Canaanite cultic practice.

Which it was. We learn from Deuteronomy 23:18 and 1 Kings 14:24 that the Canaanites had qedeshim, sacred prostitutes, both male and female, who would enact the role of a god or goddess in an ecstatic, sexual ritual. Campaigns against cultic prostitution were undertaken by King Solomon and King Josiah. Similar forms of cultic prostitution were found in Babylonia, as recorded by Herodotus, and elsewhere in the Ancient Near East. Especially since Leviticus 18:22 follows Leviticus 18:21, it seems clear that what's being forbidden here is what the Bible is always interested in forbidding: idolatry.(p.65)

Michaelson's conclusion is that:

All I have to do, to remove the false stigma of 'God versus Gay,' is to read the verse closely, literally, and attentively. Leviticus 18:22 is a prohibition on male anal sex in the context of idolatry. Nothing more. (p.66)

> **Matthew Vines – Leviticus forbids same-sex activity involving anal penetration because it involves a man being feminised and thereby degraded.**

In *God and the Gay Christian* Vines also sees Leviticus as concerned with anal penetration. Drawing on the work of Saul Olyan[32] he argues that Leviticus forbids same sex activity involving anal penetration because it would involve a man being degraded by being treated as if he were a woman and hence someone of an inferior gender. (p.88)

Vines accepts that Leviticus does not distinguish between active and passive partners, but argues that this does not undermine his interpretation because:

> Philo condemned both partners in male same-sex intercourse, and social status was very much on his mind. He rebuked the passive partner for becoming feminized and the active partner for enabling that feminization. That equality of treatment regardless of role is unique among ancient law codes, but so is the declaration of Leviticus 24:22 that the Israelites 'are to have the same law for the foreigner and the native born.' The law treated foreigner and native-born as social equals which helps explain why both male partners are condemned. Old Testament scholars Richard Elliott Friedman and Shawna Dolansky[33] have argued that Leviticus prohibited all male same-sex intercourse 'since by cross-cultural perception such intercourse would necessarily denigrated the passive partner and violate his status under God's Law.' (p.90)

Vines goes on to observe that this view of Leviticus undermines the idea that it is concerned with the anatomical complementarity of men and women and explains why lesbianism is not mentioned:

---

[32] Saul M Olyan 'And with a male you shall not lie the lying down of a woman,' *Journal of the History of Sexuality* 5:2, 1994, pp.183-186.
[33] Richard Friedman and Shawna Dolansky, *The Bible Now*, Oxford: OUP, 2011, p.35.

In fact, the entire, question of how bodies fit together doesn't seem to be on the radar. The concern we see instead is centred on the proper ordering of gender roles in a patriarchal society.

That understanding also sheds light on why Leviticus contains no parallel prohibition of female same-sex relations. If the issue were anatomical complementarity, female same-sex relations should be condemned on an equal basis. And yet the text is silent on this matter. But from the standpoint of gender roles, the absence of such a prohibition makes more sense. (p.90)

> **Keith Sharpe – Leviticus is concerned about men acting as if they were women and thereby undermining patriarchy.**

Sharpe takes the same approach as Vines. In *The Gay Gospels* he too sees the text as concerned with a prohibition of anal penetration based on a patriarchal view of the relations between men and women. He writes that 'what the author of Leviticus is concerned with is anal penetration' and that:

> This prohibition of anal intercourse between men has absolutely nothing to do with same sex love. As discussed above, penetrative sex in the culture of Ancient Israel is all about domination and possession of females by males. What the male author of Leviticus is so anxious about is not the act of anal intercourse itself but rather what it means for Ancient Israelite society. And what it means for that society is men acting as if they were women. He sees this as a terrible confusion of categories and a grave challenge to God's divine ordering in which males do the dominating, possessing and penetrating. It is therefore a huge threat to the social fabric and to the patriarchal privileges which that social fabric affords to males. (p.19)

What this means, says Sharpe, is that:

...the use of Leviticus 18:22 to condemn gay sex is highly problematic for homophobic religious leaders because the text by implication actually permits same-sex erotic activity, so long as no penetration takes place. Only if one male penetrates another does the activity turn into the crime of 'males acting as females', and only then does it come under the scope of this law. Furthermore. what this law is designed to protect is not heterosexuality but a supposedly divinely ordained sexual hierarchy which privileges males and treats women as virtually subhuman; something that we would now regard as totally unacceptable, completely immoral and definitely unchristian. (p.20)

c. The prohibition of ritual homosexual prostitution.

Steve Schuh – Leviticus is referring to homosexual acts that are expressions of pagan religion.

Steve Schuh in his article 'Challeging conventional wisdom' also sees idolatry as the key to understanding the Levitical prohibitions. He sees the contexts of these prohibitions as being the sort of cultic activity referred to in passages such as Deuteronomy 23:17-18, 1 Kings 14:22-24, 15:11-14, 22:41-46 and 2 Kings 23:4-25 and his conclusion is that:

...idolatry is not just the primary context in which homosexual acts appear in the Old Testament – it is the only context. The homosexual acts prohibited in Leviticus 18 and 20 are described in the immediate context of idolatry and therefore very likely refer to ritual acts of male homosexual prostitution, as evidenced by at least five historical, biblical references. They appear besides other examples of idolatry intentionally, for they were, like child sacrifice, and the sex rites of fertility cults, primary expressions of pagan religion. (pp.5-6)

71

d. The prohibition of homosexuality among the people of Israel within the land of Israel

> Jacob Milgrom – the prohibition of homosexuality in Leviticus applies only to Jewish men living in Israel.

Another Jewish scholar, Professor Jacob Milgrom, does not see the prohibitions in Leviticus as being as specific as Greenberg or Michaelson suggest, but he does agree that they are limited in extent. In his commentary on Leviticus[34]

> Does the Bible prohibit homosexuality? Of course it does (18:22, 20:13), but the prohibition is severely limited. First, it is addressed only to Israel, not to other nations. Second, compliance with this law is a condition for residing in the Holy land, but is irrelevant outside it (see the closing exhortation 18:24-30). Third, it is limited to men; lesbianism is not prohibited. Thus it is incorrect to apply the prohibition on a universal scale. (p.196)

Milgrom's explanation for the omission of lesbianism is that in sexual relations between women 'there is no spilling of seed'. This means that 'life is not symbolically lost, and it is for this reason, in my opinion, that lesbianism is not prohibited in the Bible.'(p.197) His overall conclusion is that while 'the Bible never approves homosexuality, neither does it prohibit most people from engaging in it.' (p.197)

---

[34] Jacob Milgrom, *Leviticus*, Minneapolis: Fortress Press, 2004.

The prohibitions are based on assumptions from a past historical context and this means they are no longer authoritative for Christians today.

> Jack Rogers – the prohibitions in Leviticus have to do with a culturally conditioned concern for ritual purity and they cannot rightly be applied to faithful homosexual Christians today.

Rogers differs from the writers we have just looked at in that he does not argue that Leviticus 18:22 and 20:13 only prohibit a certain type of sexual activity or only prohibit it in a certain geographical location. However, what he does argue in *Jesus, the Bible and Homosexuality* is that these verses have to be read in the light of a specific historical context and its assumptions about the importance of ritual purity.

As he sees it, the function of the 'Holiness Code' in Leviticus, of which the two verses relating to homosexuality are a part, was to help the people of Israel to define their identity over against their non-Israelite neighbours. The statement in Leviticus 18:22 'You shall not lie with a male as with a woman; it is an abomination' needs to be read against this background:

> The Hebrew word *toevah*, translated as 'abomination' refers here to something that makes a person ritually unclean, such as having intercourse with a woman while she is menstruating. Ritual purity was considered necessary to distinguish the Israelites from their pagan neighbours. (p.69)

Jesus, however, was not concerned with ritual purity, but purity of heart, as Matthew 15:10-11 and 18-20 make clear. This means, says Rogers, that:

> When we see Jesus as the fulfilment of the law (Matt. 5:17), we understand that our challenge is not to meticulously maintain culturally conditional laws, but rather, with Jesus, to love God and love our neighbour (Matt.22:36-40). When these texts in

Leviticus are taken out of their historical and cultural context and applied to faithful, God worshipping Christians who are homosexual, it does violence to them. They are being condemned for failing to conform to an ancient culturally conditioned code that is not applicable to them or their circumstances. (pp.69-70)

> **James Brownson – the probibitions in Leviticus are based on the assumptions of a particular historical context and are not relevant to committed Christian gay and lesbian relationships today.**

Brownson likewise argues in *Bible, Gender, Sexuality* that the Levitical prohibitions are rooted in the assumptions of a particular historical context in a way that means they are no longer binding today. He declares that in Leviticus:

> Male-male sex is...linked with the behaviour of alien nations, with idolatry and cultic prostitution, and with the degradation of distinctively male honor. It may also be the case that, since the ancient world assumed that men held the 'seed' for future generations, that female-female sex was left out because there was no 'seed' involved. When all these considerations are taken together, Leviticus concludes that 'lying with a male as with a woman' is an 'abomination' to both God and Israelite sensibilities, and its presence could not be tolerated within Israel. (p.272)

In his view, however, these concerns seem 'distinctly out of place' in relation to contemporary same-sex relationships between committed Christians. As he sees it:

> We can appreciate the way the ancient writer is seeking to preserve the integrity of Israelite life in Leviticus without assuming that the same concerns are relevant to life today...the religious, purity, procreative, and honor-shame contexts that form the underlying logic of the Levitical prohibitions,

74

understandable and coherent as they may be in their own context, simply do not apply to contemporary committed Christian gay and lesbian relationships.(p.273)

Richard Treolar – the assumptions underlying the prohibitions in Leviticus are problematic for Australian Anglicans today.

In his essay in *Five Uneasy Pieces,* Dr Richard Treolar argues that the assumptions underlying the Levitical prohibitions raise serious theological problems for Australian Anglicans today.

He notes that the command to 'be fruitful and multiply' which underlies much of the teaching of Leviticus 'has had to be reinterpreted and qualified by the demand for ecological stewardship in an age in which we have begun to recognise that creation cannot bear the consequences of anthropocentric reading strategy, any more than our geo-political environment can bear the consequences of an ethno- or religio-centric one.' He also suggests that the Levitical idea of 'holiness as differentiation' with its clear distinction between the Israelites and the indigenous people of the land is 'intolerable' in an Australian context in view of the treatment meted out to the indigenous inhabitants of Australia and the Torres islands and that 'in a world teeming with displaced persons' to see exile as the punishment for pollution of the land as Leviticus 18:24-30 does is 'as theologically untenable and morally repugnant as positing HIV/AIDS as some sort of divine (or quasi 'natural') judgment on homosexuals.' In the light of such problems taking the witness of Scripture fully seriously may, he says, involve exercising a 'hermeneutic of resistance' or 'improving upon some portion of Scripture' as Christians have already done in relation to texts relating to slaves and women. (p.27)

Andrew Mein – the prohibitions in Leviticus are based on the idea of the superiority of men over women.

Mein argues in article 'Threat and Promise' that the key issue underlying the Levitical prohibitions is the Old Testament understanding of gender roles and that for this reason the Levitical texts are of little use for us today. He quotes with approval Gareth Moore's comment on Leviticus 18:22:

> What this law depends on, and what it expresses, is the idea that God wills male superiority over the female; it also depends on and expresses a conception of sexual penetration as a symbolic actualization of the superiority. Most modern Christians reject absolutely both of these ideas, officially at least. (p.26[35])

This being the case, Mein declares:

> ...the Old Testament texts which directly address homosexual acts are not a great deal of help to us. They reflect the moral outlook of an unfamiliar and alien culture, and are thoroughly bound up with ancient Israel's broader understanding of family, sexuality and religion. If as contemporary Christians we are uncomfortable with the Old Testament's hierarchical view of sex and marriage, we may legitimately be uncomfortable with the condemnation of homosexual acts we find within it. (p.26)

The issue of inconsistency

> **Alan Falconer, J Mary Henderson and Marjory A MacLean – observing some but not all of the prohibitions in Leviticus could be viewed as inconsistent.**

The presenters of the revisionist case in the Church of Scotland report observe that the Levitical prohibition of male homosexual intercourse forms part of 'a long list of sexual and other practices' which 'make a person ritually unclean.' They declare that no one suggests:

---

[35] The quotation is from Moore, op.cit, p.80.

...that Christians are required to observe all these prohibitions, or that the death penalty should be applied when the holiness code demands it. Jesus himself had no qualms about making himself ritually unclean when compassion moved him to touch people with leprosy or a woman with vaginal bleeding. It could be regarded as inconsistent to select some, but not all, of the Levitical prohibitions as universally applicable. (p.1/68)

> **Adrian Thatcher – consistency demands obeying all the injunctions in the Old Testament and executing gay people.**

In similar fashion, Thatcher contends in *The Savage Text* that if, like the Congregation for the Doctrine of the Faith of the Roman Catholic Church, we see the judgement against homosexuality in Leviticus 20:13 as still binding today then we need to at least be consistent in our application of the Old Testament text:

> Surely if this injunction is to be obeyed, all 613 injunctions in the Old Testament are equally binding? Shellfish and much else 'shall be an abomination unto you' (Leviticus 11:12). Which abominations are still abominable now and which not? Perhaps the Vatican would prefer to have gays killed, as this text expressly requires? This is precisely what it did to 150 'Sodomites' in Spain between (1570 and 1630), and many more at other times and in other places. Just to make plain the Inquisition's disapproval, the Spanish Sodomites were burned alive 'without benefit of strangulation.' [36]

Deuteronomy 23:17-18

As the comments from Michaelson and Schuh on Leviticus 18 and 20 quoted above show, some revisionist scholars hold that Deuteronomy 23:17-18 refers to men engaging in cultic prostitution and that this

---

[36] Thatcher, op,cit. p.22.

practice is what lies in the background of the prohibition of same-sex relations in Leviticus.

Other revisionist scholars, however, disagree with this view. For example, **Deryn Guest** notes in her comments on Deuteronomy 23:18 in *The Queer Bible Commentary* that the idea that Deuteronomy refers to cult prostitutes 'has largely been abandoned' by Old Testament scholars for lack of supporting evidence. However, she does agree that it may be referring to non-cultic male homosexual prostitutes. (pp.139-142) For another example, **Stephen Greenberg** declares in *Wrestling with God and Men* that the view that these verses in Deuteronomy are 'a prohibition of the sacred prostitution presumed to be part of Canaanite worship' has been 'challenged by contemporary scholars' on the grounds that there is no evidence that the religion of Israel's neighbours included sex acts and that it is questionable whether the sexual activity in Mesopotamian rites included 'sex between male prostitutes and male celebrants.' (pp. 177-178)

Romans 1:26-27

Romans 1:26-27 have traditionally been seen as not only describing both gay and lesbian sexual relationships as sinful, but also as providing a clear theological explanation of why such relationships are sinful, namely that they are the outworking of humanity's rejection of the witness to God borne by the created order. Revisionist scholars have challenged this traditional view of theses verses in a variety of different ways.

They have argued:

- That these verses represent a Jewish viewpoint which St. Paul himself rejected;
- That Romans 1:26 does not refer to lesbianism;
- That the homosexual activity that St. Paul was objecting to was not the same as faithful Christian homosexual relationships

today because it was rooted in pagan idolatry or involved pederasty;

- That St. Paul was referring to homosexual activity engaged in by people who were naturally heterosexual and therefore what he says is not relevant in the case of people who have an innate homosexual orientation;

- That St Paul regarded homosexual activity as shameful and unusual, but not sinful;

- That St Paul's argument in Romans 1 can no longer be accepted by us today because we no longer accept his belief that humanity was originally monotheisitic and later turned to idolatry, because he lacked the knowledge we now have about the innate nature of homosexual sexual orientation and because we no longer accept the assumptions about male superiority, shame and honour, or the problematic nature of sexual passion that underlie his argument;

- That what St Paul was doing was challenging cultural prejudice against the passive partner in pederastic relationships.

Because revisionist writers have frequently combined a number of these arguments, the material below is organised by author rather than by the type of argument they have used.

> **Renato Lings - Romans 1:18-32 is the citation of views which St. Paul himself rejects.**

The most radical solution to the interpretation of Romans 1 is that offered by Renato Lings. Building on Douglas Campbell's 2009 study *The Deliverance of God:*[37] Renato Lings argues *in Love Lost in Translation* that Romans 1:18-32 are Paul's citation of the views of an unnamed Jewish preacher in Rome, views which Paul himself rejects in Romans 2. His conclusion is that:

---

[37] Douglas Campbell, *The Deliverance of God: An Apocalyptic Re-reading of Justification in Paul*, Grand Rapids: Eerdmans, 2009.

If the verses 1:18-32 are to be taken as an indirect citation of the views of an unnamed opponent in Rome, it is a bitter irony of history that they have been attributed to Paul himself, turning the apostle into a fierce critic of sexual activity between members of the same sex and making him contradict his own Gospel message. In actual fact, and given his primary concerns in Romans, it seems far more likely that Paul distances himself from one or more recently converted zealots with Jewish backgrounds who spend too much time quoting the book of Wisdom to condemn idolatry, including certain orgies occurring in Roman temples. (p.565)

The view that Romans 1:26-27 do not represent St. Paul's own theology is one that does not appear to be shared by other revisionist writers. A more common approach is to suggest that for a number of different reasons what Paul is condemning in Romans 1 cannot be directly compared to faithful committed Christian gay relationships today. The following examples illustrate this approach.

> **Jay Michaelson - Romans 1 sees homosexuality as 'unnatural' because it violates the naturally active role of men in sexual activity.**

Michaelson writes in *God vs. Gay?* that what Paul is saying in Romans 1 is that:

...the Romans turned their backs on God, and as a result were *given over* to various forms of immorality, including sex that Paul understood as unnatural (*paraphysin*) because it violated the natural roles of men (active, dominant) and women (passive, submissive). Paul is not singling out homosexual activity as a sin (it is a consequence, not a cause), not referring to gay people as we understand them today (who cannot be 'given over' to homosexuality), not referring to loving and sacred forms of same-sexual expression (since he specifically describes the lusts as 'shameful'), and possibly not referring to adult homosexuality at all (since pederasty was the predominant form of homosexuality in Rome, and Paul uses the general term *arsen*). That is the extent of the condemnation. (p.84)

> **Tobias Haller – St Paul does not refer to lesbianism but to male homosexual activity involving orgies and pederasty.**

In *Reasonable and Holy* Haller rejects the idea that Romans 1:26 has anything to do with lesbianism. He maintains rabbinic parallels show that this verse has to do with Gentile women who engage in 'non procreative intercourse' with their husbands in which there is 'the insertion of the penis in an unusual place.' This was also the way the passage was understood by writers in the Early Church such as Clement of Alexandria. (pp.63-68)

He further maintains that Paul's critique of male same-sex sexuality was probably addressed:

> ....to what he perceived as approved among the Gentiles: either the orgies of the idolatrous cults or male 'pederasty;' that is, the Greek idealization of the 'normal' upbringing of a young man under the erotic tutelage of an adult. The Greeks did not approve of life long sexual relationships between men, which were conceptually mapped against mixed-sex marriage or prostitution. The idea of a grown man taking a passive role was deeply offensive to the culture. There may well have been covert relationships based on equality rather than mapped against the uneven male-female marriage relationship in Graeco-Roman society – but these rarely rose to public awareness. In his time, Paul critiqued what the Greeks approved: orgy and pederasty. (pp.69-70)

Haller's overall conclusion is that:

> Romans 1, a description of the total collapse of good order among idolaters, has no application to the question of faithful,

monogamous same-sex relationships between Christian men – and says absolutely nothing about such relationships between women. (p.67)

> **Dale Martin - St Paul puts forward the mythological idea that homosexuality is the result of idolatry and objects to homosexuality because it involves sexual passion and transgresses the hierarchy of men over women.**

In his book *Sex and the Single Savior*[38] Dale Martin also sees idolatry as the key to understanding Romans 1. Because the Gentile world has given itself over to idolatry God has in turn given the Gentiles over to the 'desires of their hearts' and these desires have resulted various forms of corrupt behaviour including the sexual actions 'beyond nature' mentioned in v 26. In Martin's view this Pauline argument is contrary to what most people believe today:

> Paul's own logic assumes a mythological structure unknown to most modern persons, Christians included. Most of us do not believe that all of humanity was once upon a time neatly monotheistic, only later, at a particular historical point, to turn to polytheism and idolatry; nor are we likely to believe that homosexuality did not exist until the sudden invention of polytheism. According to his etiology of homosexuality, Paul must not have believed that it ever existed among the Jews, at least those who abstained from idolatry. Importantly, when Paul finally indicts the Jews in Romans, he does not accuse them of idolatry or homosexual immorality; Jewish immorality is revealed, at most, in adultery and dishonesty regarding the property of temples (2:22). This is perfectly consistent with Paul's assumption that homosexuality is punishment for idolatry and polytheism: the Jews have not been punished because they have not, in general, been guilty of that particular

---

[38] Dale Martin, *Sex and the Single Savior*, Louisville: Westminster, John Knox Press, 2006.

sin. If we were to follow Paul's logic, we would have to assume that once idolatry and polytheism were forsaken, homosexuality would cease to exist, which is probably what Paul believed; after all he never even hints that any Jews or Christian engages in homosexuality. (p.55)

On the issue of what St Paul thought was actually wrong with homosexual activity in itself Martin offers two suggestions. Firstly, it involved sexual passion ('were consumed with passion' v27) and for Paul this was always wrong. 'For Paul, homosexuality was simply a further extreme of the corruption inherent in sexual passion itself. It did not spring from a different of desire, but simply from desire itself' (p.59). Secondly, it transgressed the proper relations between men and women. 'Doubtless, Paul also objects to same-sex intercourse due in part to his assumption about the cosmic hierarchy of male over female. While this is not made explicit in Romans 1, it is probably assumed.' (p.59)

> **Steve Schuh – Romans 1 is not about lesbianism, but is probably about idolatry leading to cultic prostitution.**

Schuh likewise contends in 'Challenging conventional wisdom' that idolatry is at the heart of what Paul is saying in Romans 1. Following the example of earlier Jewish writings such as the *Wisdom of Solomon*, what Paul is doing from Romans 1:18 onwards is describing the impact of idolatry on the human condition. First human beings become idolaters, then as a result their worship becomes corrupt, and finally their corrupt worship expresses itself in sexual immorality. (pp.8-10)

That, for Schuh, is where Romans 1:26-27 fit into the picture. As he sees it, Romans 1:26 is not about lesbianism but about females engaging in non-coital sexual activity with men and then men engaging in sex with men, both in the context of pagan cultic activity and both possibly in the context of prostitution (for Schuh the 'payment' (*antimisthia*) referred to in 1:27 may possibly be literally payment for sex). (pp.10-12) Schuh's conclusion is that in 1:26-27:

Following the expected storyline...Paul unveils a third, dramatic panel in his triptych of the pagan rejection of God and God-honouring worship. His descriptions of idol-making and idol-worship flow seamlessly into an instantly recognizable portrait of ritualized sexual immorality – very likely female and male cult prostitution – for 'the idea of making idols was the beginning of fornication [*pornei*], and the invention of them was the corruption of life (Wisdom 14:8-12, NRSV). (p.12)

> **Jack Rogers – Romans 1 is about idolatry resulting in inordinate desire and the violation of Hellenistic-Jewish expectations about how people ought to behave.**

In *Jesus, the Bible and Homosexuality* Rogers also argues that the key issue which Paul is addressing in Romans 1:18-32 is not sexuality but idolatry. However, unlike Schuh who focuses on pagan cultic activity as the background to Romans 1, Rogers takes idolatry in the broadest sense of giving allegiance to anything other than God 'Paul is writing about idolatry, that is, worshipping, giving our ultimate allegiance to anything in the creation instead of God, the Creator.'(p.73) The reason that Paul I writing about this is to make the point that:

> We are without excuse, especially when we judge others. Why? Because in God's sight we are all given to idolatry. Paul is driving home the point that is at the heart of Reformation theology: no one is righteous before God. (pp.73-74)

Rogers further argues that what Paul is criticising in Romans 1:26-27 is not:

> ...wrongly oriented desires, but about inordinate desires – going to excess, losing control. Idolaters fail to give God glory and gratitude. God then allows them to lose control in erotic passion, which brings them dishonour. (pp 75-76)

In Rogers' view when Paul talks about same-sex relationships being 'against nature' he is not talking about 'a violation of the order of creation,' instead he is referring to 'the conventional view of people and how they ought to behave in first-century Hellenistic-Jewish culture.' (p.74) In addition when he talks about the behaviour of women in Romans 1:26 he is reflecting the contemporary view of male sexual dominance:

> The text does not say that women had sex with other women. They could have been condemned for taking the dominant position in heterosexual intercourse, or for engaging in non-procreative sexual acts with male partners. The issue is gender dominance, and in that culture women were to be passive and not active in sexual matters. (p.75)

Rogers' conclusion is that what Paul says in Romans 1 'is not appropriately applied to contemporary gay or lesbian Christians who are not idolaters, who love God, and who seek to live in thankful obedience to God.' (p. 76)

James Brownson – St Paul is concerned in Romans 1 about excessive lust, the violation of gender roles, the non-procreative nature of homosexual relationships and the violation of the ancient world's understanding of the natural order of things.

Brownson puts forward similar arguments to Rogers, but without a specific reference to the issue of idolatry. After looking in detail at Romans 1, he argues in *Bible, Gender, Sexuality* that there are 'four forms of moral logic' that underlie Paul's teaching about homosexual relationships in this chapter:

> First, Paul viewed these relationships as an expression of excessive lust that is not content with heterosexual relationships but is driven to increasingly exotic forms of stimulation leading to the loss of purity of heart. The notion that someone might not be significantly attracted to persons of the

opposite sex – but to persons of the same sex – is never even considered by early Jewish or Christian writers. [39]

Second, he viewed these relationships as shameful, particularly because they treated a man as a woman, inherently degrading the passive partner, and more generally because they violated understood gender roles in the conventions of the ancient world.

Third, because same-sex relationships are unproductive, Paul regarded these relationships as selfish and socially irresponsible, neglecting the obligation of procreation.

Finally, Paul regarded these relationships as 'unnatural' because they violated ancient society's understanding of the natural order, the commonly accepted synthesis of understanding one's individual disposition, larger social values, and the surrounding physical world.(pp.266-267)

He later goes on to suggest that cultural changes since New Testament times means that the moral logic underpinning Romans 1 and other biblical passages critical of homosexuality cannot be said to 'clearly and unequivocally forbid all contemporary forms of committed same-sex intimate relationships.' Such relationships, he maintains, 'were never considered by the biblical writers, which leaves us with the need to discern more clearly how the church should respond to these relationships today.' (p.277)

---

[39] Brownson notes the argument of Neil Elliott that in talking about excessive lust St. Paul may have been alluding to 'the incredible greed, violence and sexual excess of Gaius Caligula, an emperor who reigned in the period not too long before Paul wrote Romans' as part of his rhetorical strategy of emphasising the corruption of the Gentile world in order to flush out feelings of self-righteousness and judgmentalism among his readers. (pp. 156-161 referring to Neil Elliott, *The Arrogance of the Nations: Reading Romans in the Shadow of Empire*, Minneapolis: Fortress Press, 2008, pp.79ff).

Matthew Vines - Romans 1 is a narrative about honour and shame.

In *God and the Gay Christian* Vines follows Brownson in seeing Romans 1:26-27 as being about the condemnation of behaviour involving excess passion in the context of a culture based on ideas of honour and shame:

> Scholars often describe the Mediterranean societies of Paul's day as 'honor-shame' cultures. Honor and shame functioned as a social currency. But what was regarded as honorable or shameful in one culture could vary in another. As we just saw, long hair was often honorable for men in Old Testament times, but norms had changed by the time of the New Testament.
>
> A focus on honor and shame can help us confirm the reason for Paul's negative statements about same-sex behavior. As New Testament professor James Brownson has written, 'What is degrading and shameless about the behavior described in Romans 1:24-27 is that is driven by excesive, self-seeking lust, that it knows no boundaries and restraints, and that it violates established gender roles of that time and culture, understood in terms of that time and culture, understood in terms of masculine rationality and honor.' (p.113)

For Vines it is ideas of honour and shame that help us to make sense of the overall argument of Romans 1:18-32:

> Even though Romans 1:18-32 cannot be understood as a narrative about 'sameness' and 'difference,' it can be understood as a narrative about honor and shame. The English Standard Version translates Romans 1:21 as 'Although they knew God, they did not *honor* him as God.' The idol worshippers failed to give God the honor he was due, so in a stroke of poetic justice, God allowed them to dishonor themselves as the penalty for their idolatrous error. In the same way, God gave them over to all the vices in verses 28-32, which compounded their shame.

87

This focus on honour and shame helps explain the statement in Romans 1:27 that those engaged in same-sex excesses 'received in themselves the penalty for their error.' Their shameful behavior was the penalty. Male passivity, female dominance, and a total lack of self-control made same-sex behavior both the height of sexual excess and the pinnacle of dishonour for many conservative moralists in Paul's day. These factors also made same-sex relations a particularly apt illustration for Paul as he described a consequence of failing to honor God: we ourselves are given over to dishnor. (pp.113-114)

For Vines seeing Romans 1 in this way means that it is not applicable to gay Christians today:

The key point to note in this analysis, which matches what we've reviewed in this chapter, is that *none of these reasons extends to the loving committed relationships of gay Christians today*. The main argument for why Romans 1 should extend to gay Christians – anatomical complementarity – is not supported by the text itself. (p.113 italics in the original)

> **Arland Hultgren - St Paul is concerned with excessive same-gender activity between people who are naturally heterosexual.**

The American Lutheran New Testament scholar Professor Arland Hultgren argues in his 2011 commentary on Romans[40] that we cannot say that Romans 1:26-27 are about 'homosexuality' or 'homosexual behavior' because 'the concepts of 'heterosexuality,' 'homosexuality' and 'sexual orientation' were unknown in Paul's day.' (p.101) He then goes on to make four additional points.

First, Paul is not talking about people with an abiding homosexual orientation. Rather he is making:

---

[40] Arland J Hultgren, *Paul's Letter to the Romans*, Grand Rapids: Eerdmans, 2011.

...a broadside indictment of the Gentiles as a whole in a world where heterosexual persons (in modern understanding) knowingly and voluntarily exchanged their normal sexual roles for same-gender activities. (p.101)

Secondly, both the 'context and wording indicate that Paul refers to excessive public same-gender sexual activity.' (p.101)

Thirdly, in the light of the difference between what was thought 'natural' in the first century and what we now consider natural in the light of the natural and social sciences, should Paul's view of what was natural and unnatural 'be considered normative in theology and ethical discourse for all time?' (p.101)

Fourthly, any discussion of homosexuality that seeks to be faithful to Romans 1 must:

> ...pay attention to the particular behaviors that Paul refers to and ask whether and where behaviors in the contemporary world would compare to them. At that point Paul's concern and judgement can be legitimately shared. (p.101)

James Alison – St. Paul is referring to bizarre cultic activity in order to highlight his readers' judgementalism.

In his article 'But the Bible says...? A Catholic Reading of Romans 1,'[41] Dr James Alison suggests that what St. Paul is referring to in Romans 1:26-27 is not homosexuality as we know it today, but rather 'bizarre cults and frenzied sexualised rites leading to castration' such as the cults of 'Cybele, Atys or Aphrodite.' Furthermore, the point of Paul's argument in Romans 1 lies in what he goes on to say in Romans 2:1

> Therefore you have no excuse, O man, whoever you are, when you judge another; for in passing judgment upon him you

---

[41] James Alison 'But the Bible says...? Text at
http://www.safesearch.net/search?q=James+Alison+but+the+Bible+says

condemn yourself, because you, the judge, are doing the very same things.

According to Alison the effect of these words

> ....is rather similar to what would have happened if Paul had said "We all know that the gentiles do idiotic things, get involved in bizarre rites and frenzies, and guess what terrible consequences this leads to: they become *gossips*, disobedient to their parents! Behave foolishly! How unlike anyone *we* know!" and then paused for the first giggles of self-recognition to break out.

> Now of course this rhetorical device of building up his listeners for a fall, and then puncturing their balloon, wouldn't work at all if Paul were claiming that his listeners had been doing the same things as the pagans – that is the bizarre cults and frenzied sexualised rites leading to castration. His point is not that his listeners have been doing these things, but that even though they haven't, and wouldn't dream of doing them, they share in exactly the same pattern of desire, and the ordinary banal wickedness which flows from that pattern, the really serious stuff, which they have in common with the pagans who do indeed do those silly things.

Because this is the point of St. Paul's argument it follows that even if it could be shown he was referring to gay and lesbian relationships of the sort we know today:

> ... even then, the one use to which his reference could not be put, without doing serious violence to the text, is a use which legitimates any sort of judging of such people. Their presence in the text would be as illustrations for an argument of this sort: 'Yes, yes, we know that there are these people who do these silly things, but that is completely irrelevant besides the hugely significant fact that these are simply different symptoms of a profound distortion of desire which is identical in you as it is in

them, and it is you who I am trying to get through to, so don't judge them.'

> **Peta Sherlock – St. Paul is referring to heterosexuals acting from greed and lust.**

In her essay 'Reading Romans as Anglicans – Romans 1:26-27,' [42] Dr Peta Sherlock declares that those who are condemned by Paul in these verses are:

> ...heterosexual people who are acting, out of greed and lust, as if they had a homosexual orientation. He seems to have no understanding of people who are genuinely, whether by genetic make up or culture, 'naturally' homosexual. (p.41)

As she reads them, Romans 1:26-27 present a:

> ...horrific description of what happens when humans do not honour God, but 'exchange the glory of the immortal God for images resembling a mortal human being or birds or four-footed animals or reptiles' (Romans 1:23). It is about the consequences of idolatry, which Paul understands to have a strong link with sexual depravity. It says nothing about a homosexual couple in a faithful, committed and loving relationship. (p.41)

> **Alan Falconer, J Mary Henderson and Marjory A MacLean – St Paul does not describe faithful Christian couples and his argument loses its force if homosexual attraction is natural.**

Those presenting the revisionist case in the Church of Scotland report acknowledge that 'most commentators agree that these verses do refer to homosexual – including lesbian – activity, which is seen as contrary to God's will for human beings.' (p.1/71) However, as they see it, Paul's argument 'loses much of its force if same-sex attraction is, in fact,

---

[42] Peta Sherlock, 'Reading Romans as Anglicans – Romans 1:26-27,' in Wright, *Five Uneasy Pieces.*

'natural', whether to the individual as part of fallen humanity or as part of the God-given diversity of creation.' (p.1/71) Furthermore they do not think Paul's language in Romans 1:29-31 properly describes 'faithful, committed, same-sex Christian couples' and they speculate that if Paul had heard the testimony given by contemporary gay people' it is at least arguable that his response might have been similar to the Jewish Christian's astonished realisation that God's Spirit – not for the first time – was unmistakeably at work in the unlikeliest of people and places.' (p. 1/71)

> **Keith Sharpe – In Romans 1 homosexuality is not sin, but a shameful activity that is the punishment for sin. It is (wrongly) linked to idolatry, it is conflated with pederasty and the fact that it is 'unnatural' simply means it is unusual.**

In *The Gay Gospels* Sharpe acknowledges that Romans 1:26-27 'looks like an unarguable condemnation of both male and female homosexuality.' (p.44) However, he argues that it is in fact a text that presents multiple problems for those who want to use it as the basis for a condemnation of same-sex relationships as sinful.

Firstly, in Romans 1 homosexuality is not the crime, but the punishment. The crime is idolatry and homosexuality is one of the punishments which God imposes for this:

> To make this crystal clear, it may be helpful to draw an analogy with obesity. Being obese is not in itself sinful in any way. What might be regarded as sinful is not obesity but the greed and gluttony which inexorably lead to it. People who criticise very overweight individuals may think they look unsightly, unattractive or even ridiculous, but their real criticism is directed towards the individual's self-indulgent lack of restraint which caused the pounds to pile on. In an exactly similar way St Paul thinks homosexuals are shameful, even ridiculous, like a man with long hair, but the sin he is targeting is the idolatry which he believes leads to it. (pp. 45-46)

In Sharpe's view there are two major difficulties with accepting St. Paul's argument here. (a) It is at odds with Jesus' depiction 'of an endlessly forgiving and merciful God who wants only to welcome people into his kingdom of justice and compassion.' (p.46) (b) It is contrary to the facts to say that idolatry results in homosexuality:

> Whereas greed and gluttony always produce obesity by the simple laws of nature and physiology there is absolutely no corresponding connection between idolatry and homosexuality. If you eat too many calories you definitely will get fat. If you commit idolatry you will not become gay. I suspect most LGBT people would be hard put to say what idolatry is, let alone be wallowing in their enjoyment of it. The idea that their gayness is due to their worship of false gods and idols is in this sense literally meaningless. (p.47)

Secondly, In Romans 1 St. Paul does not describe homosexuality in terms of sin. He has a list of sinful acts worthy of death in Romans 1:28-32 but homosexual activity is not among them. He sees homosexuality as shameful rather than sinful:

> What he does believe is that homosexual lust brings disgrace and social embarrassment. The Greek word he uses for 'shameful' is 'aschemosyne'. Being given over to homosexual behaviour is for Paul an embarrassment or a social impropriety rather than something inherently sinful. It is like being found naked in a public situation, 'being caught with your trousers down,' as we might say nowadays. Literally it means 'not according to form,' and it is related to the English word 'scheme.' Aschemosyne is something not in the scheme of things, something which is 'bad form' as used to be said. It dishonours you, robs you of respect, brings you into contempt and ridicule, but it does not define you as evil. (pp.48-49)

Thirdly, St. Paul conflates homosexuality with pederasty. In Romans he was not thinking of 'consensual loving same sex relationships between two equal individuals' but instead mainly had in mind 'the widespread practice in Gentile societies, especially Greece and Rome, of pederasty.' (p.49) According to Sharpe:

> Such activity was broadly acceptable as customary and unexceptionable. Often this practice involved a degree of violence, coercion, or at least an absence of consent, and was not uncommonly directed against boys who would now be defined as clearly underage. These facts, of which St Paul was manifestly aware, make it even odder for modern ears to hear that he thought God deliberately caused it to happen. Again this forces us to put a question mark over the extent to which we can simply accept what St Paul believed as either correct or moral, even if we regard ourselves as Christians or followers of Jesus. These facts also imply that this Pauline text has absolutely nothing to say about the morality of consensual same sex love between adults. (p.49)

Fourthly, St. Paul did not see homosexuality as wicked because it was 'unnatural':

> The Greek phrase used by St Paul in this passage translated as 'unnatural' is 'para physin,'which although often translated as 'against nature' actually means 'beyond nature. Again we can learn a lot about what Paul had in mind by looking at where else he uses the same phrase. For instance he uses it to refer to grafting a wild branch onto a cultivated tree (a metaphor for God's plan of including gentiles in the plan of salvation for Jews). He sees this an unusual (*para physin*) because cultivated branches are usually grafted onto wild trees rather than the other way round. He naturally saw the Jews as cultivated and the Gentiles as 'wild.' This does mean of course that he sees God in this instance as acting 'unnaturally'! More importantly for the present argument, however, is that it implies homosexuality is unusual rather than wicked. (p.50)

Two final approaches to Romans 1 are offered by Adrian Thatcher and Sarah Ruden.

> **Adrian Thatcher – Romans 1 may not refer to lesbianism, describes homosexuality as shameful rather than sinful, forbids us to judge others and it based on premises Christians no longer accept.**

In *The Savage Text* Thatcher acknowledges that the traditional approach to Romans 1:26-27 has been to see these verses as teaching that 'sexual acts between people of the same sex are sinful.' However he rejects this approach for a number of reasons which echo points made by other revisionist writers on Romans whom we have looked at above.

First, we cannot be sure that Paul is referring to lesbian activity in 1:26. Secondly, the text says that male homosexual activity is shameful but not that it is sinful. Thirdly, Romans 2:1-3 forbids us from condemning the activity of anyone else. (pp.17-18) Finally, Christians today no longer accept the premises of Paul's argument:

> Paul thinks that before Christ the Gentiles were well capable of recognizing and worshipping the one true God. Forsaking Hebrew monotheism they became Gentile polytheists, making images 'like to corruptible man, and to birds, and four footed beasts, and creeping things' (Romans 1:23). But historians of religion agree that monotheism did not come first, and that Jews were not immune from polytheism themselves. 'In sum, modern people, even Christians do not believe the mythological structure that provides the logic for Paul's statements about homosexuality.'(p.19)

Thatcher also contends that since the New Testament:

> ...does not deal with contemporary cases where people of the same sex make lifelong vows of commitment to each other based on their love for each other it is disingenuous to use this

scripture or any other to proscribe same-sex marriages and civil partnerships. (p.17)

> **Sarah Ruden – St Paul is challenging prejudice against the victims of pederasty.**

Dr Sarah Ruden argues in her book *Paul Among the People*[43] that in Romans 1 Paul acts in a revolutionary way by challenging the first century cultural prejudice against the passive partner in pederastic homosexual relationships. She writes that:

> Paul could have, like generations of Greek and Roman moralistic and satirical commentators, lit into passive homosexuals, into the victims. But in Rom 1 he makes no distinction between active and passive: the whole transaction is wrong. This is crucially indicated by his use of the Greek word for 'males,' *arsenes,* for everybody; he does not use the word for 'men' as the NRSV translation would have us believe. The Classical *and* New Testament word for a socially acceptable, sexually functional man is *aner.* In traditional parlance, this could mean an active but never a passive homosexual. But Paul places on a par all the male participants in homosexual acts, emphasizing this in Romans 2:1...and clearly implying that they are *all* morally degraded and that they *all* become physically debilitated from the sex act with each other. Such effects were unheard of among the Greeks and Romans when it came to active homosexuals: these were thought only to draw their passive partner's moral and physical integrity into themselves. (pp.66-67)

Ruden sees Romans 2:1, 'in passing judgment on another you condemn yourself' applying to those who judged only passive same-sex partners and pictures Paul:

---

[43] Sarah Ruden, *Paul Among the People*, New York: Image Books, 2010.

...flushed and sweating in his rage as he writes that everyone is responsible for what pederasty has made of society: especially those who, egging one another on in an insolent, boastful clique, damage others with active sodomy and then blame then. These acts are 'the very same things' no matter who is doing what to whom. (pp. 67-68)

Ruden's conclusion is that:

> Paul's audience knew what justice was, if only through missing it. They would have been surprised to hear that justice applied to homosexuality, of all things. But many of them – salves, freedmen, the poor, the young – would have understood in the next instant. Christ, the only Son of God gave his body to save mankind. What greater contrast could there be to the tradition of using a weaker body for selfish pleasure or a power trip? Among Christians, there would have been no quibbling about what to do: no one could have imagined homosexuality's being different that it was; it would have to go. And tolerance for it did disappear from the church. (p.71)

In her view this means that Paul is nowadays ironically labelled a 'bigot' for his opposition to homosexuality when what he was doing was in fact 'challenging centuries of execrable practice in seeking a more just, more loving society.' (p.71)

Ruden doesn't make a contemporary application of her reading of Romans 1 and 2, but it would seem to leave open the possibility of a Christian recognition of a non-pederastic, non-exploitative form of same-sex relationship since this is not what Paul is critiquing.

1 Corinthians 6:9-11 and 1 Timothy 1:10

In 1 Corinthians 6:9-11 there is a vice list which includes the two terms *malakoi* and *arsenokoitai* and in 1 Timothy 1:10 there is another vice list in which the term *arsenokoitai* is used. Traditionalists have argued that in 1 Corinthians *malakoi* and *arsenokoitai* are terms for the passive and active partners in male homosexual sexual activity while in 1 Timothy *arsenokoitai* is a general term for male homosexual sexual activity. Revisionist writers have challenged this argument in various ways. As can be seen below, they have argued instead:

- That the meaning of the terms is uncertain and translations should reflect this fact
- That *malakoi* on its own refers to men who are sexually decadent, men who are effeminate, men characterised by moral weakness, the passive partners in pederasty, or male prostitutes;
- That *arsenokoitai* on its own refers to men who are pimps, men who economically exploit others by means of sex, men who engage in homosexual activity that involves adultery, men who have sex with boy prostitutes, or men involved in cultic prostitution;
- That the two terms together refer to pederasty, incest, male prostitution cultic homosexual activity and hedonistic sexual activity involving male prostitution, or the trading of boy slaves.

It has also been argued that whatever the exact translation of these terms, the other terms used in the vice lists suggest that the these terms cannot rightly be used to refer to faithful same-sex relationships today.

A feature of the revisionist discussions of 1 Corinthians 6 and I Timothy 1 is that writers who agree on their understanding of one of the two terms may disagree on their understanding of the other term. In order to reflect this, in the material below authors presenting similar arguments are grouped together, but they have not been grouped under sub-headings that would suggest that they are in complete agreement.

> **Holly Hearton - malakoi and arsenokoitai refer to decadence and pimping.**

Professor Holly Hearton's commentary on 1 Corinthians in *The Queer Bible Commentary* notes that there are two key Greek words in 1 Corinthians 6:9, *malakoi* and *arsenokoitai*. She suggests that the first of these word is a general term referring to decadent sexual behaviour and that the second refers to pimping. Her conclusion is that:

> It is important that these two words be heard in context; they should not be singled from other vices in verses 9-10, which include greed, drunkenness, thievery and idolatry. If *malakoi* is understood as decadence and *arsenokoitai* as pimping, then the entire list of vices can be seen to revolve specifically around behaviours that involve excess and exploitation, behaviours that ultimately place one's own interests at odds with God's covenant relationship with humankind. Within the context of 1 Corinthians, this vice list is framed by Paul's complaints against lawsuits between believers and those visiting prostitutes. Both of these activities fall under the heading of excess and exploitation. The list is intended to be illustrative of these moral flaws. It is not specifically directed towards homosexual activity, nor, indeed, sexual activity in general. (p.614)

> **Renato Lings - malakoi and arsenokoitai refer to moral weakness and sexual abuse or exploitation.**

Lings argues in *Love Lost in Translation* that the idea that the word *malakoi* has to do with sex is relatively recent. He maintains that in classical usage the word *malakos*, from which the plural *malakoi* is derived, originally meant 'soft' and subsequently acquired 'derogatory nuances' such as 'feeble,' 'morally weak' and 'cowardly'. In his view 'in the moral sphere discussed by Paul, the latter categories seem to match *malakoi* in 1 Corinthians 6:9.'(p.501)

He further argues that the word *arsenokoitai* 'is unlikely to allude to men involved in homoerotic relationships in general given that the usual Greek terms for two male lovers are *erastes* and *eromenos*, among others.' He holds that 'a more credible alternative is to view *arsenokoitai* as a specific reference to men who practise abusive sex or commit economic exploitation, including theft and kidnapping young people of either sex into economic slavery.' (p.519)

> **Matthew Vines - malakoi and arsenokoitai refer to moral weakness and economic exploitation involving sex.**

Vines writes in *God and the Gay Christian* that the word *malakos* literally meant 'soft' and that in moral terms 'was used to describe a lack of self-control, weakness, laziness, or cowardice.' (p.119). Most uses of the term were 'not related to behavior' and when it was it was more frequently applied 'to men who succumbed to the charms of women' rather than to the passive partners in same-sex activity.(p.120)

Turning to *arsenokoitai* he declares that if the root term *arsenokoites* referred to male same-sex behaviour at all then it possibly referred to pederasty. However, given the infrequency with which the word was used 'the most we can say with confidence is that it may refer to some kind of economic exploitation involving sexual behavior. While that may have included same-sex behavior, it would likely have been exploitative forms of it.' (pp.125-6)

For Vines the argument that when *malakos* and *arsenokoites* are put together they refer the passive and active forms of male same-sex activity 'rests on speculation' since these two words 'were never used as a pair by other ancient writers.' (p.126). Furthermore:

...even if Paul *had* intended his words to be a condemnation of both male partners in same-sex relations, the context in which he was making that statement would still differ significantly from our context today.

As we have seen, same-sex behavior in the first century was not understood to be the expression of an exclusive sexual orientation. It was understood as excess on the part of those who could easily be content with heterosexual relationships, but who went beyond them in search of more exotic pleasures. (p.126)

Dale Martin - malakoi and arsenokoitai refer to effeminacy and economic exploitation involving sex.

In *Sex and the Single Savior* Martin argues that it is 'linguistically invalid' (p.39) to try to determine the meaning of *arsenokoites*, from which *arsenokoitai* is derived, on the basis of etymology. Instead we have to look at how the word is used 'in as many different contexts as possible.' (p.39) Referring to the evidence of the *Sibylline Oracle* 2:70-77, the second century *Acts of John* and the treatise *To Autolycus* by the second century apologist Theophilus of Antioch (pp.40-42) he suggests that:

> ...a careful analysis of the actual context of the word *arsenokoites*, free from linguistically specious arguments from etymology or the word's separate parts, indicates that *arsenokoites* had a more specific meaning in Greco-Roman culture than homosexual penetration in general, a meaning that is now lost to us. It seems to have referred to some kind of economic exploitation by means of sex, perhaps, but not necessarily homosexual sex. (p.40)

On *malakos* Martin argues by contrast that that the meaning of the word is clear. It meant effeminate:

> There is no question, then, about what *malakos* referred to in the ancient world. In moral contexts it always referred either obviously or obliquely to the feminine. There is no historical reason to take *malakos* as a specific reference to the penetrated man in homosexual intercourse. It is even less defensible to narrow that reference down further to mean 'male prostitute.' The meaning of the word is clear, even if too broad to be taken

101

to refer to a single act or role. *Malakos* means 'effeminate.' (p.47)

> **Jack Rogers – malakoi means soft or effeminate and arsenokoitai means those involved in sexual exploitation.**

Rogers accepts Dale Martin's argument that we should not see *arsenokoites* as a term that simply refers to those who have sex with other men. He cites Martin's conclusion that a study of Greek writings both Christian and secular shows that the term probably refers to 'some kind of economic exploitation, probably be sexual means: rape or sex by economic coercion, prostitution, pimping or something of the sort.' (pp.70-71[44])

Rogers further argues that *malakos* literally means 'soft' and often connotes effeminacy, which in that culture was treated as a moral failing' and that the fact that in 1 Timothy 1:10 the plural of *arsenokoites, arsenokoitai* , is followed by a reference to 'slave traders, a group who exploited others, adds weight to Martin's evidence for *arsenokoitai* as sexual exploiters of some sort, since the vices in the lists were often grouped according to their similarity to other vices in the list.' (p.71)

> **James Brownson – 1 Corinthians is referring to pederasty and 1 Timothy to men who make use of boy prostitutes.**

Brownson argues in *Bible, Gender, Sexuality* that what 1 Corinthians 6:9 and 1 Timothy 1:10 are referring to is pederasty and prostitution. In relation to 1 Corinthians 6:9 he declares that 'most scholars' recognise that the combination of the words *malakoi* and *arsenokoitai*:

---

[44] Rogers is quoting D B Martin *'Arsenokoites and Malakos: Meanings and Consequences'* in R L Bawley (eds), *Biblical Ethics and Homosexuality*, Louisville: Westminster John Knox Press, 1996, p.121.

...reflects widespread assumptions throughout the ancient world about male-male homosexual activity: almost all the documents discussing male same-sex eroticism assume a distinction between active older men (commonly referred to in Greek as *erastai*) and passive younger males (commonly referred to as *eromenoi*) – in other words, the practice of pederasty. The *malakoi* ('softies') are younger passive *eromenoi*, and the *arsenokoitai* ('men bedders') are the older active *erastai*. (p.274)

In relation to 1 Timothy 1:10 he states that the list of vices it contains include three interrelated Greek terms, *pornoi*, *arsenokoitai* and *andropodistiai*. In this verse:

...we see kidnappers or slave dealers (*andropodistai*) acting as 'pimps' for their captured and castrated boys (the *pornoi*, or male prostitutes), servicing the *arsenokoitai*, the men who made use of these boy prostitutes.

As he sees it, when we take this original social context of 1 Corinthians and 1 Timothy seriously:

...we again recognise a gap between what these vice lists are rejecting and what is happening in committed same-sex relationships today. In the ancient world, these pederastic relationships were transitory rather than permanent and committed; they were driven by the desires of the older partner rather than being mutual and shared; and they were often characterized by abuse, slavery, and prostitution. One can readily agree that all sexual relationships that have these characteristics are rightly rejected by Christians, and one can still question whether committed gay and lesbian relationships should be painted with the same brush of rejection. (p.75)

Keith Sharpe - malakoi and arsenokoitai refer to pederasty

Sharpe also sees the terms *arsenokoitai* and *malakoi* as referring to pederasty. However, in line with his interpretation of the prohibitions in Leviticus as being concerned with the feminisation of Israelite males, he argues in *The Gay Gospels* that pederasty is condemned because it involves feminisation:

> The *arsenokoitai* harms the *malakoi* by corrupting him and robbing him of his manliness. The malakoi harms himself by behaving as a woman. They both deserve death, now or in the world to come. What is crucial for LGBT people today, however, is that the *arsenokoitai* and *malakoi* are not excluded by Paul because they are homosexuals. There is not even any condemnation of pederasty as a sexual act. The sole concern is that men should not be identified with the despised category of women. (p.65)

William Johnson - malakoi and arsenokoitai refer to hedonistic sexual behaviour, prostitution and slave trading.

Johnson maintains in *A Time to Embrace* that 1 Corinthians 6:9-10, and 1 Timothy 1:10 refer to hedonistic sexual behaviour, prostitution and slave trading.

On 1 Corinthians he writes:

> The linking of *arsenokoitai* and *malakoi* here suggests precisely the hedonistic sexual practices that were widespread in the Roman Empire, Such practices were almost always performed by social superiors upon social inferiors; that is, there was nothing essentially loving, exclusive or covenantal about these encounters. They were premised on Roman understandings of class and status. As I have noted in the previous chapter, a Roman citizen could sexually penetrate his wife, a woman of lower social standing, his slave, a prostitute – anyone who was his social inferior.

In specifically linking 'male prostitutes' [*malakoi*] and 'men-who-have-sex-with-men' (*arsenokoitai*) Paul is referring to the sort of male prostitution in which men who were not slaves, but free, sold themselves to other men who were seeking sexual gratification. To sell oneself in this way was considered demeaning, and in denouncing such behavior Paul was not being especially countercultural. Many Romans themselves, especially those influenced by Stoicism, had come to question such sexual hedonism and exploitation. (pp.132-133)

On 1 Timothy he declares that what is in the background is the selling of boys into sexual slavery:

Slave boys were usually captured during military campaigns, when the Romans took many prisoners of war. It was commonplace for the Romans to castrate their young male prisoners to preserve their soft features for as long as possible. If they survived this mutilation, they quickly went to market as sexual slaves. Eventually, enough Romans came to consider slave-boy castration problematic that they crafted laws banning the practice, though it persisted despite these efforts. This fact alone testifies to the lucrative nature of slave-boy castration and thus the difficulty of stamping it out. This is almost certainly the situation which prompted 1 Timothy to place in the very same phrase 'fornicators, men-who-have-sex-with-men, and slave traders. This hardly the kind of behavior involved in exclusively committed same-gender love. (p.133)

> **Robert Geiss – arsenokoitai probably refers to cultic prostitution while malakos means effeminate.**

In his book *Same Sex in Scripture*[45] Dr Robert Geiss argues that the background to the use of the term *arsenokoitai* in 1 Corinthians 6:9 and 1 Timothy 1:10 probably lies in the condemnation in the Old Testament

---

[45] Robert Geiss , *Same-Sex in Scripture*, Lanham: University Press of America, 2009.

of the cultic prostitutes, or *qedishism,* referred to in Deuteronomy 23:17-18.

> Given the passages to which arsenokoitai led us we have been able to postulate a background to the term of cultic prostitution, pagan idolatry, where anal penetration was for the purpose of deific appeasement. That would automatically exclude a blanket condemnation of same-sex since none of these practices accompany every situation of same-sex behaviour. While a process of inference does allow as reasonable that *arsenokoitai* in Corinthians refers to the *qedishim* of Old Testament ignominy, we cannot say so with certainty. We do know quite categorically, however, that it does not refer to any behavior that the civilized West today knows as same-sex. Fertility goddesses have long gone the way of other myths and dehumanizing superstitions. (p.32)

Geiss also argues that the term *malakos* means 'effeminate' rather that 'homosexual' or 'pervert' and that:

> ...since we do not know what *arsenokoitai* actually means, to claim *malakos,* as meaning 'effeminate,' meant in the Corinthians passage the passive partner in a male-male act is to take one obscure term and seek to clarify another by it. Darkness, however, does not make anything brighter. (p.33)

Steve Schuh - malakoi and arsenokoitai refer to homosexual acts in the context of pagan religion

In 'Challenging conventional wisdom' Schuh also argues that pagan religious practice involving homosexual prostitution is what lies behind the vice list in 1 Corinthians:

> The vice list – which catalogues, in order, prostitutes, idol worshippers, adulterers, *malakoi* and *arsenokoitai* – is immediately followed by a discussion about prostitution that involves temple imagery and allusions to idol foods. Paul

contrasts union with Christ to union with a prostitute, perhaps alluding to the 'sacred marriage' rites of fertility cults. The immediate juxtaposition of *malakoi* and *arsenokoitai* with prostitutes and idolaters in the text – and the likely origin of the vocabulary itself in the Levitical prohibitions – only reinforces this idea and is consistent with the Old Testament cultural context for homosexual acts as expressions of pagan religion. (p.8)

> **Jay Michaelson - in 1 Corinthians the terms malakoi and arsenokoitai refer to cultic homosexual prostitution, and in 1 Timothy arsenokoitai refers to homosexual activity involving adultery.**

In *God vs. Gay?* Michaelson holds that the meanings of the terms *malakoi* and *arsenokoitai* remain unclear. However, he says, if we ask what Paul is writing about in 1 Corinthians 6:9-11 the answer is that he is writing about the Corinthians propensity to settle their disputes in the secular courts. In this context:

> He's critiquing an entire society, and 'shaming' Christians for continuing to associate with it. Paul specifically mentions 'idolaters' in between *pornos* (sexually immoral) and *moichos* (adulterers), *malakoi* and *arsenokoitai*. Is this just an accident? Surely not. Surely what Paul is talking about is an entire 'pagan' culture in which idolatry and lasciviousness went hand in hand. Paul was painting, with a broad brush, a society of depravity. People sinned sexually in every possible configuration: adultery, general immorality, general looseness of morals, and some kind of cultic homosexuality or prostitution as well. Just as in Romans, where these transgressions were the signs of a society that had turned away from God, here they are listed as signs of a society whose judges are not to be trusted and whose values are not to be emulated. (p.89)

In this 'litany of lusts,' writes Michaelson:

> ...we do not see anything resembling stable, sanctified same-sex relationships. Here the situation is similar to that of the Sodom story. Whoever Paul is describing, they are lust-filled, immoral people who have turned their backs on God. Now, is that true of lesbians and gays today? Not all of them. Therefore, they can't possibly accord with these obscure Greek terms. (p.91)

On 1 Timothy 1:10 Michaelson claims that the crucial thing is the juxtaposition between *arsenokoitai* and adulterers (*moichos*). In his view this means that the verse is not really talking about homosexuality but rather adultery:

> As in the language of Romans about being 'given over to shameful lusts,' the parallel structure between *arsenokoitai* and *moichos* suggests that it is extramarital lust that is being condemned here. Just as an adulterer is not a 'heterosexual' but rather someone who violates the sanctity of marriage by having sex with a woman, so too *arsenokoitai* are not 'homosexuals' but those who violate the sanctity of marriage by having sex with a man. The issue is less the physical act itself than the context: sex outside of marriage. (p.91)

Alan Cadwallader - malakoi and arsenokoitai refer to incest.

Dr Alan Cadwallader contends in his article 'Keeping Lists or Embracing Freedom'[46] that the terms *malakoi* and *arsenokoitai* in 1 Corinthians 6:9 refer to the incest described in 1 Corinthians 5:1. This is because 'the wife of a man's father is, in this sense, an extension of the father' and having sex with her therefore comes under the condemnation of same-sex relations in Leviticus 18 to which *arsenokoitai* refers. Such behaviour also involves an attack on the manliness of the father, which is why the term *malakoi* is used. (pp.58-60)

---

[46] Alan Cadwallader, 'Keeping Lists or Embracing Freedom: 1 Corinthians 6:9-10, in Context,' in Wright, *Five Uneasy Pieces*.

What this means, declares Cadwallader, is that the vice list in 1 Corinthians 6:9-10, has:

> ...no pertinence to contemporary definitions and debates about homosexuality in society and the Christian community, even at the level of the familiar argument about cultural differentiation between male-to-male sexual expression in the ancient world and today's expression of same-sex love and fidelity. The vice list is a rhetorical device in the larger unit of chapters 5 and 6 that refers to the specific offences of incest. [47]

David Gushee - the uncertainity about the meaning of the terms should have been acknowledged in English translations.

Gushee emphasises what he sees as the uncertainty about the meaning of *arsenokoitai* and *malakoi* and the damage done by contemporary English translations:

> How might the history of Christian treatment of gays and lesbians have been different if *arsenokoitai* had been translated 'sex traffickers' or 'sexual exploiters' or 'rapists' or 'sexual predators' or 'pimps'? Such translations are plausible, even if not the majority scholarly reconstruction at this time. And they are at least as adequate, or inadequate, as homosexual – a term from our culture with a range of meanings including sexual orientation, identity and activity – not a word from Paul's world.

> It might have been nice if in our English Bibles the genuine uncertainty about how to translate Paul's neologism *arsenokoitai*, or the two words *malakoi* and *arsenokoitai* together, at least had been mentioned in a footnote.

> But alas...most of the translations we got, read as if every homosexual person was being condemned - to eternal fire. This

---

[47] Ibid, pp.63-64.

overly confident translation decision then shadowed the lives of all LGBT people, most sadly gay and lesbian adolescents rejected by their mothers and fathers (and pastors and youth ministers) as hell-bound perverts.

Very high-level scholarly uncertainty about the meaning and translation of these two Greek words, together with profound cultural and linguistic differences, undermines claims to conclusiveness of *malako*i and *arsenokoitai* for resolving the LGBT issue.

I deeply lament the damage done by certain questionable and sometimes crudely derogatory Bible translations in the lives of vulnerable people made in God's image. (pp.79-80)

> **Alan Falconer, J Mary Henderson and Marjory A MacLean – we have to take the other terms in the passages into account.**

Finally, those presenting the revisionist case in the Church of Scotland report declare that we have to take into account the other terms used in the lists of offenders in these passages when interpreting the significance of the terms *malakoi* and *arsenokoitai* for today. They ask whether, regardless of how we translate these terms, we can:

> ...honestly put loving, faithful, committed same-sex partners, one or both of whom may have responded to a call to Christian ministry, in the same category as 'idolaters, adulterers, thieves, drunkards, murderers, slave traders and perjurers'? (p.1/69)

Jude 7

Jude 7 declares that 'Sodom and Gomorrah and the surrounding cities' indulged in 'unnatural lust' and for this reason were punished with 'eternal fire.' 'Unnatural lust' has traditionally been seen as a reference to the homosexual lust displayed by the inhabitants of Sodom in Genesis 19. However, revisionist writers have questioned whether 'unnatural lust' is a reference to homosexuality. The majority view amongst revisionist scholars is that Jude 7 refers instead to the desire for sex with angels. However, there are also revisionist writers who feel less confident that Jude 7 should be interpreted in this way. As we shall see below, the revisionist contributors to the Church of Scotland report think the matter is unclear whilst Jay Michaelson argues that Jude is concerned with combatting heretical teachers rather than condemning homosexuality, but is silent about the precise nature of the sexual immorality to which Jude 7 refers.

The desire for sex with angels

James Brownson

Brownson writes in *Bible, Gender, Sexuality* that in Jude 7 Sodom and Gomorrah 'serve as an example of 'unnatural lust' because of the desire of the residents for the angelic visitors.' However, 'the language used in Jude cannot be understood to focus on same-sex eroticism.' (p.269)

Jack Rogers

In *Jesus, the Bible and Homosexuality* Rogers criticises the claim by the traditionalist writer Thomas Schmidt that Jude is referring to homosexuality. In Rogers' view Jude 6 and 7 contain 'a lot of discussion about sex between humans and angels (angels with human women, and human men with male angels) that is labelled as 'sexual immorality' and 'unnatural lust.' However, 'for Schmidt, or anyone else, to make the leap that this text somehow condemns present day Christians who are homosexual strikes me as bizarre.' (p.72)

Michael Carden

Carden argues that Jude uses the consequences of the pursuit of sex with angels by the inhabitants of Sodom as a warning against the sexual libertines who are disrupting the community to which he is writing. He writes in his book *Sodomy* that:

Jude 7 uses Sodom's destruction to warn the community against following the libertine ecstatics. Jude accuses the Sodomites of sexual immorality and pursuing 'other flesh,' *heteras sarkos* (which the NRSV has translated as 'unnatural lust'). The preceding v. 6 also refers to the angels of Genesis 6 'did not keep their own position but left their proper dwelling and were punished.' The Sodomites are compared with them, and it would appear that both are used as examples of any who 'defile the flesh, reject authority, and slander the glorious ones' (Jude 8). Certainly both the Sodomites and the angels rejected authority and defiled their flesh by pursuing sexual unions across the angelic/human barrier. But, as in the *Testaments* and *Jubilees*, the important referent for Jude is the disruptive lawlessness of *porneia* arising from following the libertines. Authority and community cohesion are the main issues here. The libertines are dividing the community and they preach nothing but surrender to *porneia*. *Porneia* breaks down community and leads to disastrous consequences as exemplified by the sons of god in Genesis 6 and Sodom and Gomorrah in Genesis 19. However, there is nothing in this reading that requires a predominantly homosexual understanding of Sodom and its sin. (p.59)

William Countryman

In his commentary on Jude in *The Queer Bible Commentary*, Professor William Countryman notes that Jude 7 literally talks about 'going after strange flesh' and declares that this 'is hardly a natural idiom for same-gender sexual intercourse.' As he sees it, both the syntax of Jude 7 and the wider argument in Jude 7-8 make it clear that Jude 7 is not about homosexuality but the desire to have sex with angels:

> Jude traces a parallel between the angels of verse 6, who had intercourse with human women and were therefore condemned to eternal punishment, and the people of Sodom and Gomorrah, who attempted to have forcible sex with the angelic visitors.

While most modern readers of Genesis 19 probably assume that the people of Sodom did not recognize the Angelic nature of the two visitors, the Genesis account does not in fact rule out Jude's interpretation.(p.749)

Countryman goes on to argue that the subject of sexual relations with angels also 'pervades the rest of the letter.' Jude, he says, describes the new teachers he is criticising 'as defiling the flesh 'in the same way' as the angels who left their place and the people of Sodom and Gomorrah (v.8), thus underlining his claim that the 'intruders' stand in the same tradition of seeking sexual intercourse with angels.' Furthermore the references in v8 to dreaming and the defiling of the flesh:

> ....suggest a religious praxis that involved visions or dreams of intercourse with angelic beings, presumably resulting in ejaculation, which would cause impurity (cf Lev.15:16-18). More importantly, however, the teachers understood the practice to demonstrate their power to command sexual intercourse with an angelic being. This would be an act of domination and would therefore defame the latter. (p. 750)

Matthew Vines

Vines notes in God and the Gay Christian that Jude 7 is cited by Christians who oppose same-sex relationships 'as a potential reference to same-sex behavior.' However, he says:

> ...the Greek phrase used in Jude 7 is *sarkos heteras* – literally other or 'different flesh.' *Hetero*, of course, is the prefix for words like *hetero*sexuality, not homosexuality. Far from arguing that the men of Sodom pursued flesh too similar to their own, Jude indicts them for pursuing flesh that was too different.

> In fact the phrase 'strange flesh' likely refers to the attempted rape of angels instead of humans. Jude 6 supports that connection by comparing Sodom's transgression with the unusual sins described in Genesis 6. In that chapter 'sons of God'

(interpreted by many to be angels) mated with human women, arousing God's ire before the flood. Jude compares the stories because the men of Sodom likewise pursued sexual contact with angels. (p.69)

Adrian Thatcher

In *The Savage Text* Thatcher contends that Jude 'condemns promiscuous sexual relations between straight and same-sex people' on the basis of talking about angels who desire to have sex with human beings:

> There are randy angels who fancy earthly women. These 'sons of God saw the daughters of men that they were fair; and they took them wives of all which they chose' (Genesis 6:2). They gave birth to a race of giants, and 'it repented the LORD that he had made man on the earth, and it grieved him at his heart' (6:6). According to the writer of Jude the sin of the randy angels was that they 'kept not their first estate' (6), that is, they did not respect the social order which placed them above men and women. The angels went 'after strange flesh' (7). That too constitutes the wrongness of same sex relations. They are strange and contradict the patriarchal order. (p.23)

According to Thatcher, this sort of argument against homosexuality is an embarrassment to thoughtful Christians today:

> Is it not truly astonishing that political, moral, and religious censure can be brought to bear on the basis of such 'evidence'? We do not inhabit the thought world where angels drop in for dinner, or get hassled by gangs of predatory men, or eye up nubile earthly women and have sex with them. (p.23)

Lewis Donelson

In his 2010 commentary on 1 and 2 Peter and Jude. [48] Professor Lewis R Donelson supports a revisionist reading of Jude, declaring that 'the sexual sin of the cities is not homosexuality.' In his view:

> Neither the syntax of going after 'the flesh of other' nor the comparison with the sins of the angels suggest homosexuality. In place here is the tradition that the visitors to Sodom and Gomorrah were angels. Just as the angels in verse 6 desired the flesh of human women, the men of Sodom and Gomorrah in verse 7 desire the flesh of angels. The problem then is sexual disorder. (p.180)

The precise nature of the 'unnatural lust' is unclear - Alan Falconer, J Mary Henderson and Marjory A MacLean

Those presenting the revisionist case in the Church of Scotland report write that 'Jude's real concern is the false teachers who have infiltrated the Church community, but he emphasises God's condemnation of them by citing those angels who did not keep to their own place in heaven, and the men of Sodom who expressed lust for Lot's male angelic visitors.' They say 'it is not entirely clear whether their lust was 'unnatural' because the visitors were male, or because they were angels, or both.' (p.1/69)

Jude 7 is about heretical teaching rather than homosexuality - Jay Michaelson

Michaelson argues in *God vs. Gay?* that Jude is concerned about heretical teachers advocating sexual license rather than about homosexuality. However, as noted above, he is silent about the precise nature of the sexual immorality referred to in Jude 7:

---

[48] Lewis R Donelson, *1 and 2 Peter and Jude*, Louisville: Westminster John Knox Press, 2010.

Jude, writing against 'ungodly people, who pervert the grace of our God into a license for immorality and deny Jesus Christ our only Sovereign and Lord,' recites several examples of Divine punishment, and then says: 'In a similar way, Sodom and Gomorrah and the surrounding towns gave themselves up to sexual immorality and perversion. They serve as an example of those who suffer the punishment of eternal fire' (Jude 7). That's it – and since Jude's homiletical purpose is to preach against heretics, he is obviously not talking about homosexuality, but rather the heretical view that the coming of Christ had obviated the need to obey the Lord (This is similar to other early Christian texts that link Sodom with various types of sexual misconduct, such as angels having sex with humans). To twist this linkage of Sodom and immorality into a condemnation of homosexuality simply doesn't make sense. (pp.70-71)

Chapter 4

Jesus' teaching and practice (I)

There is no single revisionist approach to what the Gospels have to say about the life and ministry of Jesus in relation to same-sex relationships. Different writers have emphasised different aspects of his life and ministry such as his silence about homosexuality, the way he welcomed everyone, the way he emphasised people's interior motives rather than their external actions, his teaching about the inclusion of eunuchs in the kingdom of God and his healing of the centurion's servant (which is interpreted as Jesus' acceptance of a gay relationship). Some writers have also argue that the authority given by Jesus to the Church to determine its own internal discipline under the guidance of the Spirit means that the Church is free to decide now to fully accept gay and lesbian people even though it has not done this in the past in the same way that Early Church was free to decide to fully accept Gentiles alongside Jews.

In this chapter we shall look at the variety of approaches taken by revisionist writers. At the end of the chapter we shall also look at two writers who have explored the idea of a 'queer' Jesus, that is to say, a Jesus who can be identified with the experiences of gay and lesbian people and other marginalised groups within society.

> **Arnold Browne – rather than speculating about Jesus' interpretation of the Old Testament laws about sexuality we should accept that our priority should be faithfulness to Jesus' call to share his life and destiny, a call which is more challenging than obedience to a set of rules.**

In his essay 'The Call of Christ' in *An acceptable Sacrifice?*, Dr Arnold Browne suggests that to ask whether Jesus took a strict or lenient view of the Old Testament law concerning homosexuality is to ask the wrong question. He argues that the issue we face when thinking about how Jesus' life and teaching relates to the debate about sexuality:

117

...is not simply a matter of deciding whether Jesus was more rigorous or more tolerant than his Jewish contemporaries in his interpretation of the laws regulating sexuality. We cannot use either a supposed strictness or an assumed leniency to fill in the gaps when we find that he is silent about same-sex relationships. (p.37)

In Browne's view, rather than try to fill in the gaps in the gospel record what we should do instead is notice that Jesus' ministry had a different focus.

Jesus priority is to call individuals into a community that shares his life and destiny, proclaiming the coming of the kingdom of God in words and actions (see especially Matthew 10:5-15; Mark 6:6-13, Luke 9:1-6). The demands of this call are more challenging than keeping any system of rules. They require more than the observance of the law of Moses, as the rich young man realized when he went away grieving, for he had many possessions (Matthew 19:22; Mark 10:22; see also Luke 18:23). (p.38)

As Browne sees it:

This priority of the call to hear and live the good news of the coming kingdom of God is expressed in a number of encounters where entering into a relationship with Jesus takes precedence over any application of the Law of Moses. For example, the woman suffering from haemorrhage is not condemned for making Jesus unclean by her touch (see Leviticus 15:19-30), but is told by him, 'Daughter your faith has made you well; go in peace and be healed of your disease' (Mark 5:34; see also Matthew 9:22; Luke 8:40). In Luke 7:36-50 Jesus welcomes the kissing and anointing of his feet by 'a woman in the city, who was a sinner.' A strict interpretation of Leviticus 5:1-5 indicates a risk of defilement upon even being touched by a sinner. This is why Jesus' host says to himself, 'if this man were a prophet, he would have known who and what kind of woman this is who is touching him – that she is a sinner.' But Jesus says to him 'her sins, which were many, have been forgiven; hence she has shown great love.' In Mark 1:40-44 (see also Matthew 8:1-4; Luke 5:12-16) the same sense of priority is seen in Jesus' touching a leper while he is still unclean (see Leviticus 13-14). Jesus himself says to the leper 'Be made clean,' even though, according to the law, it is the prerogative of the priest to pronounce a leper clean. Jesus then sends the cleansed leper to the priest to make his legal offering 'as a testimony to them.' In this way the man he has healed becomes a witness to the precedence of Jesus' saving word over any application of the law. (pp.38-39)

The significance of these encounters is that they clearly express:

...Jesus' sense of the inadequacy of the regulations of the law. His transgression of its boundaries between the clean and the unclean clearly horrified some of his contemporaries. However, even the law of Moses must give way to the prior claims of Jesus' call to respond to his proclamation of the coming kingdom of God. Our fundamental question should not be about his severity or tolerance as a legal interpreter. Our concern should be our faithfulness to his call to share his life and destiny. (p.39)

Browne's conclusion is that:

The call to follow Christ before all other considerations led early Christians like St Paul to see all rules, even the law of Moses, even the Ten Commandments, as being of secondary importance. So too for us wrestling with the issues of same-sex relationships. Our primary concern should be our faithfulness to Jesus call to share his life and destiny rather than the adoption of either a supposed strictness or an assumed leniency to fill in the gaps when we find that he is silent about same-sex

119

relationships. Through the personal encounters with our Lord familiar to us from the Gospels, we have a powerful expression of Jesus' sense of the inadequacy of the regulations of the law. His call on our lives is more profound and challenging than the keeping of any system of rules – as the diversity of interpretation within the New Testament, in the light of different circumstances demonstrates. As we respond to the experience and lives of fellow disciples, brothers and sisters in Christ, who are gay, it is his voice to which we must be attentive. (p.45)

Jack Rogers – Jesus welcomed everyone.

Rogers highlights the way in which Jesus welcomed everyone regardless of who they were. He writes in *Jesus, the Bible and Homosexuality*:

> Jesus welcomed every kind of person into God's community – especially the outcast, the alien, the marginalized, the forgotten, and the foreigner. Reading the Bible through the lens of Jesus' redemptive life and ministry we see over and over again, God's radically inclusive grace that welcomes all who have faith. (p.128)

He cites three texts as examples of the way in which 'Jesus' teachings illuminate God's extravagant welcome,' (p.128) the parable of the Good Samaritan in Luke 10:25-37, Jesus comments on different kinds of eunuchs in Matthew 19:10-12 and the story of Philip and the Ethiopian eunuch in Acts 8:26-39. What he sees in all these passages is a call to welcome and accept those who are different, including those who belong to sexual minorities:

> Look what Jesus does in each of the three passages. In Luke 10:25-37, Jesus is asked a legalistic question about differing interpretations of the holiness code and he immediately expands the circle of those who are our neighbors to include the Samaritan – a hated, alien, outcast. In Matthew 19:10-12, Jesus

120

is asked a question about laws concerning heterosexual marriage, and he immediately broadens the conversation to include sexual minorities. In Acts 8:26-39, the Holy Spirit, the Spirit of Christ, intercedes three times to guide Philip to reach out to a black, African, Gentile eunuch so that he too could be included! In each case, the formerly marginalized are welcomed and honored just as they are. That is the gospel message. That is Jesus' call to us – to love God with all our heart, soul, strength and mind, and to love our neighbor as ourself.

Jesus is the center of Scripture. It is to Christ that the church witnesses. Jesus taught that to love God and love our neighbor is the heart of the gospel. Jesus welcomed society's outcasts. He reached out to women, children, people of all races and ethnicities, the poor, the disabled, the sick, Gentiles, and, yes, sexual minorities. When we read the Bible through the lens of Jesus' redemptive life and ministry, we can see that both the Old and New Testaments command us to accept those different from ourselves. (p.135)

Keith Sharpe – the story of the healing of the centurion's servant shows that Jesus commended the faith of someone he knew was in a sexually active gay relationship.

In *The Gay Gospels* Sharpe highlights the significance of the story of the healing of the centurion's servant recorded in Matthew 8:5-13 and Luke 7:1-10.

He claims that the word *pais* (RSV 'servant') used in Matthew 8:6 'normally refers to someone young and only by way of either endearment or condescension to an adult' and that it could also be used 'for the boy slaves who were kept for sexual purposes, a practice not only common but one also regarded as normal amongst Romans.'(p121) He also argues that the word *'entimos'* (RSV 'dear') used in Luke 7:2 'implies that the boy was very dear to the centurion, that there was a really close emotional bond between them.' (p.121)

121

and that the word *'parakaloon'* (RSV "beseeching him') used in in Matthew 8:5 'betokens a real desperation that anybody watching life painfully flowing out of a lover would feel. The most probable answer is that the boy was a sexual slave but the centurion had grown very fond of him.' (p.121)

Sharpe's overall conclusion is that:

> This was to all intents and purposes a same sex loving relationship. It might have started in the exploitation of a slave but had apparently grown into a reciprocal relationship of love, care and concern. It may well be that the centurion was actually gay, in the sense of having a fixed sexual orientation which meant he would fall in love with males rather than females. (pp.121-122)

In Sharpe's view Jesus must have known about the nature of the relationship. 'If you believe Jesus was the Son of God it is difficult to believe also that he was naïve or stupid.' (p.122)

Sharpe follows the work of Theodore Jennings in his 2003 book *The Man Jesus Loved* [49] by arguing that in this story Jesus extends the kingdom's welcome to 'disreputable Gentiles' in line with Matthew 21:32 which talks about tax collectors and prostitutes entering into the kingdom of heaven before the Jewish chief priests and elders:

> The (Gentile) gay centurion combines in one person the distinctive characteristics of the tax collector (servant of the Gentile Roman oppressor) and the prostitute (he is a pederast and sexually disreputable from a Jewish point of view). What the gay centurion does is very courageous. In his desperate love he risks rejection and ridicule to try to get help for his boyfriend from a most unlikely source. When Jesus commends him for his 'faith' he does not mean a set of codified catechistic ideas the centurion has learned and memorised but rather: *The loving*

---

[49] Theodore Jennings, *The Man Jesus Loved*, Cleveland, The Pilgrim Press, 2003.

concern that draws one to take risks, to become vulnerable in hope, to reach out in yearning for well-being, to refuse to give disease or madness or paralysis the last word, to suppose that divine power is not on the side of calamity but on the side of wholeness: Jesus calls this outlook faith.

This is why the gay centurion will go to heaven and why those who obsess about mere legal compliance, ritual cleanliness, doctrinal orthodoxy and moral rectitude will not. (p.123 quoting Jennings p. 143)

> **Jay Michaelson – Jesus' silence about homosexuality indicate that the Old Testament prohibitions have been superseded and his healing of the centurion's servant his attitude to 'family values' and his teaching about eunuchs constitute a clear message of radical inclusion.**

Michaelson begins his chapter on the Gospels in *God vs. Gay?* by noting that Jesus says nothing about homosexuality. For him this silence is highly significant.

> We cannot simply pass over this silence, or attribute it, as some have done, to a tacit acceptance of the Old Testament's existing rules. Jesus wasn't tacit about the values that mattered most. If regulation of homosexual behaviour was one of them, the Gospels would not be silent. On the contrary, the silence equals supersession. The Old Testament's proscriptions on male anal sex are connected to prohibitions on idolatry; they are about ritual purity, not ethical law. For Christians, the distinction is central. While the Hebrew Bible remains authoritative for moral teachings, it is not binding on Christians for ritual ones – if it were, Christians would have to avoid shrimp and lobster, wear fringed garments, and perhaps offer sacrifices instead of hymns. (p.74)

As well as noting the significance of Jesus' silence, Michaelson also notes the significance of Jesus' healing of the centurion's servant, his general stance towards 'family values' and his attitude towards eunuchs.

On the first of these, Michaelson declares that the story has an 'unmistakeable same-sex subtext.' In his view:

> ...the relationship between a centurion and his favored servant is assumed to be a romantic one. The centurion's servant is a *pais*, a boy companion, not a *doulos*, a mere slave. And it was common practice for Roman centurions to have younger male servants who acted as concubines as well. (p.75)

This means that 'Jesus is being asked to heal not just the centurion's servant, but also his lover' and as Michaelson sees it:

> In addition to Jesus' silence on homosexuality in general, it speaks volumes that he did not hesitate to heal a Roman's likely same-sex lover. Like his willingness to include former prostitutes in his close circle, Jesus' engagement with those whose conduct might offend sexual mores even today is a statement of radical inclusion and of his priorities for the spiritual life. (p.75)

On the second, he declares that we need to remember that:

> ...Jesus and the apostles would, by the standards of their society, themselves be considered quite 'queer,' not in a sexual sense, but in terms of gender roles and societal expectations. Think about it: this was someone who told people leave their parents and follow him (Luke 14:16) to reject societal expectations of familial life and devote oneself to a different kind of community, a 'family' marked by love and spiritual fellowship (Matthew 12:50). This is a savior who lived his life on the margins, and who deliberately flouted the conventions of his day. Jesus was a boundary crosser. He violated Israelite purity codes, accepted a former prostitute into his inner circle, spoke with women when

others did not (John 4:27), and preached that precisely those who were most oppressed were most beloved of God. (p.76)

On the third, he suggests that the 'eunuchs from birth' referred to in Matthew 19:12 might mean 'men who are congenitally not attracted to women – people we might today call homosexual.' Even if this is not the case, he says:

> ...it is striking that Jesus specifically recognizes, and does not judge, the presence of sexual/gender diversity among people. Some people are eunuchs, of whatever type, and they are able to refrain from marriage. Others are not, and they are permitted to marry, though it is still better not to do so: 'The one who can accept [celibacy] should accept it' (Matthew 19:12). As in the story of the Ethiopian eunuch in Acts 8:26-40, God's emissary does not withhold the gospel from the gender-variant person who desires to hear it. (pp.76-77)

Michaelson's concluding observation is that:

> It would have been understandable, and perhaps more appropriate, for a Jewish teacher in occupied Palestine to emphasize ritual purity and conventional family structures. He could easily have rejected the centurion's probably sexual companion, not to mention Mary Magdalene; no one would have been surprised. Whatever Paul or the priestly writer of Leviticus has to say, let's remember that in addition to Jesus' silence on homosexuality, his actions send a clear, radical message of inclusion. (p.77)

> **William Johnson – Jesus' teaching about eunuchs and his healing of the centurion's servant invite the Church to move beyond legalism to welcome gay and lesbian people and the power of the keys given to the Church means that it has the authority to do so.**

In *A Time to Embrace* Johnson also emphasizes the significance of Jesus words about eunuchs and his healing of the centurion's servant. He begins his comments by asking 'How are we to square the laxity with which today's churches treat Jesus' teachings on divorce with the strictness the church applies to gays and lesbians, a subject about which Jesus never said a word?'(p.139)

'If anything,' writes Johnson, 'Jesus' explicit teachings should invite us to push beyond legalisms in dealing with gay and lesbian people.' This is because 'in all his dealings Jesus pushed beyond the surface in order to embrace the humanity of each person whom he encountered,' (p.139), something that is made clear in his comments on eunuchs in Matthew 19:11-12 that follow on from his teaching on divorce.

Johnson argues that at one level Jesus' comments about eunuchs are:

> ...merely a statement of the degree of religious devotion demanded by Jesus. Some (though not all) are called to put aside sexual relations for the sake of following God's reign. To this extent, it is a statement of ethical rigor. (p.140)

However, he says, there is something more going on in this statement.

First of all, according to Jewish law:

> ....a eunuch was a sexually nonconforming person. In the conventions of the day, a eunuch was a person who was neither male nor female and thus was excluded from the 'male and female' community of Genesis. Because of this perceived lack of purity, such a person was barred from the religious assembly (Deuteronomy 23:1; Leviticus 21:20). (p.140)

126

Jesus, however, speaks:

> ...of these sexually nonconforming persons in a remarkable way. Not only does he defy convention by including them within the religious community; he also considers them a symbol of the highest and best devotion that individuals in that community could achieve. (p.140)

Second, Jesus' words implicitly fulfil the promise made in Isaiah 56:4-5 that if eunuchs 'hold fast to the covenant they will be given a name that will never be cut off.' This promise, suggests Johnson, forms part of the background of the story of Philip and the Ethiopian eunuch in Acts 8. In this story the eunuch asks Philip if there is anything to prevent him from being baptized:

> The answer is, that under a strict reading of the law, there is everything to prevent his baptism: his nonconforming sexuality bars him from the covenant. But under the new dispensation of the Spirit, this man's sexuality and his personhood are able to be blessed. If gays and lesbians hold fast to the covenant today, are we willing to stand with Isaiah in promising that they will not be cut off from their community?' (p.141)

According to Johnson, a further instance where 'Jesus pushes the envelope regarding Jewish sexual mores' is Matthew 8:5-13. Like Sharpe and Michaelson, Johnson suggests that the centurion's servant 'may not have been not only a slave but more specifically a sex slave'. Johnson comments that:

> We cannot know for sure what the nature of the centurion's relationship with his slave was, and it does not matter for the purposes of the argument. What matters is that Jesus does not rebuke the centurion, either for having a slave or for how he treated the slave. This is astonishing in itself. Instead, Jesus' focus is on something else altogether: he praises this pagan centurion's faith and uses it as an object lesson for the ways of the 'kingdom.' (p.141)

This shows, says Johnson, 'that belonging to the covenant is about more than conforming to social conventions –even to sexual conventions. It is about allegiance to God and the people of God.'(p.142)

Johnson further argues that Jesus call in the Sermon on the Mount for the disciples to 'do' and 'teach' the commandments of the Old Testament law in the light of God's coming kingdom (Matthew 5:19) is directly relevant to the question of 'ethics for gay and lesbian Christians.' This is because:

> The dynamism in the life lived before the biblical text means that the church is empowered to exercise a sanctified discretion in ordering its corporate life. Having been given the 'keys to the kingdom' means that the church is empowered to exercise a sanctified discretion in ordering its corporate life. Having been given the 'the keys to the kingdom' the church is empowered to judge ethical cases with wisdom as they arise. They are encouraged to make decisions with 'binding' and loosing (*luo*) effects in the community. (p.142)

The Church made this sort of decision in the first century when it decided to admit Gentiles without requiring that they first become Jews and in making a decision today about gay and lesbian people it 'makes eminent sense' for the Church to ask 'what would Jesus do?':

> Do we really believe that Jesus would condemn gay couples who are sincerely seeking to live a life committed to one another? After all, Jesus was the one who taught his followers that the promises of Scripture were being brought to completion in his own life and ministry, and he also admonished them to bring the law to completion in their own lives by loving their neighbors (Matthew 5:43-45). (p.143)

> **Tobias Haller – Jesus said nothing about same-sex relationships. He was interested in internal motives rather than external activity and the stories of Jesus' anointing by the women in the house of Simon the Pharisee and his encounter with the Canaanite women with the sick daughter show that Christians should not spend their time worrying about the sins of others but should accept that Jesus welcomes all into the kingdom.**

Haller also focusses on the question 'what would Jesus do?' He argues in *Reasonable and Holy* that in seeking an answer to this question we must acknowledge that Jesus said nothing about explicit same-sex relationships. Criticising the work of Gagnon he argues that:

> ...the assertion that *porneia* was understood to include male-male sexual intercourse, or that references to Sodom or *abomination* or *dogs* must be similarly understood – or was so understood by Jesus and the apostolic church - do not stand up to close scrutiny. (p.134)

In the absence of any explicit evidence, says Haller, we have to look for guidance to the way in which Jesus approached other moral issues. When we do this, we find that Jesus' emphasis was on internal motive rather than external activity, as shown by his statement on ritual washing in Mark 7:1-23:

> Morality, he says, is not about what goes into one from the outside, but about what comes out of one, from the heart. In this, Jesus is advocating an ethic of disposition or intent, as opposed to an ethic based primarily upon a list of externally exercised do's and don'ts, which finds its most primitive form in moralities based on taboo and purity. (p.137)

We also find that in his teaching on the 'golden rule' Jesus 'refines the specifics of the Decalogue down to the pure gold of love for God and neighbor, with the subjective touchstone of doing as one would be done by' and that in his teaching on the Sabbath Jesus emphasises that the

Sabbath 'exists not as an end in itself, but as a means to the rest and refreshment and betterment of human beings.' Similarly, writes Haller, marriage exists for people, 'stemming from the deep human need for an instituted and regularized companionship.' (pp.138-139)

On the basis of this understanding of Jesus' teaching Haller then offers the following story as an 'imaginative exercise' that is 'in keeping with the gospel':

> Some lawyers came to Jesus and said to him, Teacher, we found two men who have set up a household and live together after the manner of a man and a woman. Shall we do unto them as is written in the law of Moses? And he said unto them, For your hardness of heart Moses gave you this law. But it was not so at the beginning, when God made companions for Adam and allowed him to choose the one suitable to him, the one who was most like him. And they said to him, But was not that Eve, the mother of all living? And he said to them, Do not be deceived, 'the Lord does not see as mortals see' – you lawyers look only on the outside and do not look to the heart. But God knows what is inside a man, and it is from inside that true love flows. And do you not know that when Jonathan looked upon David his soul was bound to him, and he loved him as his own self, and gave up his life for his friend? David spoke rightly when he said that there is no greater love than this. If these two should set up their lives together what is that to you? Love the Lord your God, and do not judge. (p.139)

Haller also draws attention to the significance of the two stories of Jesus' anointing by a sinful woman in the house of Simon the Pharisee (Luke 7:36-50) and his encounter with a Canaanite woman with a sick daughter (Matthew 15:22-28).

On the first story, Haller comments that the story presents 'two models for our encounter with Christ, and Christian ministry.'

Some will prefer to spend their time worrying about other people's sins and whether the church can tolerate them. They will seek to obstruct their service, thinking all the while that they protect God's body from the touch of unclean hands, from those who, if only the truth were known, would not be allowed to serve. They are simply being good housekeepers of the household of God – like Hyacinth Bucket making people take off their shoes before entering her spotless house.

Others will get on with the hopeful works of faith and love, of justice and compassion – the kind of good housekeeping that accepts the fact that there will be some cleaning up to do from time to time, because so many people have been made welcome in the house. Is there any question at all which of these Christ would rather have us do? (pp.141-142)

On the second story, Haller suggests that Jesus' initial reluctance to accede to the woman's request may have had to do with his wanting to test the faith of the disciples, to see if they would persist in their normal attitude of wanting to get rid of 'troublesome people' (see Mark 6:36, 10:13, 9:38). He then asks:

To what extent do the heirs of the apostles continue their efforts at exclusion and dismissal? Or will they finally get the message of Jesus' wish to fulfil the prophecy of Isaiah that all will be drawn into his kingdom, even the formerly hopeless eunuchs and unclean foreigners (Isaiah 56:4-6). All, all, belong to the Bridegroom, and his Bride is not fully clothed until every soul God loves is included in her. (p.147)

> **Dan Via – John 10:10 indicates that God wills abundant sexual life for gay and lesbian people and in recognising this the Church would be being led 'into all the truth' by the Spirit just as Jesus promised.**

In *Homosexuality and the Bible – Two Views*, Via appeals to Jesus' saying in John 10:10 that he has come to bring people life in abundance as one of his key arguments for the acceptance of gay and lesbian relationships. He declares:

> Human life is bodily and sexual and God wants all of God's human creatures to have life in abundance. Obviously John's Gospel makes no express connection between abundant life and the full actualization of anyone's sexuality. But 'abundant life' precisely because of its nonspecificity, is all –encompassing. It can exclude no aspect of human life. And since God wills abundant life for all of God's creation, God's own, on what grounds could we deny that God wills abundant bodily (sexual) life for gays and lesbians as well as heterosexuals? (p.34)

Via acknowledges that this position involves superseding 'the few explicit biblical texts that forbid homosexual practice', but he argues that to do this would simply be 'to appropriate what Scripture promises in the Gospel of John.' In John Jesus tells his disciples:

> ...that after he is gone both the Father and he will send the Spirit to remind them of all that he has taught them (14:26, 15:26). More than that, he has many things to say to them that they are not able to bear now. However, when the Spirit comes, he will lead the disciples into all the truth, into implications of Jesus' redemptive mission and message that have not yet come to explicit expression – because they are not yet ready to bear or receive these things.

> Again there is no explicit reference to homosexuality. But 'all the truth' is as encompassing as 'abundant life.' Nothing can be excluded. So why should not a new posture towards

homosexuality be understood as a hitherto unrecognized and unacknowledged aspect of all the truth that comes in Jesus, a truth that illuminates an aspect of human existence hitherto constricted by both church and society? (p.39)

Marcella Althaus-Reid and Robert Goss – the queer Jesus in the gospels of Mark and Luke.

A final approach to the issue of how Jesus relates to the debate about same sex relationships has been to see Jesus as 'queer.' This does not mean that Jesus himself is seen as having been a practising homosexual, rather, like the analogous claim that Jesus was 'black,' it means that Jesus can be identified with the experiences of gay and lesbian people and other groups in society who are marginalised and oppressed.

A good example of this approach is provided by the commentaries on Mark and Luke *in The Queer Bible Commentary*.

In her commentary on Mark, Dr Marcella Althaus-Reid writes about a transvestite In Buenos Aires who suffered multiple deaths 'by ostracism, by being abandoned by her family, by being denied a job, by being denied her right to her own identity and to love, and to have a good life with dignity.' In a similar way:

> Jesus' life according to Mark is also signed by a multitude of deaths. These are the deaths of a queer man. First of all, Jesus is a man who has departed from his family. In a way, he lost his family and social location. Second, he suffers from economic death. How? He is a poor man, rendered invisible by the economic power of his time, a nobody. And finally, torture and death by crucifixion ends his messianic mission. The crucifixion made him redundant. He becomes an unemployed God, a devalued, misunderstood God outside the market. In everything Jesus did, God's abundant presence was there but nevertheless, for society he was a failure. (p. 520)

However, throughout the Gospel Jesus also has multiple 'resurrections' in the sense that his mission continues and the challenge presented to us by the lack of a resurrection narrative at the end of the Gospel is whether we have faith that the queer Jesus will resurrect after the final death on the cross:

> ...the cross is the attempt to kill once and for all the multiple resurrections of a queer Jesus, to fix him once and for all on a stable cross so that no queer God would do what queer Gods do, that is, to exceed the border limits of a fatigued heterosexual foundational epistemology which has reduced religious experience and human love. But will the queer Jesus resurrect? I belong to a community of people who think that yes, the resurrection of the queer God is not only possible, but already a reality. The queer God is present in every group or individual who still dares to believe that God is fully present among the marginalized, exceeding the narrow confines of sexual and political ideologies. For God comes out from heterosexual theology when the voices from sexual dissidents speak out to the churches, daring to unveil sexual ideologies from theology, and daring to love with integrity in a world where love has also become a commodity. In fact, in every community of excluded people and in every inch of the struggle for sexual and economic justice, the queer God manifests Godself with full glory, grace and power. (p.525)

In his commentary on Luke, Dr Robert Goss writes that 'to say Jesus the Christ is queer is to say that God identifies with us and our experiences of injustice...Jesus the queer Christ is crucified repeatedly by homophobic violence.' (p.544) He goes on to say that we should also understand the resurrection in queer terms:

> Resurrection is God's ultimate queer surprise. It is the metanarrative for all the parables by which Jesus shocked his audience: the Prodigal Son, the Good Samaritan, and the Great Supper. What God did in the resurrection of Jesus, God was

doing from the beginning of creation and in the ministry of Jesus. It is the coming out of God as unconditional love and grace. It is the complete translocation of Jesus's dead body. (p.544)

For Goss the key thing about Luke's resurrection accounts is 'how God places queer folk back into the story of the ongoing presence of the risen Christ.' (p.544) Building on the work of Michael Kelly[50], Goss offers a queer reading of these accounts in which the message of the resurrection is brought to the mainstream Church by the queer women and the queer disciples from the road to Emmaus:

> The queer Church travels back to the mainstream Church, bringing the message of the power of Christ's resurrection discovered in their embodied erotic experiences. They embody the risen Christ, and the recognition of their embodiment of the queer Christ motivates them to return to the larger community to bear witness to the queer Christ in their own lives. They now have the power to transform the despondent and disembodied community so that they can recognize the presence of the risen Christ embodied in queer disciples. It is only their embodied return that prepares the community to welcome and hear the risen Christ in their midst.
>
> Luke comprehends the stories of irregular women and the two outside disciples as the catalyst to recognize the presence of the risen Christ within its midst. Outside women and men find the presence of Christ in the empty tomb, in exile, in their vulnerability, in the scriptures and the breaking of the bread, and in the truth of their erotic lives. The Christian churches can only be reawakened to embodiment of an erotic spirituality as it listens to the stories of women and queer folk. The churches can be resurrected to an embodied Christ who is enfleshed in the

---

[50] Michael Kelly, *The Erotic Contemplative*, Vol 6, Video Talk, Oakland: Ero Spirit, 1994.

erotic lives of women and queer folk. The story of Jesus the Queer Christ will continue in queer lives; they will translate that story into the diverse languages of the many queer sub-communities in Acts and into the future. (pp.546-547)

Chapter 5

Examples of same-sex relationships in Scripture? (I)

As well as arguing that the passages in Scripture which have traditionally been as prohibiting same-sex relationships do not do so, and that Jesus' teaching and practice give support to the acceptance of same-sex relationships, revisionist writers have also argued that Scripture contains examples of significant same-sex relationships, such as the relationships between David and Jonathan and Ruth and Naomi, that are known about, that are accepted rather than condemned, and that play an important role in the development of the biblical story. In addition it has been argued that it is possible to read the Old Testament in a way that sees God as involved in a same-sex relationship with David and to read the gospels in a way that sees Jesus as being same-sex attracted and in a gay relationship with the Beloved Disciple.

In this chapter we shall look at material from revisionist writers that puts forward these ideas.

David and Jonathan

The account of the love between David and Jonathan in 1 Samuel 18:1-2 Samuel 2:27 has generally been seen as the clearest example of a same-sex relationship in Scripture. However, revisionist writers disagree about whether or not it was a sexual relationship.

(a) We can be sure it was a sexual relationship

> **Stephen Greenberg – the Books of Samuel depict the relationship between David and Jonathan in erotic terms.**

Greenberg writes in *Wrestling with God and Men* that in spite of 'the rabbinic insistence on the platonic nature of this biblical friendship, the narrative description of Jonathan and David's relationship in the Books of Samuel is guardedly but surely erotic.' (p.100) In his view:

The story would seem to make most sense if Jonathan were gay, but David not. Jonathan is, after all, a son who disappoints his father in just the ordinary ways. Though he manages in battle, we find him not very aggressive or interested in military prowess. He doesn't think strategically. Moreover, he is smitten at first sight by the young David and immediately dresses him in his own clothing. The erotics of this gesture are difficult to explain away. Lastly, his love of David is deemed perverse and shameful by his father. (p.104)

Greenberg concedes that it might be possible to read the story in a non-sexual way. However, he says, 'while such a reading is possible, it avoids a more direct and obvious power in a narrative in which love is mentioned over and over again regarding a relationship between the two men.' (p.105)

> **Adrian Thatcher – the biblical accounts of the relationship between David and Jonathan only make sense if they were lovers.**

Thatcher declares in *The Savage Text* :

The long narratives describing the relationship between David and Jonathan in 1 and 2 Samuel make little sense unless they were lovers. Imagine a male candidate for ordination today confiding to his bishop that his love for another man was 'wonderful, passing the love of women' (2 Samuel 1:26). And if he is an honest Roman Catholic ordinand he will certainly be deemed to 'present deep-seated homosexual tendencies' which will 'gravely hinder' him 'from relating correctly to men and women.' (p.33)

Theodore Jennings – David was the lover of both Saul and
Jonathan and there was also an erotic relationship between
David and God.

In his book *Jacob's wound – homoerotic narrative in the literature of
Ancient Israel* [51] Professor Theodore Jennnings goes further and
suggests that not only were David and Jonathan lovers, but so were
David and Saul, and that his relationships with them made possible an
erotic relationship between David and God in which God learned what
it meant to love.

Jennings argues that:

> In terms of the relation between the narration of David and his
> (human) male lovers and the story of his relationship with
> YHWH, we may notice that David is introduced to the warrior-
> leaders of Israel after, and because of, his prior selection by
> YHWH. But the narration of David's love affairs with Jonathan
> and Saul comes to an end before the eroticism of the
> relationship between David and Adonai receives further
> narrative elaboration. It is as if David first had to learn or
> practice what it means to be the beloved before he could be
> depicted as the beloved of Adonai.
>
> In this case David's relationships to Saul and Jonathan prepare
> him for the consummation of his being the beloved of YHWH.
> (p.74)

Jennings further contends that 'YHWH seems to be changed in the
course of the narrative.' At the start of 1 and 2 Samuel 'YHWH has been
a distant and inattentive deity. When he does pay attention, he seems
astonishingly arbitrary and unpredictable as well as extremely
dangerous.' At the end of the narrative, however. 'we hear of YHWH's
steadfast love.' What has changed? The answer, says Jennings, is that:

---

[51] Theodore Jennings, *Jacob's wound*, New York & London, Continuum, 2005..

It appears that David has tamed the ferocious desert chief. And David has done this precisely in the way he has deal with his other lovers. For in truth the exemplar of steadfast love in this story is not YHWH but David, and the way that has been practised and demonstrated is through David's behavior with his other lovers, Saul and Jonathan.

Although it may seem strange to say it, it would seem that YHWH has learned love from David, has learned what it is to love all the way – precisely in relation to David – and has learned steadfastness in love from David. Through being the Lover of precisely this beloved one, YHWH has become a better lover, one who can be trusted, one who can be relied upon, one in whom one can have faith.

Apart from the narrative we have been reading, it would be hard to imagine Adonai as a god who could be loved. And apart from David's relationships to Saul and Jonathan, it would be hard to imagine the love between David and YHWH. Homoeroticism therefore is the very fulcrum of biblical religion. (p.75)

Keith Sharpe – David was the lover of Saul and Jonathan.

In *The Gay Gospels* Sharpe also argues that David was the lover of both Saul and Jonathan.

He quotes I Samuel 20:30 'Then Saul's anger was kindled against Jonathan, and he said to him, "You son of a perverse, rebellious woman, do I not know that you have chosen the son of Jesse to your own shame, and to the shame of your mother's nakedness?' and sees this as suggesting a gay relationship between Saul and David:

It is probable that the implication here is by having an erotic or even sexual relationship with David, Jonathan is uncovering 'his father's nakedness' because Saul has already had sexual relations with David. And by so uncovering his father's

140

nakedness Jonathan also uncovers the nakedness of another with whom Saul has had sexual relations; his wife, Jonathan's own mother. Saul's outburst does not seem to make any sense unless he has also 'known' David 'in the biblical sense.' So at the same time as he is effectively calling his son a queer he is also revealing that he too has had a homosexual liaison with David. (p.143)

On the relationship between David and Jonathan Sharpe writes:

This was actually love between two men in the fullest sense, grounded in homoerotic desire but overlain with deep emotion and enduring commitment. It is a covenant which is kept and fulfilled by both men until the end of their days. Tom Horner (1978) in his celebrated book *'Jonathan loved David'* likened their relationship to that between Gilgamesh, King of Uruk, and Enkidu, his inseparable companion, whose love was well known throughout the Middle East in ancient times. Describing Gilgamesh's inconsolable distress when his lover dies, Horner comments: *No mourner in the history of the world – except perhaps Alexander at the passing of his friend Hephaestion – has ever been more broken up over the loss of his (or her) beloved friend.*

David's words of utter devastation when Jonathan is killed follow precisely in this tradition of male love. And, significantly, at no point in the narrative is there any word of criticism from the Hebrew God. On the contrary, the Lord lavishes favours upon David, leading him to the throne where he will become the greatest king of Ancient Israel. And from the line of David will eventually be born in Bethlehem the Saviour of the world. If ever a man was blessed by God it was David. And this despite his involvement in at least two homosexual affairs. This is truly an inspirational story for all gay people everywhere. (p.145)

(b) It is not clear whether this was a sexual relationship

> **Jay Michaelson** - the Relationship between David and Jonathan may not have been sexual, but it was a relationship of romantic love with erotic overtones.

Michaelson is wary about saying that this was definitely a sexual relationship. However, he declares in *God vs. Gay?*:

> At the very least, surely we would all agree that what Jonathan felt for David can be described as a romantic love with erotic overtones, whether or not it blossomed into sexual activity. And surely that is more important. As we explored earlier, the very notion that 'homosexuality' can mean both an orientation toward romantic connection and a physical sex act is part of the problem. It reduces love to sex, and reduces gay people to what we do with our genitals. What matters here is that Jonathan loved David, that this love was an essential part of the story of David's ascent to kingship – and that, understood traditionally, this part of God's plan. Jonathan's love for another man is not some bit part in the drama of the Bible. If Jonathan had not loved David as he loved his very soul, there would be no Messiah. (p.101)

As he sees it, if we allow the Bible to tell its own story about this relationship:

> ...what emerges is a touching and perhaps tragic tale of one man's love for another, a deep, passionate, embodied love that ultimately shaped the most important drama in human history: the line of David leading to the messianic redemption. David and Jonathan's romance prepares David for his relationship with God, seals the transmission of the Israelite monarchy to the Davidic line, models a relationship with God that all of us might reflect upon, and alters the very course of human history. What also emerges is a biblical universe with multiple configurations of, and approaches to, sexuality, homosociality,

142

eroticism, and same-sex romantic love. LGBT people find themselves in history, and everyone who has experienced love finds another prism through which this universal human emotion can be refracted. The story expands our horizons regarding the emotional capacity of human beings – and this is of importance to us all. (p.101)

> **Ken Stone – we cannot reach a definite conclusion about whether David and Jonathan had a sexual relationship.**

Professor Ken Stone maintains in his commentary on 1 and 2 Samuel in *The Queer Bible Commentary* that the fact that David and Jonathan both marry women and have children does not mean that there could not have been a sexual relationship between them, 'the relations David and Jonathan have with women are no impediment to a reading in terms of male homoeroticism.' (p.207)

However, he also concedes that it may be anachronistic 'to assume that the deep affection Jonathan and David clearly have for one another in the text would automatically signify a sexual relationship in the ancient world.'(pp.207-208) It may he says, seem self-evident to many modern readers:

> ...that one's sexual relationships, whether heterosexual or homosexual, are also the relationships in which intimacy and affection are most deeply expressed and in which one finds close companionship. Yet most of the explicit references to sexual activity in 2 Samuel have nothing at all to do with emotional intimacy or affection but are concerned instead, as we shall see, with power, property or procreation. Thus it is quite possible that David's lament over Jonathan actually testifies to a world in which the lives of most people were characterized by, on the one hand, ongoing sexual relations with people of the opposite sex; and, on the other hand, affectionate and emotionally intimate relations and companionship with

persons of the same sex which, however, did not necessarily entail sexual intercourse. (p.208)

Stone's conclusion is that in the end 'it is neither necessary nor possible to reach a single, definitive conclusion about the nature of the relationship between David and Jonathan.' (p.208)

> **James Harding – rather than trying to decide about the precise nature of David and Jonathan's relationship we should think afresh about the importance of loving friendship.**

In his essay 'Opposite Sex Marriage a Biblical Ideal?' in *Pieces of Ease and Grace* James Harding notes that David's statement in 2 Samuel 1:26 that Jonathan's love surpasses that of women leaves open a lot of questions:

> Is this love sexual or non-sexual, or erotic, but without explicit sexual expression? Is Jonathan's non-sexual love for David being compared with women's sexual love for him? Is it the love a man shows for siblings, parents, children, or other members of the household or clan? Is the comparison then between the love of women, who are perhaps little more than political pawns, and the love of Jonathan, which was founded on a decision to honour his covenant with David above the ties of kinship that should have bound him to be loyal to his father (cf 1 Samuel 20:30-34)? Does 'love' here bear primarily emotional nor political connotations, or have these distinctions become indistinguishable? Is the comparison between a love given with no ulterior motive and a love given only for some form of advantage? Is David implying that Jonathan's love was that between equals, in contrast with relationships with women that had been of culturally determined inequality? Is David comparing the kind of love that might obtain among women in an all-female context with the kind of love that might obtain between men in all-male context, such as on the field of battle?

Is it between a genuine mutual, mutual affection of the two warriors and the lack of mutual affection in the context of political marriages? (pp.44-45)

Rather than try and resolve these questions, Harding suggests that we should accept that it is Jonathan's sacrificial love for David that is praised in David's lament in 2 Samuel 1 and that this should lead us to think afresh about the Christian virtue of love:

What then if we were to think through the Christian virtue of love anew, taking *loving, sacrificial friendship* as the most basic relationship, a form of loving friendship whose model is divine love, and whose human embodiment fulfils the human need for companionship expressed in Gen 2:18? If we were to think in those terms, perhaps opposite-sex marriage might be understood as one among many manifestations of that kind of love. It might also free us to think *of many different kinds of opposite-sex and same-sex relationships*, not all, or even a majority, of which need be sexual. For a good deal of the problem is that a fixation on one form of opposite-sex marriage has made it harder to see clearly how loving friendships, *whether sexual or not*, and love that is lived and embodied in a *celibate* life, might be honoured in a Christian context. (p.46)[52]

Ruth and Naomi

Revisionist scholars have seen the relationship between Ruth and Naomi as depicted in the Book of Ruth as a lesbian relationship of a 'marriage like' nature and they have argued that it provides an example of how lesbian and gay relationships are able to survive and flourish in patriarchal and heterosexist societies.

---

[52] James Harding provides a detailed study of the biblical material on David and Jonathan and how it has been interpreted in his book *The Love of David and Jonathan – Ideology, Text, Reception*, Sheffield: Equinox Press, 2013.

> **Theodore Jennings – the story of Ruth and Naomi shows how love between women can thrive in the face of patriarchy and heterosexism.**

Jennings writes in *Jacob's Wound* that the story of Ruth and Naomi :

> ...may help us to see how the love of women for one another has managed to survive and even thrive under conditions of patriarchy and heterosexism. The obligations of the patriarchal structures are in fact complied with: Boaz has a son. But by this means the women find a shelter within which their love for one another can flourish. It is, after all, this love – the love of these two women for each other – that is the entire motivating force for the plot that unfolds; that is the romantic heart of this short story. (p.230)

As Jennings sees it:

> It is difficult to see how any tale from antiquity could have been more explicit in dealing with 'women loving women' or with what is more prosaically termed a lesbian relationship. Yet, of course, men like Boaz have no clue about what is going on. He doesn't know that he spent the night not only with Ruth but also with her co-conspirator. Boaz is pleased to be chosen over younger, more attractive mates, never suspecting the motive of economic security. He thinks a son has been born to him, but the village women know better; they know that Ruth has succeeded in giving Naomi a son. Boaz doesn't even name the son; the women do that for him. Boaz gets a son and more land and so never suspects what was and is going on. (p.230)

In his view the story of Ruth and Naomi:

> ...serves to depict what it means to have steadfast love, what it means to 'cleave to one another,' what it means to be knit together as one soul. It shows what it means for the love of two persons of the same sex to love one another in ways that

'surpass' the more structured heterosexual relationship within patriarchal culture. (p.233)

> **William Johnson – the story of Ruth indicates that there can be a one flesh union between two men or two women.**

In *A Time to Embrace* Johnson notes that one of the most important covenants in our society is the covenant of marriage and then goes on to argue that 'the language used in the book of Ruth gives us a clue that covenant loyalty, as conceived within the precepts of biblical religion, is about something other than the narrow construct of 'gender complementarity'.' (p.145) Ruth makes a commitment of covenant loyalty to Naomi that echoes the language of one flesh union used in Genesis 2:24 and this points us to the fact that when

> ...two men or two women find each other and make this one-flesh commitment to one another, there is just as much reason to rejoice as when Adam first beheld Eve. When anyone finds a suitable life partner, it is appropriate for the community to give them its blessing. For they have become one bone, one flesh – united in the same family. (p.147)

> **Ruth Mathieson – the story of Ruth is one that provides room for gay, lesbian and transgender people.**

Ruth Mathieson argues in her essay on 'Ruth and Naomi' in *Pieces of Ease and Grace* that both the marriage of Ruth and Boaz and the 'marriage-like' relationship of Ruth and Naomi 'make room for gay, lesbian and transgender people.' (p.32)

Mathieson points out that the marriage between Ruth and Boaz 'involves the reinterpretation of the biblical injunction not to marry Moabite wives.' This reinterpretation:

> ...is made possible by bringing together the Mosaic laws about the levirate practice and redemption of the land for impoverished kinsmen and applying them to Ruth and Naomi's

147

situation. The legal process in which this happens is witnessed and affirmed by the elders and the whole people. Nevertheless, the initial bringing together of the two laws is done by Ruth, one of the excluded minority. This provides a biblical precedent for modern day minorities to participate in the reinterpretation of biblical laws which may currently exclude them from the church and prohibit them marrying. (p.32)

She goes on to argue that:

Ruth and Naomi's relationship has a marriage-like quality. Ruth makes a life-long commitment to Naomi (1:15-18), which is sustained throughout the book of Ruth until the closing scene when 'a son has been born to Naomi' (4:17). They are concerned for one another's welfare. Ruth goes out to glean, acting as a breadwinner and their relationship is recognised in a positive way by Boaz and not immediately 'solved' by marriage. Even the threshing floor scene does not negate the marriage-like commitment between Ruth and Naomi. Practising deception around the identity of a woman for future well-being and preservation of the male line is also found in biblical marriages, including those of the patriarchs in the book of Genesis. (pp.32-33)

Her conclusion is that:

Both the marriage of Ruth the Moabite and Boaz of the family of Judah and the marriage-like quality of the relationship of Ruth and Naomi provide a biblical precedent of re-interpreting the Scripture to favour inclusion rather than exclusion, goodness (*hesed*) over purity. (p.33)

> **Mona West – Ruth is a book which provides 'Queer' people with strategies for survival.**

In her commentary on Ruth in *The Queer Bible Commentary* Dr Mona West argues that it is a book which provides 'Queer' people with strategies for survival 'in a society and a culture that invoke and create laws with narrow definitions of family and procreative privilege in order to exclude us and perpetuate hatred and violence against our community.'(p.190)

First, Ruth's words of commitment to Naomi in Ruth 1:16 provide Queer people with 'an act of self-determination, refusing to accept a marginalized status based on heterosexist patriarchal definitions of marriage, family and procreation.' (p.191)

Secondly, the arrangement made by Boaz in chapter 2 for Ruth to be allowed to glean invite Queer people:

> ...to join forces to create communities in which all of us have access to goods and services. Like Boaz, those of us with some privilege (those of us who are white, male able-bodied, educated and have economic resources) can use these privileges to resist oppressive structures and go above and beyond the law to ensure that the less fortunate in our communities are provided for.(p.192)

Thirdly, in chapters 3 and 4 Naomi, Ruth and Boaz decide to 'create their own family and define their own understanding of kinship and responsibility to one another within the context of the inheritance and kinship laws of ancient Israel.' Their actions are similar:

> ...to the ways in Queer people of today create families: a bisexual man and two lesbians live together with their biological child; a gay man is a sperm donor for a lesbian couple and is part of the parenting of their child; three gay men live together as lovers and family for twenty years; a lesbian mother and her lover live two doors down from her lesbian daughter and her lover. (p.193)

In addition, the ways that Ruth and Boaz manipulate the laws surrounding kinship to facilitate their marriage parallel the ways 'that we in the Queer community manipulate laws to overcome barriers that deny the legality of our relationships.' (p.194)

Finally, the blessing pronounced upon Naomi by the women of Bethlehem in 4:14-15 can be claimed as a blessing for Queer unions 'we claim with them that our unions, our love, our families with or without children, are life-giving and procreative.' (p.194)

> **Keith Sharpe – the story of Ruth and Naomi is a paradigm for the survival of lesbian relationships in a male dominated society.**

Sharpe sees the relationship between Ruth and Naomi in the same way as West. He writes in *The Gay Gospels* :

> It is probable that the story of Ruth and Naomi is a paradigm for how lesbian relationships survive in male dominated society. The men are so focussed on fulfilling the exacting demands of the male role within the structures of power that they simply do not notice the female relationships being enjoyed all around him.
>
> In this story the two women cleverly manipulate the situation in which they find themselves to arrive at the ideal outcome for their partnership. Naomi is greatly respected by everybody and Ruth is loved and accepted into Naomi's community. Almost everybody seems to know what is really going on. Even the ageing Boaz may simply be turning a blind eye because the arrangement suits him so well. It really is extraordinary that he does not object to Naomi's 'intrusion' into his marriage with Ruth, and even more bizarre that he says nothing when the townswomen name his son. One wonders what the other men around Boaz thought but the Bible is silent on this point. Presumably if they were troubled the reader would have been told. And of course the other significant silence is the Lord's. There is no comment or condemnation from Yahweh either. (p.158)

Sharpe also declares that Ruth and Naomi were in what we would now call a gay marriage:

The vow that Ruth makes to Naomi when she refuses to be left behind in Moab captures perfectly the essence of marital love, which is of course why it is used so often at weddings. That it is so often used indeed confirms precisely the marital love these two women felt for each other. (pp.159-160)

Jesus' relationships

Turning to the New Testament, it is argued by a number of revisionist writers that John's gospel describes a gay relationship between Jesus and the 'beloved disciple' referred to in 13:22-25, 19:26-27, 21:7 and 21:20-23), and that there are also other pieces of evidence that can be read as suggesting that Jesus was sexually attracted to other men rather than to women.

> **Theodore Jennings – Jesus and the Beloved Disciple were boyfriends or lovers.**

In his book *The Man Jesus Loved* [53] Jennings argues that in the fourth gospel:

> The singling out of one who is loved by Jesus makes clear that some kind of love is at stake other than the love that unites Jesus to the rest of his disciples. The text itself suggests that we should recognize here some form of love that certainly does not contradict the more general love of Jesus for all, but which sets it apart from this general love. A reasonable conclusion is that this difference points us to a different sphere or dimension of love: love characterized by erotic desire or sexual attraction. (p.22)

---

[53] Theodore Jennings, *The Man Jesus Loved: Homoerotic Narratives from the New Testament*, Cleveland, Pilgrim Press, 2003.

In Jennings view there is substantial similarity between the relationship between Jesus and the Beloved Disciple and that between a lover and a beloved in a Hellenistic gymnasium. In contemporary terms we would say that they were boyfriends or lovers.

> **Robert Goss – Jesus and the Beloved Disciple were in a homoerotic relationship.**

Goss also suggests a gay relationship between Jesus and the Beloved Disciple. He writes in his commentary on John in *The Queer Bible Commentary* that:

> For nearly two millennia, men attracted to the same sex have intuited a homoerotic relationship between Jesus and the Beloved Disciple. They have correctly read the relationship between Jesus and the Beloved Disciple as a rare instance of homoerotic desire, finding moments of grace and self-acceptance in this relationship. (pp 560-561)

For many queer folk, he declares, the story of the fidelity of the Beloved Disciple to Jesus:

> ...serves as a reminder how faithful we have been to the Christian tradition despite its exclusions, its violence and its crucifixions of our folk. We have remained faithful to a tradition whose institutions have consistently rejected us and targeted us for cultural assault. The gay writer and scholar Donald Boisvert speaks about how meaningful the image of Jesus and the Beloved Disciple is. 'It is, however, a beautiful image, a deep and touching affirmation of our central place as gay men in the heart of God.' We may not be loved by the churches but we certainly have a place in the heart of God. (pp.561-562)

> **Keith Sharpe – John's gospel indicates that Jesus and the Beloved Disciple had a mutual homoerotic attraction and there is other evidence both from the gospels and 'Secret Mark' that suggests that Jesus sexuality was focused on men.**

Sharpe likewise suggests in *The Gay Gospels* that the evidence of John's gospel indicates that Jesus and the Beloved Disciple shared 'a mutual homoerotic attraction based on reciprocal desire and delight.' (p.101)

He writes:

> At the Last Supper we have a picture of real affection involving bodily intimacy, which is seen recognised and approved by the other disciples. It is very telling that Peter assumes that if Jesus has told anyone who the traitor is, it will be the Beloved Disciple. Jesus' concern on the cross for this man mirrors exactly the concern of any dying lover for the future welfare of the beloved. He wants him taken care of and instructs his mother accordingly. Neither here nor anywhere else does Jesus express love for his mother. He simply wants her to look after the Beloved Disciple. Moreover, neither Mary nor the other women present appear to be at all surprised. Like Peter they seem to take this relationship for granted. At the empty tomb, the Beloved Disciple's behaviour is what you would expect from a lover in such traumatic circumstances. He has recently witnessed the cruel torturing to death of his partner, and he can hardly bear to contemplate seeing the body. And then only the Beloved Disciple senses that the stranger on the shore is the risen Christ, as if the love he has shared with Jesus has endured through to the new life. Later Jesus seems to endorse this intuition. His concern for the Beloved Disciple is presented as eternal, literally undying. This man is to be the oOne and only human soul to be put beyond Petrine care and to be tended directly by the Son of God. Could there be a more powerful expression of love. (p.101)

In his view:

> To all intents and purposes what we have here in John's Gospel looks like a real love story. It would be perfectly natural for such an intensely loving relationship to encompass physical erotic activity, although of course the Biblical text does not describe any such acts. But then neither does it in the case of relationships which we know were sexual, so this means nothing. (pp.101-102)

Sharpe also draws attention to the story of the rich young ruler whom Jesus 'loved' (Mark 10:17-22), the naked youth in the Garden of Gethsemane (Mark 14:50-52) and the document known as 'Secret Mark' (actually a letter by Clement of Alexandria) discovered in 1958 which gives us an alternative version of Mark. Sharpe notes that there is uncertainty about whether these texts, and those referring to the Beloved Disciple, refer to one person or several, but he argues this does not really matter:

> What matters is that we have before our eyes extensive material evidence, much of it sanctified as divinely inspired gospel text, that Jesus' sexuality was predominantly, possibly exclusively, male focused.
>
> Two thousand years of tradition based on heterosexist ideology have sought to suppress these facts. Clement's letter makes clear that there were earlier versions of Mark's gospel which reported openly on Jesus' gayness. Gradually these versions were denounced by authority figures such as Clement and homophobic prohibitions were introduced into the Church. Over time the publicly accepted version of Mark is left with only tiny homoerotic fragments. Only in the Gospel of John with story of the Beloved Disciple do we still have a substantial narrative implying that Jesus was homoerotically inclined. However, the uncovering and reassembling of all the pieces of textual evidence which the Christian tradition has sought to

keep hidden leaves us with a picture of the Son of God with which LGBT people can readily identify. (pp.115-116)

> **Adrian Thatcher – Mark 14:51-52 may refer to someone who was gay and with whom Jesus can a close relationship.**

In *The Savage Text* Thatcher also points to the story recorded in Mark 14:51-52 of the young man who fled naked from the scene of Jesus' arrest as another example of a possible reference to a gay character in the Gospels. He quotes Jennings' statement that this text is 'an apparent allusion to the typical recipient of homoerotic attention (the nude youth) in Hellenistic pederastic culture at a decisive moment in the passion of Jesus, and with the suggestion of a particularly close relationship between Jesus and this youth' and comments 'Jesus, we may speculate, was just the sort of company with whom a sexually exploited young man could relax and feel accepted.' (p.33 [54])

> **Dale Martin – it is possible and legitimate to read the gospels from a homoerotic perspective.**

In *Sex and the Single Savior* Martin invites us to consider what happens 'if we read the gospels though the eyes of the male homoerotic gaze?' His answer is that:

> We may note, for starters, that there is practically no place in the Gospels where Jesus is said to 'love' a woman in particular. The closest is when the Fourth Gospel tells us that Jesus loved Martha, her sister, and Lazarus (John 11:5), perhaps a *ménage a quatre*? Jesus' attraction to specific men, on the other hand, is explicit. Though he at first treated the 'rich young ruler' a bit abruptly, Jesus then 'looked on him and loved him' (according to Mark 10:21). Even the people standing around surmised from Jesus' weeping that he must have loved Lazarus a great deal (John 11:36). And of course there is 'the disciple whom Jesus loved' who is regularly close to Jesus, who lies practically on top

---

[54] The quotation is from Jennings, *The Man Jesus Loved*, p. 113.

of him at the last dinner, whom Jesus loves so much that he seems unwilling to allow him even to die (13:23-25); 21:20-22). For those unable to imagine anything erotic going on here, just consider what people would think if we took the 'beloved disciple' to be a woman (as has in fact been imagined, presumably by heterosexuals); in that case, most people wouldn't be able to resist the consequent erotic imaginings. Finally, we have Jesus' last discussion with Peter in the Fourth Gospel, in which Jesus teases and flirts with Peter like a schoolgirl: 'Do you *really* love me? Really? Really? Then prove it!' (21:15-19). (pp.99-100)

Martin also identifies what he calls 'other sites of the sensual in the Gospels' all of which have to do with men:

> Thomas is invited to penetrate the holes in Jesus' body (John 20:24ff). Jesus dips his 'little piece' (*psômion*) in the gravy and places it in the hand of Judas (John 13:26). And though Jesus allows a woman to wash his feet (and we biblical scholars – who know our Hebrew – recognise the hint), when it is his turn he takes his clothes off, wraps a towel round his waist, and washes the feet of his male disciples, again taking time out for a special seduction of Peter (John 13:1-11). In contrast, when Mary later wants a hug, Jesus won't let her even touch him (John 20:17). (Jesus' *noli me tangere* is the Gospel version of Paul's homosocial slogan 'it is better for a man not to touch a woman' in 1 Corinthians 7:1). (p.100)

Martin goes on to explain that these references indicate that we do not need to think of Jesus as actually 'having sex' in order to 'see him as erotic and sensual.' For Martin this is because:

> Any sexually experienced person knows that the most intense eroticism may be had by denying oneself consummation. Flirtation, titillation, intimacy, love taken to the edge of orgasm, are often more sexually intense than mere intercourse. May that

156

explain the intensity of Jesus' passion? *If* we take him to be an ascetic after all (although as we've seen, that is not at all certain), do we nevertheless see in him the erotic passion and desire of the sexually charged ascetic? But in that case *again*, Jesus is certainly not a normal man – not even a 'normal' *gay* man. He ends up again looking very singular –very queer. (p.100)

Martin is at pains to point out that what he is not saying is that the 'gay' Jesus is the 'real Jesus' (p.101). In line with his non-foundationalist approach to biblical interpretation that we noted towards the beginning of this report, the point he is making is rather that it is possible to interpret Jesus in many different ways (including homoerotic ways) and that it is perfectly legitimate to do so.

We have a right to think about the sex of Jesus, the sexuality of Jesus, the desires of Jesus, the singularity of Jesus. What none of us has the right to do, I am arguing, is to insist that he or she will supply *the* method of interpretation that will bring interpretation to an end and silence the imagination of others. (p.102)

Part 2
Traditionalist Approaches

Chapter 6

The nature of the Bible and its use in the debate about human sexuality (II)

Like the revisionist scholars surveyed in chapter 1, a number of traditionalist scholars have offered reflections since 2003 on the nature and interpretation of the Bible and how these relate to the debate about same-sex relationships. Again like their revisionist counterparts, these scholars have taken a variety of different approaches to these topics and so their material too is organised by date of publication rather than grouped under subject matter.

Robert Gagnon (2003) – The primacy of Scripture means that those who seek to overturn its core values need, including the restriction of sex to intercourse between men and women, to meet an extraordinary burden of proof.

In his 2003 debate with Dan Via, Professor Robert Gagnon declares that as well as being a biblical scholar who employs 'historical-critical methodology', he also believes, 'in keeping with the historic stance of the church,' that Scripture is 'the primary authority for faith and practice.' (p.42)

If that primacy is to count for anything, he writes, 'it must count for core values. ' Such values are those which are held:

1. pervasively through Scripture (at least implicitly)
2. absolutely (without exceptions), and...
3. strongly (as a matter of significance)

This applies all the more to instances in which:

4. such values emerged in opposition to contrary cultural trends and...
5. have prevailed in the church for two millennia

The 'biblical limitation of sex to intercourse between male and female, with its attendant opposition to all same-sex intercourse' is, he says, such a value. (p.42)

In Gagnon's view, the authority of Scripture puts the onus of proof on those who would seek to reject its core values:

> If the authority of Scripture means anything, those who seek to overturn its core values must meet an extraordinary burden of proof. The evidence must be so strong and unambiguous that it not only makes the witness of Scripture pale by comparison but also directly refutes the reasons for the Bible's position. For example, it would not be enough to prove that (1) the only models for homosexual behaviour in antiquity were exploitative, or (2) modern science has demonstrated the homosexuality is congenital and fixed. One would also have to prove that the Bible condemned homosexual practice (3) primarily on the grounds that it was exploitative (e,g, because it abused boys) , or (4) on the grounds that all participants in homosexual behavior experienced desires for the opposite sex. As we shall see, none of these points can be substantiated. (p.42)

Walter Kaiser (2009) – Scripture is the norm for making ethical decisions

---

Professor Walter Kaiser writes on 'The Use of the Bible for Ethical Decisions'[55] in his book *What does the Lord Require? – A Guide for Preaching and Teaching Biblical Ethics.*

He begins by explaining what is meant by 'biblical ethics'. A biblical ethic, he says is one which:

> ...begins with the light of Scripture: 'Your word is a lamp to my feet and a light for my path' (Psalm 119:105). Thus for

---

[55] Walter Kaiser, *What does the Lord Require?,* Grand Rapids: Baker Academic, 2009.

Christians, biblical ethics is the reflection on human acts and conduct from the perspective given to us in Holy Scripture from our Lord. Though it contains sixty-six books written by some forty human authors, the Bible itself speaks of this compilation as one book (John 10:35, 17:12, 1 Timothy 5:18). The apostle Paul claimed that 'all Scripture is God-breathed and is useful for teaching, rebuking, correcting and training in righteousness, so that the [person] of God may be thoroughly equipped for every good work (2 Timothy 3:16-17) – including such works as ethical and moral living that are pleasing to our Lord. (pp.9-10)

He then goes on to explain what it means for a person to use Scripture when making or evaluating ethical decisions. In his view Scripture constitutes the 'norm' for such decisions:

Scripture is the 'norm' (a word coming from the Lain word *norma* which originally meant a 'carpenter's square,' a tool that determined whether a corner or line was square and straight) we can use to show that an action or a decision is right or wrong, just or unjust. Scripture can be used in four different ways in this connection; it can act (1) as a guide, (2) as a guard, (3) as a compass, and (4) as a principle. Accordingly, *guides* point out the route we should take, while *guards* warn us against wrong decisions or paths. *Compasses* help us gain our orientation, and *principles* gather the abstract ideas that encapsulate a number of examples found in Scripture. (p.10)

For Kaiser, then, 'Our knowledge...with which to evaluate ethical issues is gathered from Scripture.' Scripture is 'our only authoritative source for hearing God's direction for acting properly and justly.' (p.10) However, in order to act rightly on the basis of what Scripture teaches we need to use our capacity for understanding, which Kaiser defines in a threefold way:

There is the understanding we have received at our birth, often called common sense. But we also have an erroneous understanding due to the fall of Adam and Eve in the Garden of Eden and the result of our own sin. Fortunately, there is also the third understanding, by which we are led in a proper way using the light of Scripture. The Psalmist rightly cries out, 'Give me understanding, and I will keep your law and obey it with all my heart.' (Psalm 119:34). (p.10)

> **John Goldingay (2010) – Scripture, tradition and human insight provide resources and norms for thinking about same-sex relationships, but Scripture is primary.**

In his essay 'How should We Think about Same-Sex Relationships?' published in his collection *Key Questions about Christian Faith,* [56]Professor John Goldingay notes that 'Christian life and theology' have traditionally been based on three sources, Scripture, the Christian tradition and human insight:

> Scripture means the Torah, the Prophets and the Writings, plus the New Testament, with some churches adding the further books in the Greek and other canons as works they read and utilize but do not reckon to treat as inherently authoritative theological resources. Christian tradition means the stream of informally recognized key figures such as Athanasius, Augustine, Thomas Aquinas, Luther, Calvin, and (for Anglicans/Episcopalians like me) Hooker, plus the agreements that many Christian churches came to make that are expressed in the historic creeds, plus convictions expressed in different denominations' confessions (for Anglicans/Episcopalians, the Thirty Nine Articles). I then use the term 'human insight' as a catch-all expression covering reason, experience (religious and other), and scientific discovery. Scripture and tradition are also repositories of human insight, but I will use this last expression simply to denote insight that comes from elsewhere. (p.318)

---

[56] John Goldingay, *Key Questions about Christian Faith,* Grand Rapids: Baker Academic, 2010.

These 'potential sources of wisdom, truth and guidance' constitute, he says 'both resources and norms.' This is because:

> They include resources that we can utilise freely by our own discretion, sources of wisdom and obligation whose inherent authority we respond to. They also include norms that we recognize and to which we surrender our discretion. Traditionally, scripture is 'the primary norm for Christian faith and life.' It is our supreme resource and norm because of its distinctive and crucial link with the story of God's activity in Israel that came to a climax in Jesus. Christian tradition and human insight are also significant resources, but they cannot trump scripture. (p.318)

For Goldingay, the role of tradition and human insight is to 'drive us back to ask fresh questions of scripture and see new insights there.' (p.319) As a recent example of this, he points to the debate about the role of women in ministry:

> Human insight made the church question the dominant Christian tradition about women in ministry and ask whether scripture really implied that there were forms of ministry that were open only to men. The conclusion of many denominations was that this was not so. They then felt free to let human insight have its way concerning the question in the conviction that it opened the Church up to implications within scripture and it could thus disagree with the dominant Christian tradition and its interpretation of scripture. (p.319)

According to Goldingay, 'one way of formulating our dilemma over same-sex relationships' is to see it as a debate over whether the same conclusion applies:

> The universal Christian tradition and its interpretation of scripture see scripture as viewing same-sex relationships as irregular and morally inappropriate. The question is whether

human insight, particularly in the Western world, is opening our eyes to other possibilities within scripture. (p.319)

> **John Goldingay, Grant Le Marquand, George R Sumner, Daniel L Westberg (2011) – Anglican conservatives see the Bible as uniquely authoritative. They seek to read it as a unity, on its own terms, in company with the Church as a whole and with an awareness of both the original context of the biblical writings and our current situation.**

Along with Professor Grant Le Marquand, Professor George Sumner and Professor Daniel Westberg, Goldingay also contributed to the 'View from the Traditionalists' in the colloquy in the *Anglican Theological Review*[57] referred to in chapter 2.

In their contribution to the colloquy these writers include a section in which they set out their approach to the interpretation of Scripture. They begin this section by declaring their overall position in relation to the Bible:

> Anglican conservatives are distinguished by treating the Bible as uniquely authoritative for basic Christian belief and practice. Our strong reluctance to set aside what we consider Scripture's direct meaning may we be the single most important factor in the opposition of Anglican conservatives to the acceptance of same-sex marriage. (p.12)

They then go on to explain their understanding of the principles of biblical interpretation. Interpreting the Bible, they say:

> ...involves reading an ancient text in a contemporary context, establishing a dialogue between very different cultures and life situations. Awareness of both ancient and modern situations and properly balancing them enables the biblical message to be clearly understood and applied. (p.12)

---

[57]'Same-Sex Marriage and Anglican Theology: A view from the Traditionalists,' *Anglican Theological Review*, Vol 93, No 1, Winter 2011.

In their view there are two 'endeavours' involved in biblical interpretation, the objective and the subjective.

First, biblical interpretation involves:

> ...trying to achieve an objective understanding of this text according to its own presuppositions and concerns. There is an analogy here to the process of gaining an objective understanding of other persons whom we love. Because of our commitment to them as persons we want to know them in reality, and not just make them a projection of our own interests. We commit ourselves to understanding them in their distinctiveness, even when we may find them difficult or objectionable. Often we find that when we do that, what seemed objectionable becomes, if not likable, at least understandable. We may then be able to learn from who they are – which does not happen either if we reject them, or if we assimilate them too quickly to what we understand and accept. The significance of modern biblical criticism lies here. It declined to be bound by traditions concerning the meaning of texts and insisted on trying to discover their inherent meaning. Exegesis focuses on the meaning of texts as acts of communication, and its interpretation, one sets aside the significance of the text for the interpreter in order to do justice to its inherent meaning. This reflects the ethical principle that someone wished to communicate something here, and we respectfully seek to understand it. (pp.13-14)

Secondly, whether we are trying to understand a text or a person:

> There was some reason for our interest in this text (or this person): something drew our attention to it, and persuaded us that it was worth the effort to understand. Moreover, being drawn in is the way into understanding the text (or the person). The subjective becomes the way into the objective. It turns out to be both an unavoidable hindrance to interpretation and its

indispensable help. The challenge to interpretation is to maximize this help and limit the hindrance. (p.14)

It is also important, they argue, to read the Bible in the company of the Church as a whole:

> One aid to our reading of the Bible is the recognition that it has been given to the whole church and not merely to individuals. We read the Bible with other eyes, and not just our own. If we are fortunate, we read it in a heterogeneous congregation. But we also read it in the company (which we intentionally bring in) of other eras (such as the fathers or the reformers); of other faith communities (such as Judaism); and of other cultures and contexts (such as liberation theology from South America, and inculturation theology from Asia or Africa). These can enable us to see things we would not otherwise see, and to recognize previous misconceptions (p.14)

As they see it, we should reject a 'full-blown 'postmodern' approach' which abandons 'the very idea of getting to the real meaning of a text.' This is for a number of reasons:

> ...we owe it to the author to try to understand what he or she meant; we also owe it to our forebears in the faith communities who took these writings into their Scriptures and invited us to live by them; and we also owe it to ourselves and to the consistency principle. If there is no meaning in the Sodom and Gomorrah story (a very different thing from saying that we may have been mistaken in understanding it), then there can be no objection to it being used as a critique of all same-sex relationships and thus used as a kind of club with which to beat people in same-sex relationships. The fact that we may sometimes be uncertain what Isaiah or Paul was seeking to communicate is no reason for abandoning the attempt to understand what they wrote. Our culture, time and place does enter into the process of interpretation, but that does not

prevent us from trying to understand a text (and a person) different from us, one that needs understanding on their own terms. (pp.16-17)

Finally, they emphasise that we need to read the Bible as a whole.

> We discern the wisdom (and the guidance of the Holy Spirit) in the pluriformity of the narratives, even when there are overlapping accounts, different accounts, slight differences in the presentation and diversity of emphasis, Deuteronomy, for instance, covers some of the same material of the law and covenant as earlier sections of the Torah, but with a different context and purpose. In the New Testament, the four gospels have much in common, but also different themes and emphases, as well as individual unique material.

> To minimize the problems of proof-texting and to secure the most faithful interpretation, we must be attentive to the witness of the whole of Scripture. We are not merely assembling full range of relevant texts on a topic. We are treating them in a way that is consistent with what we know of the basic theological themes and principles, and especially in accordance with the teaching and witness of Jesus Christ, the incarnate Word of God. (p.17)

David W Torrance (2012) – The Bible as a whole not only contains but is the Word of God.

In the context of debate about same-sex relationships and the ministry in the Church of Scotland, David Torrance argues in his essay 'The authority of Scripture: is the Bible the Word of God or does it only contain the Word of God?' [58] that we need to recognize that the Bible has to be viewed as a unity:

---

[58] David Torrance, "The authority of Scripture: is the Bible the Word of God or does it only contain the Word of God?' in David Torrance and Jock Stein (eds)

The Bible is a unity. When we recognise its unity and how all Scripture points to Jesus Christ, then we begin to understand how all parts of the Bible, even those which at first seem less important or even offensive have a part to play in the total testimony. When we view the Bible as a whole as God intends, then we readily recognise that whereas all Scripture is inspired, 'no part is to be regarded as the Word of God in isolation from the rest. It is only in its relation to all the rest of Scripture that each particular part is the true and authentic Word of God.' (p.67) [59]

Holding that Scripture as a unified whole is the Word of God, Torrance is critical of those who argue that the Bible only contains the Word of God so that some parts of it are God's Word while others are not:

Those who adopt a progressive position and wish to accept same sex relationships, are generally willing to accept that the Bible is against same sex relationships, but seek to insist that the Bible only 'contains' the Word of God. Hence they argue that some things in the Bible, such as the prohibition of same sex relationships, are not the Word of God.

Some of a liberal persuasion wish also to say that the Bible was the Word of God and authoritative for the day in which it was written, but it is not always and necessarily authoritative for us today. They say that modern science has enabled us to understand much about creation of which the Biblical writers were unaware. They say it can guide us in our understanding of scripture and help us to determine what is the Word of God and authoritative. Is this not to adopt the same position as those who say that the Bible only 'contains' the Word of God? (p.74)

Embracing Truth – Homosexuality and the Word of God, Haddington: Handsel Press, 2012,
[59] The quotation is from C E B Cranfield, *The Bible and the Christian Life*, Edinburgh: T &T Clark, 1985, p.10.

The problem with these approaches, Torrance maintains, is that it involves human beings seeking to put themselves in the place of God:

> If we argue that the Bible only 'contains' the Word of God so that some things in the Bible are not the Word of God, then are we not seeking to place ourselves (as we said previously) above the Word of God so that we can make judgements upon it? In judging are we not, whether we know it or not, claiming to be superior to what we are judging, namely the Word of God, and in fact unwittingly seeking to place ourselves in the position of God? If we seek to argue that it is with the help of the Holy Spirit that we are judging what is and what is not the Word of God then we are still claiming to be superior to the Word. We are still claiming to be in control. We are judging and the Holy Spirit is simply our helper in judging what is and is not the Word of God! As Christians, this is an impossible position to hold. How can we at one and the same time listen to, and seek to obey God's Word and stand in a position of judgement over it? (pp.74-75)

In Torrance's view, 'While we must use our minds to the full with all their faculties of reason we must at one and the same time listen to the Word of God addressing us in the Bible and acknowledge its authority.' If the Church fails to do this its authority and its ability to witness effectively to Christ will be undermined:

> The Church owes her authority to the Word of God as witnessed to in Scripture. The Church's authority is the authority of a servant, commissioned to proclaim the Word of God. She has no independent authority of her own. 'The church is called, empowered, and guided to her proclamation by Holy Scripture, and that involves the assertion that Holy Scripture is the Word of God.' If and when the Church questions the authority of the Bible and seeks to elevate herself to a position where she can determine what is and what is not the Word of God, she loses her empowerment. The Church loses her authority to speak to

170

the world. She will inevitably speak with a divided voice, being uncertain about what is truly the Word of God. The Church will lose her identity in Christ. Society and the world will not generally be attracted to the Church or wish to listen to the Church. For the most part the Church will simply say what the rest of the world already thinks and says. The Church in these circumstances ceases to be 'the salt of the earth' proclaiming to the world the mind of Christ. (p.75)[60]

> **John Richardson (2012) – There are three types of law in the Old Testament, the cultic, the cultural and the moral. The New Testament sees sexual issues as coming under the last category and therefore sees sexual behaviour that was wrong in the Old Testament as still wrong.**

In his book *What God has made clean*[61] John Richardson also addresses the question of the continuing relevance of the Old Testament law for Christians in order to address the question of why Christians should continue to observe the Old Testament prohibition on homosexual activity when they no longer observe its prohibition on eating prawns.

He argues that in the Old Testament there are three types of laws, the cultic (which have to do with sacrifices, the sacrificial priesthood and the temple), the cultural, such as the food laws and circumcision (which serve as boundary markers distinguishing Israel as a distinct people belonging to God) and the moral law (such as the laws concerning murder and adultery) which have to with morally right or wrong behaviour. The cultic laws have been fulfilled through the sacrificial death of Christ and the cultural laws have been replaced as boundary markers by baptism and union with Christ (which is why the food laws and circumcision are no longer a requirement for Christians). However, the moral laws still need to observed, as the Sermon on the Mount

---

[60] The quotation is from Karl Barth, *Church Dogmatics* I/1, London and New York: T&T Clark, 2004, p.122.
[61] John Richardson, *What God Has Made Clean*, The Good Book Company, 2ed, 2012, Kindle edition.

makes clear, even though their observance is not the cause of our salvation and we are freed by Christ from the condemnation that follows from failing to obey them.

Having made these points he then asks: 'What can we say, then, about understanding and applying the Law in a Christian context? And what does this mean for the laws on prawns and the laws on homosexuality?'

He gives two answers to this question.

> First, as Law these are both things to which we have died in Christ. We no longer live under either of these laws but under grace, no longer having our relationship with God defined by them and freed from the condemnation that breaking them would bring. Nevertheless as Scripture both these laws point to Christ and are fulfilled in him.

> Second, then, we must determine the application of these laws in the New Testament context by asking how they are fulfilled in Christ. Regarding food laws, the question has been answered already. But although it should be clear that we can eat prawns and still belong to the Covenant community of God's people, some may still ask why we are not also allowed to engage in homosexual acts. Admittedly they are condemned in the Old Testament, but can we not suggest that, as with food laws, the coming of Christ renders all sexual acts 'clean'?

In order to answer this, he says:

> ....we need to demonstrate in which category of the Law the pronouncements on homosexuality belong – cultic and cultural (and therefore superseded by Christ's work on our behalf and our union with him) or moral (and therefore both transcended by him and yet to be applied in our lives). And this means looking at the basic biblical attitude to sexuality.

Having reviewed the evidence, he concludes that in the New Testament sexual issues come into the category of moral law:

...there is no indication in the New Testament that sexuality per se belongs to any other category than the moral. There is no point at which sexual practices are analysed either from a cultic perspective (and hence as fulfilled in Christ's priestly ministry) or from a cultural one (and hence as part of the now-obsolete barrier between Jew and Gentile).

Where the New Testament does take up themes on sexuality from the Old Testament it generally assumes that what was wrong then is wrong now. If there is a difference, it consists in raising the standards of moral behaviour required of God's people. Thus concubinage, divorce and polygamy may have been tolerated once, but are tolerable no longer (1 Corinthians 7:26, Matthew 19:7-8, 1 Timothy 3:2).

Even more so than under the Old Covenant heterosexual marriage is consistently presented under the New Covenant as the proper context for sexual activity, outside of which is only adultery and fornication. The remedy to sexual sin may be speedy marriage (as suggested in 1 Corinthians 7:26) or rigorous abstinence (as demanded by the Sermon on the Mount – see Matthew 5:27-30), but there are no sexually active alternatives to marriage envisaged. Marriage is to be welcomed, fornication is to be fled from (1 Corinthians 6:18). These are the two options for the New Covenant people.

Gordon Kennedy, Jane McArthur, Andrew McGowan (2013) – five core methods for interpreting Scripture and six observations on using the Old Testament law for ethical guidance.

Another Scottish reflection on Scripture is provided by Gordon Kennedy, Jane McArthur and Professor Andrew McGowan who set out 'The Traditionalist Case' in the report of the Church of Scotland's Theological Commission on Same-Sex Relationships and the Ministry.

173

They argue that 'the key to understanding and interpreting Scripture' is to recognise the integral relationship between Word and Spirit:

> It was the Holy Spirit who brought the Scriptures into existence (origins), it was the Holy Spirit who enabled the church to recognise Scripture as Scripture (canonicity), it is the Holy Spirit who helps us to understand the meaning of Scripture (illumination) and it is the Holy Spirit who enables the preaching of Scripture (empowerment). This being the case, the 'text' must be read in an attitude of prayer and worship, seeking the mind of the Holy Spirit, recognising that the Spirit will never contradict what has been given to us in Scripture. (p. 1/90)

They also identify five 'core methods' that are necessary for the proper interpretation of the Scriptures:

> First, there must be an examination of the original Hebrew and Greek texts by grammatico-historical exegesis. Second, there should follow a thorough investigation of the literary, social cultural and historical background to the text. Third, the text should be examined in context, taking into account the place of the text in the canonical book, and in the Bible as a whole, seeking to understand the intention of the author and the theological structure of the argument being presented. Fourth, there ought to be a recognition that difficult passages must be read in the light of clearer passages. Fifth, like the Reformers we should begin with a commitment to the fundamental unity of Scripture as the Word of God and hence part of our interpretation will involve comparing Scripture with Scripture. (p 1/90)

They acknowledge that even when these interpretative principles are employed Christians will still disagree:

> There are many subjects on which honest and faithful exegetes have come to differing conclusions. In the New Testament, for example, there are strands of teaching on baptism, on the

relations between church and state, on eschatology, on marriage and divorce, on women's ordination and many other matters, where Christians have gone to Scripture, believing it to be the Word of God and reached contradictory conclusions. These are differences 'within the family' and should not bring about separation of fellowship. (pp.1/90-91)

However, they say, the situation with regard to homosexual activity is 'entirely different.' This is because:

In both Old and New Testaments, homosexual acts are universally condemned. There is not one positive reference to homosexual acts in the entire Bible, rather such acts are regarded as sinful. This is what makes the issue of homosexual acts quite different from all of the matters on which Christians legitimately disagree. To give approval to homosexual acts within a Christian lifestyle is not, therefore, a matter of the interpretation of Scripture but is rather a rejection of the teaching of Scripture. (p.1/91)

Like Richardson, Kennedy, McArthur and McGowan also consider the issue of how Christians should understand the Old Testament law when seeking to make use of it for guidance on moral and ethical matters. They make six observations about this:

(a) The Old Testament in all its parts, has authority and relevance for Christians in all times and places, albeit that we recognise the distinction made in the Westminster Confession of Faith between the moral, ceremonial, and judicial aspects of the law.

(b) On the matter of the law, there is a unity between the Scriptures of the Old and New Testaments. This unity is not in any way undermined by the fulfilment of the law in Christ (Romans 10:4). Jesus himself indicated that not even the smallest letter or stroke of a pen would pass from the law until heaven and earth disappear (Matthew 5:18). Indeed, the apostles recognised that the underlying purpose of the law might be applied to new circumstances (1 Corinthians 9:7-12), as the *Confession* underlines.

(c) The priority of God's grace in giving the law further unites both Testaments. The law of God is not viewed as a burden to weigh people down but as a gracious gift to be celebrated (see Psalm 19 and 119). Having made his covenant with Israel through Abraham, God gives the law 430 years later through Moses. The giving of the law does not undermine the promises made in the covenant, rather it is a spelling out of how the covenant people ought to live before God (Galatians 3).

(d) The mission of Israel is central to our understanding of the Old Testament. God has chosen, elected, the people of Israel to achieve his purposes of grace and redemption in the midst of the other nations and to be a blessing to all the nations. God's election of Israel leads directly to an ethical demand upon the elect people. The mission given to Israel will be achieved through obedience to the law.

(e) The function of the law in relation to Israel must be understood. Having brought his people up from slavery in Egypt, God calls them to be a priestly nation, a holy people. The gift of the law serves the people in their priestly and holy service offered to the nations. Israel, through obedience to the law becomes a light to the nations.

(f) Israel is a model, or paradigm, for all nations and peoples of the earth. The role of the law within Israel similarly serves as a model for the lifestyle and ethics of the nations. The law cannot thus be confined to Israel but has a relevance to all peoples.(pp 1/96-97)

All this being so, Christians are called to 'strive to understand the objectives of the law within Israel' in order to be in a position 'to hold on to the objective of the law as given while applying the law to the changed situation in which we find ourselves.' (p.1/97)

Michael Brown (2014) – the Bible only mentions homosexuality very rarely because it is a 'heterosexual book.'

Dr Michael Brown notes in his book *Can you be Gay and Christian?* [62] that gay Christians point out that out of a total of more than thirty one thousand verses in the Bible there are between six and eight 'clobber passages' which are used to show that Scripture condemns homosexuality:

> In other words, out of tens of thousands of verses in the Scriptures, less than one in a thousand deal with the issue of homosexuality. How important can it actually be? And why in the world does the church make such a big deal about something that God's Word hardly addresses? Isn't this evidence of homophobic attitudes in the church rather than a careful representation of God's heart as expressed in His Word? (pp.82-83)

Brown's response is to say:

> Those are definitely fair questions, but the reality is that the evidence goes in the exact opposite direction. In other words, without any doubt, the Bible is a heterosexual book. From Genesis to Revelation the Bible presents and presupposes heterosexuality as the divinely intended norm. (p.83)

According to Brown, it is because the Bible is a 'heterosexual book,' in the sense of being a book that presupposes a heterosexual norm, that it does not mention homosexuality all the time. He gives the analogy of a new cookbook which features healthy desserts that don't contain sugar:

> In the introduction to the book the author explains her reasons for avoiding sugar products, telling you that you will find sumptuous, sweet dessert recipes – but all without sugar. And so, throughout the rest of the book, the word *sugar* is not found

---

[62] Michael Brown, *Can you be Gay and Christian?* Lake Mary: Front line, 2014, pp.82-83.

a single time – not once! Would it be right to conclude that avoiding sugar was not important to the author? On the contrary, it was so important that every single recipe in the book makes no mention of sugar.

It is exactly the same when it comes to the Bible and homosexuality. There are a few strong very clear references to homosexual practice – every one of them decidedly negative – and then not a single reference to homosexual practice throughout the rest of the Bible. Was it because avoiding homosexual practice was not important to the authors of the Scriptures? To the contrary, the only relationships that were acceptable in God's sight or considered normal for society were heterosexual relationships, so homosexual practice was either irrelevant (because it had nothing to do with the God ordained relationships of marriage and family and society) or, if mentioned, explicitly condemned. (p.84)

Developing the point further Brown writes:

The Bible is a heterosexual book, and that is why it does not need to constantly speak against homosexual practice. It is heterosexual from beginning to end, and my heart truly goes out to 'gay Christians' trying to read the Bible as 'their book.' For them it cannot be read as it is; it must be adjusted, adapted, and changed to fit homosexual couples and their families. In short 'gay Christians' must read God-approved homosexuality into the biblical text since it simply isn't there.

And this is the pattern throughout the entire Bible in book after book.

- Every single reference to marriage in the entire Bible speaks of heterosexual unions without exception, to the point that a Hebrew idiom for marriage is for a man 'to take a wife.'

- Every warning to men about sexual purity presupposes heterosexuality, with the married man often warned not to lust after another woman.
- Every discussion about family order and structure speaks explicitly in heterosexual terms, referring to husbands and wives, fathers and mothers.
- Every law or instruction given to children presupposes heterosexuality, as children are urged to heed or obey or follow the counsel or example of their father and mother.
- Every parable. Illustration or metaphor having to do with marriage is presented in exclusively heterosexual terms.
- In the Old Testament God depicts His relationship with Israel as that of a groom and a bride; in the New Testament the image shifts to the marital union of husband and wife as a picture of Christ and the Church.
- Since there was no such thing as in vitro fertilization and the like in biblical times, the only parents were heterosexual (it still takes a man and a woman to produce a child) and there is no hint of homosexual couples adopting children.

The Bible is a heterosexual book, and that is a simple, pervasive, undeniable fact that cannot be avoided, and, to repeat, this observation has nothing to do with a disputed passage, verse or word, it is a universal, all pervasive, completely transparent fact. (pp.88-89)

Chapter 7

The interpretation of the key biblical passages (II)

Genesis 1-3

Like their revisionist counterparts, traditionalist writers have not all said the same things about the opening chapters of Genesis. However, they have all emphasised that these chapters teach that God created human beings as male and female and that the complementary relationship between men and women with heterosexual marriage as its social expression is the basis for biblical sexual ethics.

The following examples illustrate these points.

> **The National Council of Churches of Singapore – God's has created human beings as male and female and this is the basis for marriage and sexual intercourse.**

The 2014 report *Homosexuality – Questions and Answers*[63] from the National Council of Churches of Singapore begins its account of the biblical approach to homosexuality by looking at what the Bible teaches about human sexuality and sexual relationships. It declares:

> According to the creation account in Genesis human beings are created male and female (Genesis 1:26). Genesis 2 tells us what this implies for human sexual relationship: the man is created for the woman, and vice versa. Genesis 2 also shows that the sexual relationship sanctioned by God is within the bounds of a monogamous marriage.
>
> This is God's original intention for sexual conduct. The sexes complement each other, and the command to procreate is a natural extension of this (Genesis 1:28). Human sexuality is a gift of God, and sex is a profound expression of love between a man and a woman within the covenant relationship of marriage.

---

[63] *Homosexuality – Questions and Answers*, Singapore: Genesis, 2014.

The Bible therefore clearly maintains that sexual intercourse is not for all: within marriage the Bible commands chastity; outside marriage it commands celibacy (Genesis 2:20-25, 1 Corinthians 6 & 7). (pp.3-4)

> **Richard Davidson – God created men and women as male and female from the beginning and Genesis 2 gives the pattern for marriage for all time.**

In his major study of the Old Testament understanding of sex and gender, *Flame of Yahweh*, [64] Professor Richard Davidson likewise notes that Genesis 1 and 2 make clear that 'God created the bipolarity of sexes from the beginning.' In his view, the idea that Genesis 1:27 teaches that humanity was originally androgynous 'cannot be sustained from the text of Genesis 1.' (p.19)

He quotes with approval the words of Gerhard Von Rad 'the plural in v27 ('he created them') is intentionally contrasted with the singular ('him') and prevents one from assuming the creation of an originally androgynous man.' (p.19)[65] This, he says, is confirmed:

> ...in the following verse (1:28), where God blessed them and commanded them to be fruitful and multiply, only a heterosexual couple, not a bisexual creature, could fulfil this command. Further confirmation of an original duality of the sexes and not an androgynous creature is the parallel passage of 5:2, where the plural them/they is again employed: 'Male and female he created them, and he blessed them and named them 'Humankind' when they were created. (p.19)

Davidson goes on to say that the distinction between male and female referred to in Genesis 1:27 is fundamental to our existence as human beings:

---

[64] Robert Davidson, *Flame of Yahweh,* Peabody: Hendrickson, 2007, p. 19.
[65] The quotation is from Gerhard Von Rad, *Genesis.* Philadelphia: Westminster Press, 1961, p.60.

To be human is to be a sexual person. 'We cannot say man without having to say male or female and also male and female. Man exists in this differentiation, in this duality.' Whether or not one agrees with Barth that 'this is the only structural differentiation in which he [the human being] exists' the sexual distinction is certainly presented in Genesis 1 as a basic component in the original creation of humankind. In Genesis 1 'heterosexuality is at once proclaimed to be the order of creation.' (pp.19-20)[66]

Turning to Genesis 2, he once again argues that the idea that this chapter describes an originally 'sexually undifferentiated earth creature' cannot be sustained from the text:

According to 2:7-8, 15-16, what God creates before woman is called *ha adam*, 'the man,' better translated as 'the human.' After the creation of woman, this creature is denoted by the same term (vv 22-23). Nothing has changed in the makeup of 'the human' during his sleep except the loss of a rib. There is no hint in the text of an originally bisexual or sexually undifferentiated being split into two different sexes. The androgynous interpretation suggests that human beings are not intrinsically sexual, a view which contradicts the anthropology of Gen 1-2. According to the biblical text *ha adam*, 'the human' formed before woman was not originally androgynous but was 'created in anticipation of the future.' He was created with those sexual drives towards union with his counterpart. This becomes apparent in the first human's encounter with the animals, which dramatically pointed up his need of 'a helper as his partner' (vv.18-20). Such a need is satisfied when he is introduced to woman and he fully realizes his sexuality vis-à-vis his sexual complement. (pp.20-21)

---

[66] Davidson is quoting Karl Barth, *Church Dogmatics* III/2, and Samuel H Dresner 'Homosexuality and the Order of Creation,' *Judaism* 40 (1991).

Davidson also observes that Genesis 2 describes how God arranged the first marriage and that 'the divinely designed marital form involved a heterosexual couple, a 'man' and a 'woman' (2:22-23). On the basis of the experience of the first couple Genesis 2:24 provides a 'succinct theology of marriage' in which the phrase a 'man and his wife':

> ...indicates a heterosexual marriage relationship of a man and a woman as the Edenic model for all time. Thus the intrinsic human duality of male and female and the heterosexual marital form involving a sexual union of a man with a woman (not man with man, or human with animal) constitute the divine paradigm for humanity from the beginning. (p.21)

> **The Evangelical Alliance – Genesis 1 and 2 teach us about a complementarity between men and women that is sexual (and therefore has procreative potential), but is also spiritual, emotional and psychological. Marriage between men and women has theological significance as a sign of God's covenant relationship with His people.**

The Evangelical Alliance Report *Biblical and Pastoral Responses to Homosexuality*[67] declares that Genesis 1:27-28 and 2:18-24 have been 'foundational for the classical Judaeo-Christian teaching that sexual intercourse is designed for expression solely within the life-long, marital relationship of a man and a woman.' p.36) In its view, these verses provide:

> ...the basic context for Christian understanding of human sexuality, procreation and marriage. Although they do not go into great detail about the distinctions between female and male they do emphasise that each was a separate, intentional creation, and that male and female were made distinct rather than 'two of the same.' (p.36)

---

[67] Andrew Goddard and Don Horrocks (eds), *Biblical and Pastoral Responses to Homosexuality.* London: Evangelical Alliance, 2012.

The report then goes on to talk about the complementarity between men and women resulting from creation:

> God's creation of the human race extends his intra-Trinitarian love outwards and opens the way to a covenant of mutual trust and care. When God sees that it is not good for Adam to be alone, he creates an 'other' – a woman – to be his companion (Genesis 2:20-25). The complementarity inherent in the resultant relationship is expressed at least partly in physical complementarity: the two who are clearly distinct and different are nevertheless intended to become 'one flesh' (Genesis 2:24). Traditional Jewish and Christian interpretation has accorded this complementarity a unique and exclusive moral status as an aspect of God's good created order, often understood in terms of natural law. It has been taken to mean that men and women are created anatomically for each other and that, since they correspond genitally and procreatively in a way that two men or two women cannot, homosexual activity lies, by its very nature, outside the realm of divine sanction. (p.36)

The report acknowledges that this argument has been criticised by Michael Vasey and Rowan Williams among others as an illegitimate leap from what is to what ought to be. It responds by saying that while 'heterosexual sex is itself hardly confined to penile-vaginal penetration and reproduction,' nevertheless:

> ...the biblical narrative on men, women and sex does not suggest that the link between heterosexual activity and procreation is merely incidental. In fact, Scripture takes the procreative capacity of heterosexual interaction per se to be a distinguishing mark of its explicit divine endorsement and something which validates it over against other, intrinsically non-reproductive, forms of sexual relating (e.g. Genesis 1:28, 9:1-15, 15:1-21, Psalm 127:3). (pp.36-37)

184

Having argued that the complementarity between men and women *is* physical, the report goes on to explain that it is not simply physical:

> Genesis 1:27 emphasises that God created human beings in His own image – male and female together – and this divine image is expressed in a relationship which may be sexual, but which is also spiritual, emotional and psychological. Being joined together in marriage becomes a fundamental expression of this – 'So a man will leave his father and mother and be united with his wife' (Genesis 2:24) – and provides the definitive biblical paradigm for human sexual love. Although this paradigm was not immediately confined to monogamous heterosexual marriage in the Old Testament, there can be little dispute that in biblical theological terms heterosexual monogamy emerges from it teleologically, as its purposed end. The Genesis creation narrative is thus later taken as the basis for monogamous heterosexual marriage by both Jesus and Paul (Matthew 19:4-6; Ephesians 5:31). It also serves as the ground of various laws and obligations designed to reinforce the singular validity and social status of such monogamy (Matthew 19:4-12; 1 Corinthians 7:4-10, Colossians 3:18-19, Titus 2:4-5; 1 Peter 3:1-7, Hebrews 13:4). (p.37)

Finally, the report notes that in the Bible marriage between a man and a woman is viewed as having theological significance:

> ...as a human covenant and form of union signifying God's covenant relationship with his people. This is a regular theme in the Old Testament prophets (eg. Hosea; Jeremiah 2:20; 3:1,20; 31:3ff; Ezekiel 16 and 23; Isaiah 50:1; 54:6-8; 62:4ff) and is given a Christo-centric and ecclesio-centric focus by Paul in Ephesians 5. Marriage is thus to mirror God's dealings with us in terms of commitment and a promise of faithful love and provision whilst other forms of sexual relationship are forbidden in Scripture as fornication (non-marital) or adultery (extra-marital).(pp.37-38)

185

> **Ian Paul – Genesis 1 and 2 describe how God created men and women in their unity and distinctiveness to represent the 'image and likeness' of God and the complementarity between them is the basis for sex and marriage. Brownson's arguments against the idea of' biologically based complementarity' are unpersuasive.**

The issue of complementarity between men and women is also covered by the account of the creation narratives given by Dr Ian Paul in his Grove Booklet *Same Sex Unions – The Key Biblical Texts.*[68]

Paul begins his exposition of these narratives by noting that these narratives 'do not integrate with each other in any simple way.' (p.7) However, they do share some key concerns with regard to the creation of humanity.

First of all Genesis 1:26-28 present:

> ....a strong binary presentation of humanity as male and female who, nevertheless, represent together the 'image and likeness' of God – unity and distinction almost alternate in these verses. The Hebrew text uses *adam* (frequently translated 'human being') in vv 26-27, and then adds the explanatory comment 'male and female' using the Hebrew nouns *zaqar* and *neqevah*.

There has been considerable debate about what it means to be the 'image and likeness' of God and we are offered two clues:

- The phrase comes again in Genesis 5:3, describing Adam's son Seth as 'in his likeness after his image.' This and other contemporary texts suggest that the central idea is of family resemblance.
- The phrase is strongly associated with God's sovereign rule over the creation. 'Let us make...so that they may

---

[68] Ian Paul, *Same Sex Unions – The Key Biblical Texts,* Cambridge: 2014, p.7.

rule' and 'He created them...and blessed them...and said...'Fill the earth and subdue it.'

So the idea appears to be that humanity (*adam*), male and female (*zaqar* and *neqevah*), reproduce, populate the earth and govern it as the offspring of the creator, ruling as his vice regents and with his delegated authority. (p.7)

Second, Genesis 2 'focuses in detail on the creation of humanity as male and female. '(p.7) In contrast to Davidson, Paul accepts the argument of feminist commentators such as Phyllis Trible that in Genesis 2 the *adam* seems at first to be an undifferentiated human rather than specifically male:

The significance of the term is made clear when *adam* is formed from the dust of the *adamah* (2:7), brought to life by the breath of God. The use of *adam* continues all the way to the start of verse 23; only then are the clearly gendered terms 'man' and 'woman' deployed (*ish* and *ishshah*).(p.7)

He then comments that the narrative in Genesis 2

...turns around the surprising declaration that it is not good for *adam* to be alone, and the subsequent quest for a 'suitable helper' (2:18, 20). The term 'helper' (*ezer*) has no particular sense of superiority or inferiority: God is at times described as the 'helper' of Israel. The term 'suitable for him' (*kenegdo*) is unusual, and has the sense of 'equal but opposite'; it is the kind of phrase you might use to describe the opposite bank of a river, combining both the sense of equality but difference and distinctiveness. The explicit sense of the narrative is that the animals are not 'suitable' since they are not the *adam's* equal. But the equally powerful, implicit sense of the narrative is that it would not be sufficient simply to form another *adam* from the ground. This 'helper' needed to be equal but opposite. There is clearly a task to be completed (subduing the earth and receiving God's blessing in being fruitful and multiplying [1:28] but there

187

is also a deep existential recognition in the (now) man's cry 'Here is flesh of my flesh!' The twin themes of similarity and difference wind their way through the story like a double helix. (p.8[69])

As Paul sees it, the climax of the narrative is the statement in Genesis 2:24 that the creation of woman out of man is the reason that a sexual bond between a man and a woman is the basis for family life:

> The breaking of a previous kinship bond and the formation of a new kinship bond are precisely located in the recognition of 'flesh of my flesh' and the uniting in sexual union that which was separated in the creation of the woman from the *adam*, who at that moment became the male (man), It is also interesting to note that the idea here of *one* man united with *one* woman is later deployed as a reforming filter in the interpretation of subsequent narratives, By the time of the NT, the permissibility of polygamy has been ruled out by reference back to the narrative of Genesis 2. (p.8)

Having offered his own reading of these narratives Paul moves on to offer a critique of Brownson's rejection of the idea that they teach the complementarity of men and women, which Paul sees as being in danger 'of setting aside the evident surface meaning of the text, that humanity is binary by gender, and that this reality is the basis of marriage.'(p.8)

Paul notes that main criticism of the idea of seeing complementarity in the Genesis narratives is the failure of commentators to agree on exactly what complementarity means. However, Paul does not find this argument persuasive:

---

[69] Paul notes in a footnote that this reading of Genesis 2 shows that 'there is a serious exegetical/narrative point behind what is sometimes seen as a cheap quip 'God made Adam and Eve not Adam and Steve,' or more precisely not Adam and another Adam. Without this the narrative makes no sense.' Fn 7, p.30.
[69] Ibid, p.8.

...just because we cannot explain absolutely or exhaustively what an idea is does not mean it is not in the text. For example, all are agreed that being made in the 'image of God' is central to the creation of humanity. But despite the clues in the text, there are many different proposals for what this means. Is it primarily about dominion? Or procreativity? Or creativity? Or rationality? Or relationality? All of these have been suggested – but this has not made anyone think that 'image of God' is not important in the text.(p.9)

Paul is also unpersuaded by the four specific objections to 'traditional readings of biologically based complementarity' offered by Brownson:

1. *In Genesis 2:4ff adam is not a binary being with one body but two centres of consciousness, so cannot be understood to be an undifferentiated being that is differentiated in the creation of woman.* Brownson appears to be extrapolating the logic of the traditionalist reading in an odd way here. There is no mention of this in the text, and no need to postulate that *adam* has two centres of consciousness in order to recognize that the text itself portrays *adam* as either undifferentiated in gender, or as needing completion, until 2:20.

2. *The focus of Genesis 2 is not on difference but on the similarity of male and female; this is seen in the rejection of the animals as 'suitable helper' since they are not similar enough, and in the man's cry of recognition.* But, as we have seen, the themes here focus on both similarity and difference. If difference was not an issue, God could simply have formed another *adam* from the dust.

3. *Male and female together as the image of God would mean that single people in general, and Jesus in particular, could not by themselves be the 'image of God,' unless Jesus was androgynous.* But in fact these problems *are* present in biblical theology. The Old Testament does treat the married state as normative, and Jesus' singleness does appear to have been quite counter

cultural – it is given its theological context by the imminent expectation of the kingdom of God. It is also interesting to note that in Paul's Christology gender is of little importance. Christ is representative and forerunner of both male and female in the people of God just as Adam is the representative of all humanity, both male and female (1 Corinthians 15:22; compare Romans 5).

4. *The phrase 'same flesh' signifies not actual flesh but bonds of kinship, since flesh is used elsewhere to designate relatives.* This proposal appears to be based on a misunderstanding of how language works. Brownson is suggesting that because 'flesh' is used metaphorically in reference to family ties, it no longer has a literal sense. This is a bit like noting that in certain subcultures 'brother' means 'friend' and concluding from this that 'brother' therefore no longer actually means 'male sibling.' (pp.9-10)

Paul's conclusion is Brownson's arguments do not undermine the traditional reading of Genesis that Brownson himself sets out at the beginning of his discussion of the matter:

> *The reason same-sex behaviour is portrayed negatively... is that God created man and woman to complement each other in the bond of marriage...[M]ale and female are both similar and different, and this complementarity of similarity and difference is foundational to human identity, and to the institution of marriage. Therefore, the only appropriate place for sexual-activity is the one-flesh union of marriage between a man and a woman.* This is clearly not all that Scripture has to say either about humanity, singleness or marriage, but it seems a fair description of the foundational role of Gen 1 and 2. (p.10, citing in italics Brownson p. 17)

> **Robert Gagnon – Men and women are made by God to form complementary sexual 'other halves' to each other and sexual activity that goes against this reality dishonours God's image in humanity.**

The issue of complementarity is also central to Robert Gagnon's essay 'How seriously does Scripture treat the issue of homosexual practice?' [70] in which he argues that Jesus himself defined Genesis 1:27 and 2:24 'as foundational for matters of human sexual ethics (Mark 10:6-8 par. Matthew 19:4-6)' and therefore 'Jesus' church must treat an offence against them as a major violation of Christian sexual ethics.' (p.156)

In this essay, Gagnon notes that there is a close connection in Genesis 1:27 between 'the image of God' and the creation of human beings as 'male and female.' He highlights two points from the language of this verse.

> First, though animals too participate in sexual differentiation and pairing, human sexual differentiation and pairing is uniquely integrated into God's image. This makes it possible for humans to enhance or to efface that image through their sexual behaviour. The alternative is to argue, falsely, that one's sexuality is wholly disconnected from God's image, thereby making it possible to engage in every kind of sexual misbehaviour, including adultery, bestiality and paedophilia without doing any harm to the imprint of God's image on the sexual dimension of human life. Secondly, a male-female sexual pairing manifests the fullness of the imprint of God's image on the sexual dimension of human life. While male and female each bear the stamp of God's image on their sexuality and have independent integrity as such, they do so in 'angular' and complementary ways. (p.157)

---

[70] Robert Gagnon, essay 'How seriously does Scripture treat the issue of homosexual practice?' in Torrance and Stein (eds), op.cit.

He then observes that Genesis 2:21-24 supplements the account in Genesis 1:

> ... with a beautiful picture of the reality that man and woman are complementary sexual 'other halves.' The sole differentiation produced by the removal of a 'side' from the original human is the differentiation of the sexes ('side' is a better translation than 'rib' of the Hebrew *tsela*...). The principle of two sexes becoming one flesh is thus grounded in the picture of two sexes emerging from one flesh (2:24). What is required in the story line of Genesis 2:21-24 is not merely a joining or merger of the two persons but a rejoining or remerging of the two sexes into one. It matters little how literally or metaphorically one takes the image. We are, after all, dealing with transcendent realities that, by necessity, require a certain amount of metaphor. The image conveys the essential point that man and woman are the two essential and complementary parts in a holistic picture of human sexuality. (p.157)

In Gagnon's view, those who suggest that Genesis 1:27 and 2:21-24 are 'merely descriptive texts and carry no prescriptive implications' for our view of human sexuality are at variance with both Jesus and Paul:

> Jesus gave priority to Genesis 1:27 and 2:24 when he defined normative and prescriptive sexual ethics and indeed predicated his 'two and two only' rule for the number of persons in a sexual bond on the twoness of the sexes at creation. Paul clearly had the creation texts in the background of his indictment of homosexual practice in Romans 1:24-27 and 1 Corinthians 6:9. (p.157)

He sees the main counter-argument against the position he has outlined as the contention that it leads to a denigration of singleness and therefore to a denigration of Jesus himself. However, he rejects this argument for six main reasons:

192

1.The truth of two primary sexes. It is axiomatic and undeniable that a male or a female is only one half of a complete sexual whole since, obviously, there are two primary sexes. This is just another way of stating the elementary point that women bring out dimensions of God's image lacking in men and vice versa.

2.The impact of sexual behaviour on God's image in humans. It is equally axiomatic and undeniable that one's sexual expression has powerful potential to honour or dishonour, to enhance or deface, one's own creation in God's image. Sexuality and divine image are interconnected in humans. Unlike some pagan conceptions of sexuality that largely disconnect sexual behaviour from religious devotion, the Judeo-Christian conception of sexuality thoroughly integrates the two dimensions so that sexual purity becomes a vital component of one's spirituality.

3.'Made in God's image' as a relative quality. It is legitimate to speak of the two sexes as complementary, and so incomplete, representations of God's image in the restricted sphere of sexuality without denying the broader integrity of an individual's creation in God's image. In a similar way one can speak of God's image as more fully represented in a community of believers than in any single individual in isolation without denying that the individual too is made in God's image.

4. The single state as a non-moral deficit. Both Jesus and Paul viewed the single state as a form of deprivation or deficit, though recognizing the value of a sexually unattached life for the advancement of God's kingdom (Matthew 19:10-12, 1 Corinthians 7:7-8, 25-40). They also recognized a distinction, as persons do today, between forgoing a valid sexual union, which is an experience of deprivation, but no sin, and wilfully entering into a structurally incompatible union, which is sin. One's status as a single sex is not a moral deficit in God's image, but a non-moral deficit since God himself ordained distinct sexes.

5. Active entrance into a structurally incongruous union is a moral violation that assaults the image of God stamped on humans. While a state of singleness violates no boundaries, a discordant sexual merger does disrupt formal or structural congruities and thus dishonour the human that God created one to be. Obvious instances of the latter that presumably even advocates for homosexual unions would have to acknowledge include attempted sexual unions involving close blood relations, three or more persons concurrently, and adult and a child, or a human and an animal.

6. Homosexual practice as a denial of the integrity of one's maleness and femaleness made in God's image. It is same sex activity, not singleness that compromises one's integrity as a sexual being made in God's image. For the logic of a same sex sexual bond is that each partner is only half his or her own sex since a sexual bond by its very nature involves bodily integration of two discrete halves. This dishonors the integrity of God's image imprinted on maleness, if one is male, and on femaleness, if one is female. The picture in Genesis 2:21-24 of a woman being formed from what is pulled out of the man/human illustrates the point that the missing element from one sex is not another of the same sex but rather one from the only other sex. The story conveys the self-evident point that on a sexual level men and women are configured bodily – and here I mean 'bodily' in a holistic sense – as open-ended to a person of the only other sex, not a person of the same sex. (pp.157-8.)

> John Goldingay – Genesis 1-2 teach that God created human beings in his image as both male and female. The creation narratives depict the relationship between men and women in egalitarian terms. A hierarchical relationship between them is the result of the fall in Genesis 3.

Goldingay writes in his essay 'What does the Bible say about Women and Men?'[71] that that image of God referred to in Genesis 1:26-27:

> ...consists in (or perhaps rather implies) humanity's being put in control of other creatures (1:26) and its being created male and female (1:27); only this second gloss on God-likeness is mentioned when the formula reappears later (5:1-2). Humanity is present only in this combination of male and female, and thus the God-likeness of humanity is present. (p.297)

In Genesis 1, he says, *adam* does not refer simply to the male. It is a generic term like 'mankind,' 'humankind.' or *'homo sapiens'* that is further defined as consisting of both male and female. This means that 'there is about humanity both a unity and a plurality, both a unity and a diversity.' It also means that there is no suggestion that the female is somehow secondary to the male:

> Only man and woman together make real humanity. Together they hear God's word, receiving God's blessing and commission to multiply as families, to exercise power in the world, and to enjoy its produce. (p.298)

In his view, Genesis 2 can be read in a similar 'egalitarian' way:

> Here, too, God forms 'a human being,' *adam* again, but not a collective, and the context here stresses the link between *adam* and the *adamah* from which it was made. In the first part of the story, effectively the creature is sexually undifferentiated. When differentiation appears, a divine awareness of the being's

---

[71] John Goldingay, 'What does the Bible say about men and women?' in *Key Questions about Christian Faith.*

incompleteness appears with it. God thus forms another human being as a companion for the first, one who stands over against the first. KJV's 'help meet for him' has misled people. 'Helper' does not suggest a subordinate God himself is often people's 'helper' in the First Testament. The image of the Holy Spirit as the one who comes alongside to be our helper and companion (John 14) may contribute to our getting the right impression in Gen 2. (p.298)

The identity of being that these two people share:

....is expressed by the picture of one of them being built up from a part of the other. Their equality may also be suggested by the part being a rib: the woman is not made from the man's head to rule him, or from his feet to be treated as his servant, but from his side, to stand alongside him 'in a partnership of love.' It is when she stands alongside him that the man becomes aware of himself as a man, in the company of a woman (*ish*, *ishshah*). He addresses her as a person over against himself (he does not name her, as if he were in control of her, in the way he did the animals). The aloneness of the sole human being need not imply loneliness, but it does imply that he faces a monumental task on his own, and a task that a man cannot accomplish, because he cannot bear children. His aloneness is overcome through the gift of another in whom he recognizes identity, yet also the differentiation of sexuality, which is a means of their communion and their procreating. (p.298)[72]

As Goldingay sees it, it is only in Genesis 3, after the first human beings have turned from God's way, 'that a hierarchical relationship between a man and his wife comes into being. 'To love and to cherish' becomes 'to desire and to dominate' (3:16).' (p.299)[73]

---

[72] The quotation is from Peter Lombard, *Sentences*. II, 18/2.
[73] The quotation is from Derek Kidner, *Genesis*, Leicester: IVP, 1967, p.71.

> **Sam Allberry – God created human beings as male and female in order enable them to fulfil the role for which made them. As Jesus underlined, God's creation of men and women is the basis of marriage and sexual union.**

In his more popular study *Is God anti-gay?* [74] Sam Allberry reflects a lot of the themes that have already been highlighted by the writers we have looked at in this section.

He states that in Genesis 1 'humanity is created in God's image and tasked with ruling the earth and its creatures.' 'In this context,' he says 'the point of the sexual difference between men and women is reproduction. Increasing in number will enable them to fill the earth and be present everywhere to rule over it.' (p.16)

In Genesis 2 'the differences between the sexes are presented in a different light.' In this chapter

> Adam is created first, and yet it is 'not good' for him to be alone. By himself he is unable to fulfil the purpose for which God created him. The remedy to this is the creation of the first woman. In contrast to the various animals Adam has just named, the woman perfectly corresponds to him. (p.16)

There are various aspects to this perfect correspondence:

> She is like him in the right way (*made of the same stuff*) and unlike him in the right way (*woman, rather than man*). It is this *complementarity* that leads to profound unity between them when they eventually come together in sexual union. (p.17)

Allberry further notes that the writer of Genesis 2 is not just talking about Adam and Eve but also about human beings in general:

> We are not being told about this first couple on the off-chance we're interested in our ancient family history. No, their story is

---

[74] Sam Allberry, *Is God anti-gay?* The Good Book Company 2013, p.15.

true for all of humankind. It sets up a pattern that we see repeated in every generation. The writer pulls back from their immediate setting to make the general observation: 'That is why a man leaves his father and mother and is united to his wife...'

What was going on with Adam and Eve explains what has gone on ever since. The perfect 'fit' between the two of them is the foundation for every human marriage since. The account is not just about their union but every marriage union. (p.17)

The teaching of Genesis is underlined by Jesus in Matthew 19:3-6. Here Jesus teaches on the basis of Genesis that human beings are created as men and women and it is for this reason that there is marriage and sexual union:

Humanity is gendered. We are not just human beings, but men and women. And this has been the case from 'the beginning.' Twas ever thus. Yes, gender is something we humans interpret and lend cultural expression to, but it is not something that we invent or fully define. It is how God created us.

Next, Jesus shows us that this sexual difference is why we have marriage. We are male and female: 'for this reason a man will leave...' It is because we are male and female that we have the phenomenon of marriage. Marriage is based on gender. Marriage would not exist without the sexual differences between men and women.

It is this sexual difference that accounts for the depth of union between the man and the woman. Eve was created out of Adam; made from his body. Their one-flesh union is therefore something of a re-union; joining together what had originally been one. (pp.19-20)

> **Gordon Kennedy, Jane McArthur, Andrew McGowan – The distinction between men and women is built into the fabric of creation. It enables procreation and the harmony and intimacy of marriage. Human sexuality has been damaged by the Fall, but through Christ it can be redeemed and renewed.**

Finally, Kennedy, McArthur and McGowan offer the following succinct summary of Genesis 1 and 2 in their contribution to the Church of Scotland report:

> All that Genesis will teach us about humanity is set in the context of creation as described in Genesis 1-2. Genesis 1 describes creation as the work of one God for his glory and Genesis 2 complements this with a more anthropocentric presentation of creation. From Genesis 1:26-27 the male female distinction is taken to reflect something of the image of God. This is built into the fabric of human creation and is not to be confused [with] or treated as a consequence of the Fall. The command given in verse 28, 'Be fruitful and multiply' would suggest that propagation of the species is commended by God, which is a result of an exercise of human sexuality.
>
> In 2:18-25 we have an explanation of the existence and power of the male-female bond within marriage. For von Rad the point of the account is to explain the human condition, the powerful attraction between male and female. Gordon Wenham helpfully adds to the work of von Rad, writing that marriage is to be between a male and a female, specifically and exclusively. This unique relationship of marriage also exists for harmony and intimacy. Marriage between a male and a female is the high standard to which relationships between male and female aspire. When commenting on this verse in Matthew 19:6, the Lord Jesus adds that any destruction of this male-female relationship, presumably by any non-married sexual activity, destroys, or seriously mars, an element of God's creative activity.

Humanity has been created male and female. There is a powerful attraction between male and female which has been built into human creation. When this attraction is expressed within marriage between a male and female, there is harmony and intimacy, a reflection of the harmony and intimacy experienced by the Triune God, whose image is impressed upon both male and female. (pp. 1/97-98 [75])

They also note that the pattern of sexual relationship established in Genesis 1 and 2 is marred though not destroyed by the Fall described in Genesis 3. They emphasise the words at the end of Genesis 3:16 'Your desire shall be for your husband and he shall rule over you' and comment:

This verse reinforces the loss of harmony and fellowship between male and female which we see played out in our lives day and daily. The consequences of the Fall, then, affects human sexuality. There is now no expression of human sexuality free from the stain of sin. This does not mean that all human sexuality is entirely sinful, or as sinful as it could be. By grace, though broken, the image of God is still borne by humans and so in Christ our sexuality can be redeemed and renewed. (1/98)

Genesis 19 and Judges 19

In contrast to a number of the revisionist writers we looked at in Part I, traditionalist writers continue to see the narratives in Genesis 19 and Judges 19 as being concerned with homosexuality. They also see these chapters as relevant to the contemporary debate about same-sex sexual activity, even though they may involve the specific issue of the desire to commit homosexual rape.

---

[75] The references are to Gerhard Von Rad *Genesis*, London: SCM, 1972, pp.84-85 and Gordon Wenham, *Genesis 1-15*, Dallas: Word, 1987, p.69.

The National Council of Churches of Singapore – Sodom was punished for the sin of homosexuality.

The report from the National Council of Churches of Singapore takes a straightforward approach. The story in Genesis 19 does involve God's punishment of homosexual sin. The report declares:

> There are a number of passages in the Bible that deal with homosexuality, whether directly or indirectly. One of the main texts is the story of Sodom and Gomorrah in Genesis 19. One of the main texts is the story of Sodom and Gomorrah in Genesis 19. Two visitors arrive and stay with Lot. But before they can retire for the night, the men of Sodom gather round Lot's house and demand that he brings the two men out so they can 'have sex with them' (19:5, NIV). There is no ambiguity in the text. The men of Sodom wanted to have homosexual intercourse with Lot's guests.
>
> Sodom was responsible for many acts of wickedness and immorality. Jeremiah presents a catalogue of Sodom's sins, including adultery, lying and unwillingness to repent (Jeremiah 23:14), But among the sins of Sodom is the practice of homosexuality. 2 Peter 2:7 interprets one of Sodom's sins as 'licentiousnesss' and Jude 7 describes the sins of Sodom and Gomorrah as 'unnatural lust.' It is therefore reasonable to conclude that homosexuality was among the many sins for which Sodom was punished. (pp.5-6)

Bill Arnold – Genesis 19 describes homosexual intent.

In his 2009 commentary on Genesis[76] Dr Bill Arnold is also clear that Genesis 19 says that that there was homosexual intent among the men of Sodom. He writes

---

[76]Bill T Arnold, *Genesis*, Cambridge: CUP,2009.

Traditionally of course the sexual connotations of 'know' (*yd*) have led interpreters to assume the offence of the men of Sodom is homosexuality (or homosexual gang rape) which gave rise to our English term 'sodomy.' Other options have been offered, such as the citizens' violation of hospitality laws, compounded by Lot's offer of his daughters as the most deplorable treatment of women. However, the use of 'know' with undeniably sexual denotation in the same context (19:8) makes it difficult to deny homosexual intent on the part of the men of Sodom, whether it is taken as the most serious offence of the text or not. Attempts to deny this are driven more by today's sensibilities rather than by the text before us. (p.184)

> **Sam Allberry – In Genesis 19 and Judges 19 it is not only the violence of the crowd but the nature of their sexual cravings that is seen as ungodly.**

Allberry is similarly clear about the meaning of Genesis 19. He notes that the fact that in later parts of the Old Testament Sodom is accused of 'oppression, adultery, lying, abetting criminals, arrogance, complacency and indifference to the poor,' but no mention is made of homosexual conduct raises the question of whether 'we have read homosexuality into the Genesis narrative.' (p.27) However, he says that 'a close look at the story' puts this doubt to rest.

First of all:

> ...although the Hebrew word for 'know' (*yada*) can just mean to 'get to know' someone (rather than to 'know' them sexually), it is clear both from the crowd's aggression, and Lot's dreadful attempt at offering them his daughters as an alternative, that they are looking for more than a quiet chat over a glass of wine. (p.27)

202

Secondly:

> ...this crowd is not a small, unrepresentative group. It is very clear that this is the whole male community: 'the men of Sodom, both young and old, all the people to the last man.' This is how the city is behaving. This is what Sodom does.

> This explains what happens next; the angels warn Lot that judgment is imminent (v13). They have discovered all they need to know. The outcry against Sodom is justified. (p.27)

Alllberry's conclusion is that the biblical evidence tells us that issue with Sodom was sex and not just violence:

> ..it was not only the violent way the crowd were attempting to satisfy their sexual cravings that was ungodly, but also the nature of the cravings as well. A parallel episode in Judges 19 indicates that it was not just pagan Sodom, but also the people of God who commit this kind of sin. (p.28)

Other traditionalist writers give more detailed and nuanced accounts of the two passages.

Willard Swartley – Genesis 19 and Judges 19 describe God's judgement on homosexual rape and inhospitality, but Genesis 19 also involves a judgement against homosexual lust.

The Mennonite biblical scholar Professor Willard Swartley declares in his book *Homosexuality – Biblical Interpretation and Moral Discernment*, [77] that the narratives in Genesis 19 and Judges 19 'are rightly said to narrate God's judgment upon homosexual rape and inhospitality and therefore hardly address – nor condemn - loving homosexual relations.' (pp.31-32) However this does not mean that these texts:

> ...do not speak to the issue of homosexual practices. In Genesis 19 it is precisely (homo) sexual lust that precludes hospitality.

---

[77] Willard Swartley, *Homosexuality – Biblical Interpretation and Moral Discernment*, Scottsdale: Herald Press, 2003, pp.31-32.

Hence, the story judges against not only Sodom's inhospitality, but also against homosexual lust, since it foreclosed the possibility of the townsmen welcoming the male strangers in a truly hospitable manner. (p.32)

Swartley acknowledges that it has been argued that 'to know' in Genesis 19:5 refers to knowing someone in a general rather than a sexual sense. However, he is not convinced:

Several scholars have argued persuasively that the Hebrew word *yadha* (to know) in 19:5 certainly intends carnal (sexual) knowledge (compare Genesis 4:25), as the use of the same verb in Genesis 19:8 makes clear, 'I have two daughters who have not known (*yadha*) a man. The view of John Boswell that Genesis 19 shows no sexual interest is, as Gerald D Coleman puts it, 'an interpretation [that] is erroneous and should sustain no credibility.' (p.32 [78])

He also notes that some later writings refer to the sexual nature of Sodom's transgression:

In about a dozen instances in later writings, especially during the intertestamental period, there are references to the sin of Sodom as sexual. Another equal number refer to Sodom's wealth without specifying the sexual aspect; some specify wealth or rebellion...Within the Old Testament itself, Isaiah 1:10 and 3:9 do not specify Sodom's sin but utilize Sodom as symbolic of people departing from the ways and deeds of God. Jeremiah accuses the prophets of Jerusalem of committing adultery and walking in lies, thus becoming like Sodom to God (23:14). Ezekiel names the sins as pride, excessive food and prosperity, and failure to aid the needy. Jude 7, however, specifies Sodom's sin as sexual immorality and unnatural lust. (p.32)

---

[78] The quotation is from Gerald Coleman, *Homosexuality: Catholic Teaching and Pastoral Practice*. Mahwah: Paulist Press, 1995, p.61.

> **Gordon Kennedy, Jane McArthur, Andrew McGowan –Genesis 19 and Judges 19 involve two sins, inhospitality and the offence of homosexual practice. In Genesis 19 both the action of the crowd and Lot's action in offering up his daughters are abhorrent and in Judges 19 neither the Levite, the old man, nor the men of Gibeah come out well.**

In their contribution to the Church of Scotland report, Kennedy, McArthur and McGowan declare that in Genesis 19:5 'we come to the heart of the sin of Sodom.' As they see it, the phrase 'that we may know them':

> ...cannot refer to any ignorance on the part of the men of the city as to the identity of the visitors, who entered publicly through the city gate. Since עדי 'to know' is frequently used in Genesis of sexual intercourse, this seems the likeliest meaning here (see 4:1, 17, 25; 24:16). The response of Lot to his request by the men of the city, indicates his understanding of their request for knowledge of the visitors to be a sexual request. (p.1/99)

It follows, that 'the sin of Sodom is sexual sin.' Although there is indeed a breach of hospitality, this not all there is:

> ...there is more, there is improper sexual desire which falls under the judgment of God. In 19:6-7 Lot's words cannot be directed against a breach of hospitality, he clearly understands the desire of the mob to be sexual. The offer of his daughters (verse 8), must be intended to shock the first audience, as it shocks us. We cannot in any way condone Lot's offer of his daughters to the mob. Lot is not free from sin. Lot is not free from sin and so is not rescued from Sodom because of his goodness or righteousness, but by the mercy of the Lord (19:16). (p.1/100)

In the Genesis story, they write:

Lot has taken a wrong turn in settling in Sodom and the consequences of this error are now played out when judgement falls upon Sodom, There is here no condoning of heterosexual violence in contrast to a condemnation of homosexual violence, both are abhorrent. With 19:9-11 the attack reaches its climax, as the mob ignore Lot and push forward seeking to tear down the door that they might achieve their wicked objectives. The two visitors save Lot, striking the men of Sodom with blindness. As elsewhere in Scripture (Isaiah 6:10, John 9), this physical blindness is accompanied by intellectual or spiritual blindness. The men of Sodom cannot see physically or spiritually where they are going. (p.1/100)

Their conclusion is that the sin of Sodom:

...is both sexual and also a rejection of hospitality. There is no justification for the attempt to suggest that the homosexual element in the story held no interest for the author. The sexual crime in view at Sodom is homosexual and it is condemned. (p.1/100)

On Judges 19 they note the similarities between this text and Genesis 19. In their view no one comes out of the story well:

...not the Levite, not the old man, not the men of Gibeah. Yes, there is an offence against the practice of hospitality here, however, this is not the only offence. The men of Gibeah demand in 19:22, 'Bring out the man who came into your house, that we may know him.' The man of the house responds in 19:24 by offering his virgin daughter and the concubine of the Levite, 'Let me bring them out now. Violate them and do with them what seems good to you, but against this man do not do this outrageous thing.' As in the case of Sodom, in Genesis 19, what lies behind this story is a sexual offence, that of homosexual practice. (p.1/105)

206

For them the key point in this text is that while Israel knew of the existence of homosexual practice:

> ...as the people of God such sexual behaviour was forbidden them and was abominable to Yahweh. Homosexual behaviour is an attack against Israel being the people of God and this element of the story in Judges 19-21 cannot be denied. (p.1/106)

> **Richard Davidson – in Genesis 19 the sin of Sodom involves homosexuality and not just inhospitality and the language used does not refer specifically to rape. In Judges 19 the sin involved is both inhospitality and rape, but the homosexual element adds an extra dimension to the horror of the story.**

In *Flame of Yahweh* Davidson notes the argument of Derek Bailey and others that the sin of Sodom was a failure of hospitality, but gives three reasons for rejecting it.

The first is the emphasis on the male inhabitants of Sodom and the gravity of their sin:

> It is important to recognise that in the Genesis narrative, initial reference to the wickedness of Sodom (13:13) utilizes the term 'men [*anse*] of Sodom' (RSV) not the more generic term 'people' (am) used elsewhere in Genesis for a reference to the general inhabitants of a city. In 19:4, the same term, *anse*, 'men of [a place],' is repeated twice in one verse, again to underscore that these are males who surround Lot's house. The immediate context also indicates that the wickedness of Sodom goes far beyond (although it does not eliminate) issues of hospitality. The narrator first describes the condition of Sodom's men as 'wicked, great sinners against the Lord (13:13), and then the same message is recorded from the mouth of God: 'How great is the outcry against Sodom and Gomorrah and how very grave their sin!' Such language could hardly describe merely a spirit of inhospitality. (p.146)

The second, the 'Achilles' heel' of the hospitality argument is the use of 'to know' in Genesis 19:

> In v. 8 the verb *yada* is used in connection with Lot's daughters and unmistakeably refers to sexual intercourse. The close proximity of its usage in v. 5 to this clear sexual meaning of *yada* in v.8 makes it very difficult to conclude that it has a different, nonsexual meaning in the former. Furthermore, 'Bailey's explanation for the reason Lot offers his daughters to the men of Sodom is simply not convincing....It is much more difficult to explain why Lot would offer his daughters to people who came only to demand to check up on two foreigners than if they wanted to abuse them sexually.' (p.147 [79])

Thirdly, there is the way that Genesis 19 fits into the wider structure of the Book of Genesis:

> James DeYoung shows how the literary macrostructure of Genesis also points to a sexual interpretation for Gen 19. Following the literary analysis of Robert Alter, he points to the three episodes just prior to the birth narrative of Isaac that delay and pose a threat to the fulfilment of God's promise of seed for Abraham – Abraham's intercession and the destruction of Sodom and Gomorrah (Gen 18-19), the incest of Lot and his daughters as the origins of the Moabites and Edomites (Genesis 19), and the sister-wife episode involving Abraham, Sarah, and king of Gerar (Genesis 20) – and shows that 'each episode relates sexual sin and its punishment....the literary structure of the text demands a homosexual meaning for the sin of Sodom. Illicit sexual enjoyment or opportunism connects all three of the episodes.' DeYoung, among others, also points out that scholars generally recognize that the narrator of the book of Judges consciously modelled his story of the disgrace at Gibeah (Judges

---

[79] The quotation is from Sakae Kubo, *Theology and Ethics of Sex*, Washington: Review and Herald, 1980, p. 74.

19) after the account in Gen 19, and since the Judges story clearly has reference to homosexual activity, one should interpret the story of Gen 19 in the same way. (p.147 [80])

Davidson further notes the view of 'most modern interpreters' that what was contemplated by the men of Sodom was 'rape or violence,' but argues that this view goes beyond what is actually in the text:

> It is likely that the specific actions contemplated by the men of Sodom included homosexual rape, but Victor Hamilton points to a fourfold problem with limiting the reference here only to homosexual *rape*. First, the verb yada, which has been translated by some versions as 'to abuse' in this passage (e.g. JB), nowhere else in the HB carries the meaning 'abuse' or 'violate.' Second, elsewhere in Scripture, specific terminology besides yada is used to describe incidents or cases of rape ('to seize,' 'to lie with,' 'to force'; cf. Genesis 34:2, 2 Samuel 13:14, Deuteronomy 22:25-27...). Third translating yada as 'rape' or 'violate' in Gen 19:5 would force a different meaning on the word than three verses later, where yada undeniably means 'have intercourse with' regarding Lot's daughters. Finally, Hamilton points out that 'such an interpretation forces these incredible words in Lot's mouth: 'Do not rape my visitors. Here are my daughters, both virgins – rape them!' In light of these problems, Hamilton concludes, correctly, I believe – 'that the incident frowns on homosexual relations for whatever reason.' (p.148 [81])

Davidson also contends that in the reference to Sodom in Ezekiel 16:49-50 'the sin of inhospitality is indeed signalled by the prophet' but 'specific terminology in the immediate context of these verses in Ezekiel

[80] The reference is to James B DeYoung *Homosexuality: Contemporary Claims Examined in Light of the Bible And other Ancient Literature and Law*, Grand Rapids: Kregel, 2000, pp.38-40>

[81] The reference is to Victor P Hamilton, *The Book of Genesis: Chapters 18-50*, Grand Rapids: Eerdmans, 1995, pp.34-35.

16 also indicates the nature of the sin of Sodom.' In addition, the fact that Ezekiel is referring not just to rape but to the 'inherent degradation' of same-sex intercourse is 'confirmed by the intertextual linkages between Ezekiel and sexual abominations mentioned in Levitical legislation.' (p.149)

On Judges 19, Davidson declares that the text is concerned with both inhospitality and homosexual rape:

> Both are part of the wicked and vile outrage that the assailants demand. Certainly the Gibeahites were inhospitable, but they also attempted homosexual rape. The two themes intertwine, as they did in the closely paralleled account of Sodom and Gomorrah in Gen 19. 'The inhospitality is reflected in their attempt at homosexual rape. Inhospitality and homosexuality are not mutually exclusive.' (p.161 [82])

However, for Davidson it is homosexual intercourse as such rather than homosexual rape that is the *nebala* ('vile thing') referred to in verses 23-24 of Judges 19. He cites with approval Robert Gagnon's rejection of the idea that the text condemns only homosexual rape and not homosexuality per se. He quotes Gagnon as asking how it is possible to argue, in the light of the clear opposition to homosexual activity in the Pentateuch and the Deuteronomic History, 'that homosexual intercourse *per se* did not add to the dimension of horror for the old man, the Levite, and for the narrator of the story?' (p.162 [83])

> **Robert Gagnon – Ezekiel 16:49-50 views the sin of Sodom as involving homosexuality.**

Gagnon argues in his article 'How seriously does Scripture treat the issue of homosexual practice' that not only is the sin of Sodom identified as sexual in nature by Philo, Josephus and other early Jewish

[82] The quotation is from Donald Wold, *Out of Order*, Grand Rapids: Baker Books, 1998, p. 85.
[83] The quotation is from Robert Gagnon, *The Bible and Homosexual Practice*, Nashville: Abingdon Press, 2001, p.95.

texts such as the *Testament of Naphtali, Jubilees* and Enoch and by Jude 7 and 2 Peter 2:6-7, 10 in the New Testament, but also by Ezekiel 16:49-50 in the Old Testament. He gives five reasons for taking this view of Ezekiel 16:

> According to Ezekiel 16:49-50, Sodom 'did not take hold of the hand of the poor and needy. And they grew haughty and committed an abomination (toe'vah) before me and I removed them when I saw it.' Is the reference to 'committing an abomination' to be identified with 'not taking the hand of the poor and needy?' The evidence indicates that it is to be identified rather with man-male intercourse.
>
> > (1) The vice list in Ezekiel 18:10-13, consisting of ten vices, indicates otherwise since it clearly distinguishes between the offence 'oppresses the poor and needy' (fifth vice) from the offence 'commits an abomination 'ninth vice.'
> >
> > (2) The two other singular uses of *toe'vah* in Ezekiel refer to sexual sin (22:11, 33:26).
> >
> > (3) All scholars of Ezekiel agree that Ezekiel knew, and shared extraordinary affinity with, either the Holiness Code (Leviticus 17-24) or a precursor document. Certainly the Levitical prohibitions of man-male intercourse are absolute...
> >
> > (4) The phrase 'committed an abomination' in Ezekiel 16:50 is identical to the phrase in Leviticus 20:13 that refers to man-male intercourse.
> >
> > (5) The conjunction in Ezekiel 18:12-13 of a singular use of *toe'vah* as a reference to a single specific offence, with a plural use of *toe'voth*, as a summary description of all preceding offences, is exactly what we find in Leviticus 18:22 (man-male intercourse) and 18:26-30.
>
> The medieval Jewish commentator Rashi also understood the text as reference to homosexual practice as have some modern

211

commentators...It is apparent then, that Ezekiel 16:50 was interpreting the Sodom episode partly through the lens of the absolute prohibition of man-male intercourse in Leviticus 18:22 and 20:13, indicating that he understood the same sex dimension of the rape to be a compounding offence. This strengthens the ideological nexus between the Yahwist's interpretation of the Sodom episode and the absolute sex prohibitions in Levi 18 and 20. (p.164)

> **The Evangelical Alliance – although Sodom was guilty of other sins there was a sexual element to its transgression.**

The Evangelical Alliance report begins by noting that while the Sodom story involves a breach of hospitality and other more deep rooted sins there does appear to have been a sexual element to Sodom's transgression:

> The story of Lot and Sodom clearly entails a gross breach of hospitality. According to justice and tradition, the men of Sodom should have protected Lot's visitors (cf. Ezekiel 16:49) but they abused them. As the texts suggests through its report that God aims to destroy the city (Genesis 19:12-14), and as Jesus later confirms when he denounces Sodom in Matthew 10:14-15, and 11:20-24, the men's actions are a manifestation of much deeper-seated sins of idolatry, pride and rebellion. These sins are strong themes of the passage but this cannot mask the fact that the abuse in question does appear to have strongly sexual connotations. (p.40)

It puts forward two arguments to support the idea that there was a sexual element to the sin in Genesis 19:

First, although the Hebrew verb 'to know' is only 'used in a sexual sense on just 15 other occasions out of 943 in the Hebrew Bible,' nevertheless this is the meaning which seems to be required in Genesis 19:

...the context here is one in which Lot himself seems to have viewed the intentions of the men of Sodom as sexual. In addition, there are clear semantic and narrative parallels between this account and that of the rape of the Levite's concubine in Judges 19:22, 25 (which quite explicitly uses the verb 'know' in a sexual way). This explains why Nissinen, who rejects some traditional interpretations of the classic texts, is clear that 'the sexual aspect of the actions of the men of Sodom cannot be gainsaid' and Gagnon concludes that 'few scholars today, even among supporters of homoerotic behaviour, adopt Bailey's argument.' (p.41[84])

Secondly, from a Christian perspective it is relevant that both 2 Peter 2:10 and Jude 7 'seem to regard Sodom's sin as at least partly to do with disordered sexual behaviour':

> ...Peter writes of those who, like the men in Genesis 19, 'indulge their flesh in depraved lust' and Jude describes the same 'sexual immorality' and 'unnatural lust' as an example of sin prone to merit the 'punishment of eternal fire.' As Robert Gagnon points out in his exhaustive study of this and other relevant texts on sexual immorality, it is noteworthy that Peter and Jude highlight the sin of lust here, rather than any failure to provide social justice or hospitality. (p.41)

Leviticus 18:22, 20:13

On Leviticus 18:22 and 20:13, traditionalist writers maintain, in opposition to the arguments of revisionist scholars, that these two verses constitute a general prohibition of male (and possibly also female) homosexual activity. The rationale for this prohibition has to do

---

[84] The quotations are from Martti Nissinen, *Homoeroticism in the Biblical World*, Minneapolis: Fortress Press, 1998 p. 46 and Gagnon, *The Bible and Homosexual Practice*, p.74.

with the violation of the order instituted by God at creation and the verses are therefore still relevant for Christian theology and practice today.

> **Jay Sklar – Leviticus 18:22 and 20:13 prohibit consensual sex between men as a violation of God's design for human sexuality.**

In his 2014 commentary on Leviticus, [85] Professor Jay Sklar states that Leviticus 18:22 is a prohibition of a man 'having sexual relations with another man.' (p.237) He goes on to explain that in this verse:

> The Hebrew uses both a verb (sakab) and a noun (miskabim) built on the same root (skb), a root associated elsewhere with having sexual relations (Genesis 26:10, 35:22, Leviticus 15:18, Numbers 5:19, Judges 21:12). The verse's meaning is well captured by the NIV *Do not have sexual relations with a man as one does with a woman.* (p.237)

Sklar further adds that Leviticus 20:13 makes clear that what is envisaged is consensual sex and that in short 18:22 tell us:

> ...sexual relations are meant to occur between a man and a woman, not between two men (and not, by implication, between two women). This was in keeping with the theological backdrop against which the Israelites would have read this law: namely the Lord's design that sexuality be expressed in a marital, heterosexual relationship (Genesis 1:27-28, 2:22-24, cf Matthew 19:4-5...). (p.238)

According to Sklar, the word *toeba* ('abomination') applied to homosexual activity in 18:22 refers to 'a thing or practice considered reprehensible in the eyes of another' and in some cases in the Old Testament it is used to refer to practices that are culturally rather than morally detestable. Thus 'the Egyptians...considered it to be *detestable*

---

[85] Jay Sklar, *Leviticus*, Downers Grove/Nottingham: IVP, 2014.

to eat with the Israelites (Genesis 43:32), while the Israelites viewed certain animals to be *detestable* as a food source (Deuteronomy 14:3).' However, the word is also used 'to refer to acts that are detestable because they go against the moral fibre of God's created world.' Such acts include 'idolatry (Deuteronomy 7:25-26; 27:15) which is a denial of humanity's Creator, or cheating others financially (Deuteronomy 25:13-16), which is a denial of the value of those created in God's image.' Homosexual activity belongs in this second category 'since it is a denial of the Lord's very intent for sexuality (cf. Genesis 1:27-28, 2:22-24), a point the New Testament underscores (Romans 1:26-27, cf Matthew 19:4-5)'. (p.238)

Sam Allberry - Leviticus prohibits homosexual activity in general and not simply cultic prostitution.

Allberry writes in is *God-Anti Gay?* that the use of the word 'abomination' in these verses does not suggest a specifically cultic context for the prohibited sexual activity:

> 'An *abomination*' is often used to describe idolatry, and so some suggest these verses are not prohibiting homosexual behaviour in general, but only the cultic prostitution associated with pagan temples. But the language used is not that specific; the passages refer in general to a man lying with a man 'as with a woman' without specifying a particular context for that act. Moreover, the surrounding verses in both Leviticus 18 and 20 forbid other forms of sexual sin that are general in nature, such as incest, adultery and bestiality.
>
> None of these have any connection with pagan temples of idolatry. These things are morally wrong, irrespective of who is doing them and where they are happening. It is also important to see that the second of these two verses (Leviticus 20:13) prohibits both male parties equally. We can't write it off as only prohibiting things like gay rape or a forced relationships.

Leviticus prohibits even general, consensual homosexual activity. (p.29)

Allberry also notes that homosexual activity is not the only sin described in Scripture as 'an abomination:'

Leviticus refers to other sexual sins in exactly the same way, and Proverbs lists deceitful speech, pride and murder as equally abominable to God. Homosexual sin is not in a category of its own in this regard. (p.30)

> **John Goldingay – homosexuality activity is incompatible with being part of God's people and the declaration that people engaging in it should be executed indicates the seriousness of the offence rather than the penalty that should be imposed. Homosexual activity is seen as imperilling the family and as failing to fit in with the way God created the world.**

The point that homosexual sin is not the only form of activity described as an 'abomination' is also made by Goldingay. He writes in *Key Questions about Christian Faith* that both Leviticus 18:22 and 20:13 describe homosexual activity:

...as *toe'bah*, conventionally an 'abomination.' In Leviticus this term is otherwise applied only to forbidden sexual relationships, though Deuteronomy applies it to religious practices such as the making of images, to forbidden foods, and to dishonesty in business. The term does not directly suggest a feeling of disgust but a conviction that these practices are to be absolutely repudiated as incompatible with membership of Yahweh's people; their repudiation is part of its purity as a people. (p.120)

He further observes that the value judgement made on homosexual acts by Leviticus is 'confirmed and underlined by the declaration that two people who engage in a homosexual act should be executed.' However, he also argues that:

Generally in the Torah, such declarations are not declarations of the penalty that the court should impose; at least, it is the rule rather than the exception that Israel does not exact the death penalty from people who are guilty of offenses to which this declaration is applied, such as murder, adultery and idolatry. To say 'such a person should be executed' is a way of underscoring the seriousness of the offense, not a way of prescribing the sanction attached to it. (p.320)

According to Goldingay, we lack the background information that would help us understand the original historical significance of the prohibitions in Leviticus. However, Leviticus itself suggests two possible rationales for its negative attitude to homosexual activity:

Both its passages appear in the contexts of prohibitions concerning certain other sexual relationships within the family; the book is concerned to avoid imperilling the family, and it implies that homosexual acts do this. The first passage also emphasizes the need for Israel to adopt different practices from the cultures around (same-sex relationships do not seem to have been disapproved of in Mesopotamia or Egypt or later in Greece and Rome; we lack evidence for Canaan). (p.320)

In addition, the broader context of Leviticus:

...shows a concern for living in light of the way that God created the world. In a slightly paradoxical sense, this applies to its teaching about animals that may not be eaten; Israelites may eat animals that fit into proper creation categories (the regulation is paradoxical because God of course created the animals that do not fit into creation categories). It applies to not having different species of cattle mate, not sowing fields with two kinds of seed, and not putting on cloth made from two different kinds of material (Leviticus 19:19). Humanity should fit into creation. Homosexual acts do not do that. (pp. 320-321)

> **Ian Paul – The prohibition of homosexual activity in Leviticus 18 has to do with the rejection of God's creation order rather than with idolatrous cultic activity, marital unfaithfulness, or an offence against patriarchy.**

Paul explains that in Leviticus 18 the prohibition on same-sex activity:

> ....is set alongside prohibitions on incest, bestiality and the sacrifice of children. The whole list of prohibited activities is called 'detestable' (Hebrew *toevah*, translated 'abomination' in the AV) in the summary comment in 18:30, but in 18:22 same-sex activity is singled out with this term, and in the following verse bestiality is similarly highlighted as a 'perversion' (NIV). As with other regulations, these are not narrowly cultic but form part of a shared, national life for all who reside in the land (18:26), including 'resident aliens' who do not participate in cultic activity. (p.14)

Paul also highlights the fact that the language used in 18:22 is very specific. In his view the use of terms *zaqar* (male) and *ishshah* (female) 'creates an echo of the creation accounts in Gen 1 and 2; it is plausible to see the serious nature of the offence as reflecting its rejection of God's creation order of 'male and female.'' Furthermore since the phrase used to refer to homosexual activity is quite general, 'there is no suggestion that the issue here is marital unfaithfulness, which is dealt with elsewhere.'(p.14)

He acknowledges that *toevah* is used 'in a cultic sense of unacceptable sacrifices, or idolatry.' However, he declares, that is not all it is used for:

> It is applied to distinct eating habits (Genesis 43:42), more general racial antipathy (Genesis (46:34), prohibited foods (Deuteronomy 14:3), magic and spiritism (Deuteronomy 18:120, remarrying someone you have divorced (Deuteronomy 24:4), and the use of dishonest weights and measure (Deuteronomy 25:16). It is quite striking that in Lev 18 and 20 the term qadesh, meaning male shrine prostitute (as in

Deuteronomy 23:17-18), is absent. The context in Leviticus is every day and particularly family life as the holy people of God. If there are hints of cultic language this is not because the prohibitions are located in cult but because the whole of life is to reflect the purity and holiness of Israel's God. (p.15)

He criticises the suggestion that the issue at stake in 18:22 is patriarchy with the objection being to a man taking a female role by being penetrated during sex. He points out that the prohibition is not against being penetrated, but against penetrating and therefore 'the verse gives no suggestion that the act is seen as a breach of manliness or the man's honour; rather the issue appears to be the failure of this act to match the divinely given creation order from Genesis.' (p.15)

> **Gordon Kennedy, Jane McArthur, Andrew McGowan –the laws in Leviticus 18 carry the authority of Yahweh Himself. Leviticus 18:22 provides a comprehensive prohibition of homosexual activity as something abhorrent to God and we should treat this prohibition with the same seriousness as the other prohibitions on sexual activity in the chapter. The imposition of the death penalty indicates the seriousness of the offence, but we should not seek to impose it today.**

In their contribution to the Church of Scotland report, Kennedy, McArthur and McGowan state that it is important not to take one or two verses of Leviticus 18 out of context, but rather to consider the whole chapter.

They note that chapters 17-22 are normally seen as a distinct section within Leviticus which can be described as 'Prescriptions for Practical Holiness' or 'Laws for Holy Living.' [86] Within this wider section a key feature of Leviticus 18 is the repeated use of the phrase 'I am the Lord

---

[86] The quotations are from Willem Van Gemeren, *New International Dictionary of Old Testament Theology and Exegesis*, vol III, Grand Rapids: Zondervan, 1997 p.797 and Gordon Wenham, *The Book of Leviticus*, Grand Rapids: Eerdmans, 1979. p.xi.

your God' in verses 2, 4 and 30 to form a theological frame for the chapter. In the words of John Hartley in his commentary on Leviticus:

> These self-introductory formulae function to locate the authority of a passage, law or summons to obedience in the name of the giver of that word, namely Yahweh. That is, a formula raises the authority of a law or series of laws above the socio-political sphere to the divine sphere. Consequently, in obeying these laws the people express their loyalty to Yahweh. (p.1/103)[87]

This means that Leviticus 18 cannot be considered as

> ...some culturally conditioned set of sexual prohibitions. The imprint of the nature and authority of Yahweh is written large over each part of this chapter. Submission to these sexual prohibitions is a response to redemption, a display of the image of God, and joyful, loving thanksgiving to Yahweh. (p. 1/103)

Leviticus 18:22, they say, provides a comprehensive prohibition of homosexual practice as something abhorrent to God:

> 'You shall not lie with a male as with a woman; it is an abomination.' This includes all homosexual practice, rather than just abusive or violent or exploitative homosexual practice. Homosexual practice is described as 'an abomination,' which means that is something 'that God abhors.' It is 'literally something detestable and hated by God.' We should not imagine that these words were written lightly, nor should they be interpreted, or dismissed, casually. (p. 1/103)[88]

Furthermore, it is arbitrary to treat homosexuality as a special case, different from the other forms of sexual activity prohibited in Leviticus 18:

---

[87] The quotation is from John Hartley, *Leviticus*, Waco: Word, 1992, p.viii.
[88] The quotations are from Hartley, op.cit.p. 297 and Wenham, op,cit, p.259.

Verses 6-18 prohibit sexual activity between close relations, verse 19 prohibits sexual activity during menstrual period, verse 20 prohibits adultery with a neighbour's wife, verse 21 prohibits offering children as sacrifices to false gods, verse 22 prohibits homosexual practice, verse 23 prohibits bestiality and the chapter concludes in verse 24-30 with exhortations to obey these laws. This demonstrates that homosexual practice is not the only expression of human sexuality which is prohibited for the people of Yahweh. In our contemporary society there is no desire to lift prohibitions on incest or bestiality and so, to remove the prohibition on homosexual practice, requires the interpreter to take verse 22 out of its context and treat it as a special case. (pp.1/103-104)

In their view, the death penalty for homosexual activity laid down in Leviticus 20:13 highlights 'the seriousness of homosexual acts.' In Leviticus 20 offences carrying the death penalty:

...are religious offences and offences against ordered family life. The death penalty is a maximum penalty which reflects the abhorrent nature of the offence, particularly that the offence is abhorrent to Yahweh.

We do not seek to apply the death penalty today, hoping that an offender may yet come to faith and repentance in the Lord Jesus Christ, acknowledging their sin and receiving forgiveness. However, we must recognise that our God considers such sexual sins as an offence against his nature and his holiness and his appointing such punishment for this sin cannot be ignored or treated lightly. (p.1/104)

> **Michael Brown – according to Leviticus homosexual activity is abhorrent to God. The prohibition against it is universal rather than limited to a context involving idolatry.**

Brown argues in detail in *Can you be gay and Christian?*:

(a) 'the prohibition against homosexuality was a universal prohibition.'

(b) 'toe'vah means 'abhorrent,' not simply taboo'

(c) 'the Leviticus prohibition is not simply limited to idolatry.'

On (a) he declares:

> ...there were laws that God gave to Israel alone, and there were laws God gave to all people, including Israel, and for the most part, using the entire Bible as our guide, it is easy to see which are which.

> Where exactly does the prohibition against homosexuality fit? Was it a law given to Israel alone, or was it a law for all people? Leviticus 18 makes it clear that for a man to have sex with another man is detestable in His sight. (p.114)

Brown reaches this conclusion on the basis of Leviticus 18:1-5 and 24-30, the explanatory passages at the beginning and end of the chapter which explain why Israel is called to obey the laws it contains. In these passages, explains Brown, the laws are said to apply other nations and not just to Israel:

> God said plainly that He judged the Egyptians and the Canaanites – idol worshipping pagans, according to the Bible – for committing these very sins, even stating that by committing these sins the very land became unclean and vomited them out. This is strong language! And that's why God tells the people of Israel not to commit these sins otherwise they too will defile the land and the land will vomit them out. In contrast God never said that He judged the nations of the world for eating unclean animals or sowing their fields with two different kinds of seeds or wearing garments with mixed fabrics. Nor did he say that the land vomited them out for doing these things. But He did say that about the sins listed in Leviticus, including homosexual practice. (pp.115-116)

Furthermore, male homosexual practice is singled out as particularly serious even among this list of universally forbidden sins:

> ...all these sins together are described as *toe'vot*, abominations, detestable things, making clear that God included incest, bestiality, homosexual practice, adultery and sacrificing children to Molech in this category...they are all 'detestable' in His sight, and together they have dreadful consequences for the nations that practice them. But only male homosexual practice is singled out in Leviticus 18 as *toe'vah*, abomination, meaning that it is a *toe'vah* among *toe'vot*, an abomination among abominations. (p.116)

His conclusion is that the prohibition against homosexual practice:

> ...was given to Israel because homosexual practice was wrong for all people in all generations, meaning it is intrinsically sinful. Why? One main reason is that God designed men for women and women for men, and to join a man with a man or a woman with a woman is to sin in a fundamental way against His purpose and design. (pp.116-117)

On (b) he emphasises the importance of the fact that there is a Hebrew verb *ta'av* derived from the same root as *toe'vah* and closely related to it in meaning. This verb is used twenty two times in the Hebrew Old Testament and means 'to detest, abhor; to act abhorrently.' Examples of its use include Deuteronomy 23:7 'You shall not *abhor* an Edomite, for he is your brother. You shall not *abhor* an Egyptian, because you were a sojourner in his land,' Psalm 5:6 'You destroy those who speak lies; the Lord *abhors* the bloodthirsty and deceitful man' and Psalm 14:1 'The fool says in his heart, 'There is no God.' They are corrupt, *they do abominable deeds*, there is none who does good.' (p.117)

Many Semitic scholars, he argues, think that the verb came out of the noun *toe'vah* , just as the noun 'paint' preceded the verb 'to paint:'

So the verb ta'av, 'to detest, abhor; to act abhorrently,' comes from the noun *toe'vah*, 'something detestable; abhorrent,' giving further support to the fact that *toe'vah* does not mean something ritually unclean but rather something abhorrent. (p.118)

It is because it means something abhorrent or repulsive that toe'vah 'could be used to describe something ritually unclean or taboo, because in certain cultures and among certain peoples, something considered taboo or ritually unclean is abhorrent to them, like pork for a religious Jew or a Muslim.'(p.118)

Turning to the use of *toe'vah* in the Old Testament, Brown notes that the authoritative Koehler-Baumgartner *Hebrew and Aramaic Lexicon of the Old Testament* states that in Leviticus 18 the phrase 'the abhorrent customs' refers to 'the abhorrent customs of the Canaanites (Leviticus 18:30), by which is meant in particular *sexual perversity.*' (p.118) [89] Brown comments 'that certainly speaks of moral violations and not just ritual taboos.'

He further observes that the uses of *toe'vah* in passages such as Deuteronomy 7:26, 12:31, 25:15-16, Proverbs 6:16-19 and Ezekiel 16:50 'hardly fall in the category of ritual taboos; instead, they speak of moral, ethical, and spiritual violations of the highest order, things that are intrinsically sinful, things that the Lord 'hates' – and they are grouped under the heading of *toe'vah*.'(p.119)

On (c) Brown points out the consequences of applying the argument consistently:

> ...the prohibition against sacrificing children to Molech in Leviticus 18:21 is followed by the prohibition against male-male sex in in verse 22, then the prohibition against bestiality in verse 23. And so, if you want to argue that homosexual acts

[89] The quotation is from Ludwig Koehler and Walter Baumgartner, *Hebrew and Aramaic Lexicon of the Old Testament Study Edition*, Vol 2, Leiden and Boston, Koln/Brill, 2001, p.1703. Emphasis added by Brown.

were only forbidden in conjunction with idolatry, you'll have to make the same case for bestiality. Anyone care to make that argument? In the same way, since the prohibition against adultery occurs in Leviticus 18:20, one verse before the prohibition against idolatrous child-sacrifice in verse 21, someone could argue that adultery is only forbidden in conjunction with idolatry. Who would want to make that argument? (pp.121-122)

In addition, in Leviticus 20:13 the prohibition against homosexuality is surrounded by prohibitions against incest and adultery with no link at all to idol worship.

In reality, he argues, the argument gets things the wrong way round:

...homosexual practice was not considered sinful because it was found in the context of pagan idolatry (or, put another way, it was not considered sinful only if it occurred in conjunction with idol worship). Rather, the opposite is true: according to the Old Testament, because idol worshipping pagans were so degraded in their sexual practices, they even included homosexual acts in their temple rituals. (p.122)

Brown's overall conclusion is:

(1)The Torah puts homosexual acts in the same class as adultery, incest, bestiality, idolatry and sacrificing children to idols, censoring them in the strongest possible terms. (2) According to Leviticus 18:24-30 God judged pagan nations for these sins. (3) According to Leviticus 20:23 God abhorred the pagan nations for committing these sexual acts. (4) The New Testament, as we will see, reinforces the seriousness of these acts, and so, for those who take Scripture seriously, these are weighty issues to consider. (pp.123-124)

> **Richard Davidson – the prohibition of homosexual activity is relevant for all time and all places and probably includes lesbianism as well. The seriousness of the offence involved is shown by the double penalty of death and being cut off for ever from God's people. The rationale for the prohibition is violation of the human beings as male and female rather than cultic concerns or a link with idolatry.**

Davidson begins his account of the Leviticus 18:22 and 20:13 in *Flame of Yahweh* by emphasising the universality of the prohibition which they contain. He quotes Roy Gane's comment on Leviticus 18:22 'the language is devastatingly untechnical, leaving no room for ambiguity' (p.149) [90] and goes on to explain that:

> The Hebrew clause *lo tiskab* [you shall not lie] consists of a negative particle followed by a qal imperfect, expressing a permanent negative command. The phrase *miskebe issa*, literally, 'the lying of a woman,' has been suggested by some to include only homosexual acts that approximate nomal heterosexual coitus and include penile intromission, but the Hebrew is clearly a euphemism for sexual intercourse (cf. the male equivalent of this passage in Judges 21:11-12). Thus this passage is a permanent prohibition of all sexual intercourse of a man with another male (zakar). This would also prohibit pedophilia, since the term *zakar* refers to any male, not just a grown man. (p.150)

He also explains that although the Leviticus 18:22 only mentions male homosexual activity a prohibition of lesbianism is probably implied as well:

> ....the prohibition of lesbian relationships is probably implicit in the general Levitical injunction against following the abominable practices of the Egyptians or Canaanites, as

---

[90] The quotation is from Roy Gane, *Leviticus, Numbers*, Grand Rapids: Zondervan, 2004, p.321.

recognised in rabbinic interpretation. All the legislation in Lev 18 is in the masculine gender (with the exceptions of female bestiality, v23). The Mosaic legislation in general is considered from a man's (male's) perspective. Even the Decalogue is addressed in the masculine singular, but this certainly does not mean that it applies only to the male gender. The masculine singular is the Hebrew way to express gender inclusive ideas, much the same as it was in English until the recent emphasis on gender – inclusive language. Since the male is regarded as the patriarchal representative of the family, laws are given as if to him (see, e.g. the tenth commandment of the Decalogue) but are clearly intended for both man and woman where applicable. (p.150)

Like other writers, Davidson notes that the death penalty is mandated for homosexual practice in 20:13, but he also draws attention to the additional sanction in Leviticus 18:29 which covers all the offences listed in the chapter: 'whoever commits any of these abominations shall be cut off from their people.' Although many scholars have equated this penalty with the death penalty, Davidson argues that being 'cut off' ('*karet*') was an additional penalty consisting of 'a conditional divine curse of extinction, obliterating the sinner (and progeny) from any role in the drama of Israel's history.' (p. 150) [91] Those engaging in homosexual activity thus faced a double penalty.

Davidson then goes on to consider the significance of the use the term *to'eba*, declaring that

the fact that among the list of specific prohibitions in Lev 18, the word *toe'ba* is mentioned only regarding homosexual intercourse gives an indication of the degree of revulsion associated with homosexual activity. Indeed, in the entire Pentateuch, the only forbidden sexual act to which the word

---

[91] The quotation is from Wold, op.cit. p.147.

toe'ba is specifically attached is homosexual intercourse. (p.151)

He rejects the idea that *toe'ba* refers simply to Jewish ceremonial impurity and that the condemnation of homosexual practice is 'based solely upon Israel's particular cultic/ritual concerns and not upon universally applicable moral/ethical considerations.' (p.151) This is because, in his view, the use of the word *toe'ba* in the Torah and elsewhere in the Hebrew Bible indicates that its meaning is not restricted to issues to do with ceremonial impurity. He quotes P J Harland's conclusion that the word is used 'to refer to something which is utterly incompatible with the will of God and which is viewed by him with repugnance because of its evil.' (p152) [92]

He also rejects the ideas that the reference to offering sacrifice to Molech in Leviticus 18:21 shows that homosexuality is prohibited because of its connection with idolatry or that this connection is shown by the repeated injunction to avoid the customs of the Canaanites (vv. 1-5, 24-30, 20:22-26).

The first idea is ruled out because (a) in Leviticus 20:13 the repetition of the prohibition of homosexuality is placed between prohibitions against incest (vv. 10-12) and bestiality (vv.14-16) rather than following the prohibition of offering child sacrifices to Molech and (b) The reference to Molech worship is not concerned with idolatry but with an offence in the area of sexuality:

> ...offering children to Molech was prohibited not only because of the idolatrous connection, but because child sacrifice threatened the sanctity of the family, or, stated differently, because Molech worship had a sexual aspect. 'The Molech cultus...consisted of a sexual element and is therefore categorized as *toe'ba* it is the sexual element that places it in the

---

[92] The quotation is from P J Harland 'Menswear and Womenswear: A Study of Deuteronomy 22:5,' *Expository Times*, 110, no.3, 1998, p.73.

list of crimes in Leviticus 18, not its idolatrous element.'(p.153)[93]

The second idea fails to note that in 18:24-30 and in 20:23 'the sexual sins described in the previous verses (including homosexuality) are defiling in their very nature and not just because they violate Israel's cultic ritual.'(p.154) It was because of such practices among the Canaanites that 'the land became defiled...[and] vomited out its inhabitants (Leviticus 18:25). Just as the land vomited out the Canaanites so God warns it will vomit out Israel if it engages in such abominations.' (p.154) In other words, the Canaanites were expelled from the land not simply because of their idolatry, but also because of their intrinsically immoral sexual practices and it is these that Israel is told not to imitate.

The fact that these Canaanites were judged because of these sexual practices shows that the prohibition of them is not limited to Jews and this is also show by the fact that the prohibitions applied to the *ger* or 'resident alien' as well as the Israelites (18:26) and by the fact that in Acts 15 they were recognised by the Early Church as applying to the Gentiles as well as to the Jews. (p.155)

Drawing on the work of Donald Wold and Samuel Dresner, Davidson contends that the rationale for the prohibitions in Leviticus 18, including the prohibition of homosexuality:

> ...rests upon the foundational principles of creation order in Genesis 1:27-28: the creation of all humanity in the image of God as 'male and female,' unique and distinct from the rest of God's creation, and the command to 'be fruitful and multiply and fill the earth.' These principles describe the order and structure of humanity in two relationships: to God and to society. All the Laws of Leviticus may be understood as violations of these principles. The activities proscribed in Lev 18 and 20 are described as 'abominations' because homosexual

---

[93] The quotation is from Wold, op.cit, p.130.

practice violates the divine order of gender set forth in Genesis 1:27 and 2:24. (p.155) [94]

Davidson also cites with approval Gagnon's argument that the refrain in Leviticus 18:22 and 20:13 'lie[s] with a male as with a woman' connects intertextually with Genesis 1:27 and 2:24 and that this connection shows that the primary concern of the prohibition in these verses is the violation of 'gender boundaries established at creation.'(p.157)[95] He also quotes, again with approval, the similar claim of B S Childs that:

> The recent attempt of some theologians to find a biblical opening, if not a warrant, for the practice of homosexuality stands in striking disharmony with the Old Testament's understanding of the relation of male and female. The theological issue goes far beyond the citing of occasional texts which condemn the practice (Leviticus 20:13)... The Old Testament views homosexuality as a distortion of creation which falls into the shadows beyond the blessing. (p.157) [96]

Finally, Davidson draws on Gagnon again for five indicators that 'the Levitical legislation concerning homosexual practice is transtemporal and transcultural.' (1) This legislation is part of a larger and consistent Old Testament witness against homosexual practice. (2) The legislation is grouped with prohibition of other sex acts that transcend the culture of Ancient Israel, incest, adultery and bestiality. (3) The death penalty for homosexual practice underscores the seriousness of the offence. (4) The language of purity is not about ritual but about ethics. (5) The New Testament appropriates the Old Testament prohibition. (pp.157-158)[97]

---

[94] Ibid, p.155, quoting Wold, op.cit. p.130, and referring to Samuel H Dresner 'Homosexuality and the Order of Creation,' *Judaism*, 40, 1991, pp.320-321.
[95] The quotation is from Gagnon, *The Bible and Homosexual Practice*, p.142.
[96] The quotation is from Brevard Childs, *Old Testament Theology in a Canonical Context*, Philadelphia: Fortress Press, 1985, p.194.
[97] The reference is to Gagnon, *The Bible and Homosexual Practice*, pp.162-168.

> **Jonathan Burnside – The prohibition of homosexual activity in Leviticus 20 is based on a set of moral distinctions according to which homosexual activity is viewed as wrong because it involves sexual activity outside marriage between two men. The imposition of the death penalty indicates the seriousness of the offence.**

In his chapter on 'sexual offences' in *God, Justice and Society – Aspects of Law and Legality in the Bible*, [98] Dr Jonathan Burnside undertakes a detailed study of Leviticus 20. He acknowledges that the fact that this chapter makes male homosexuality a capital offence has meant that it is often read as a 'text of terror.' However, he argues that it should not be read in a negative way because what it is actually concerned with is:

> ....setting out a positive vision of what the Bible sees as necessary to well–ordered sexual relationships in order to optimize relational order. Relational order consists of the following dimensions: (1) covenantal order, (2) species order, (3) gender order, (4) generational or 'descent' order, and (5) kinship order. Leviticus 20 indicates that sexual relationships are not meant to be – and cannot be – haphazard and arbitrary. On the contrary, Leviticus 20 assumes that there is a contrast between covenantal sex, expressed as the covenant of heterosexual marriage, and casual sex, which refers to every other kind of sexual relationship since these do not express heterosexual marital commitment. Relational order, covenantal sex, and sexual faithfulness are seen as the answer to the questions of how to channel sexual energy in a way that creates community. Leviticus 20 is thus a detailed study of the place of sexual relations in relational order. It also depicts the relational consequences of sexual chaos. Leviticus 20 shows that the shockwaves spread out and impact on the following relationships: (1) the betrayed husband or wife, (2) the

---

[98] Jonathan Burnside, *God, Justice and Society,* Oxford: OUP, 2011.

cohesion of the community, (3) the future of the nation, and (4) the relationship between the people and God, all of which are interconnected. (p.348)

According to Burnside, Leviticus 20 is structured around the commands in the Decalogue (Exodus 20:3-14) not to worship other gods, to honour your father and your mother and to not commit adultery. Offering your children to Molech (20:2-5) is a sexual offence which contravenes the command to offer worship only to God. The other sexual offences in the chapter are then listed under the two headings of cursing father and mother (v. 9) and adultery (vv. 10-21). (pp. 349-350)

Cursing father and mother comes into the picture, he says, for two reasons.

First, respect for parents was shown by obtaining the father's consent for a marriage. This being the case:

> If respect for parents is part of the normal sequence of heterosexual marriage, and if sexual deviancy is understood as a departure from what is normative, then it follows that the biblical characterization of adultery, and other sexual relationships opposed to marriage, will include the idea of disrespecting or cursing parents. (p.351)

Second, it may also 'reflect the reality that in practical terms, parents are deeply affected by the sexual misbehaviour of their children (including adultery) because they are the ones who, in most cases, have to deal with the emotional, organizational and possibly lineage implications.' A biblical example of this is the effect on David of Amnon's sin in 2 Samuel 13:20-21. (p.352)

The reason adultery is then used as a further heading for a range of sexual offences is because 'adultery is the paradigm case of consensual relations outside marriage.'(p. 352)

In verses 10-16 of chapter 20 there are a series of sexual offences carrying the death penalty, starting with straightforward adultery and finishing with bestiality, all of which represent increasing deviations from the norm of sexual activity between a man and woman in marriage. Homosexuality comes into the list in verse 13 'because it is no longer one man and one woman but *one man and another man*.' (p.363)

Burnside notes that the language of Leviticus 20 may be suggesting that the death penalty is a suitable rather than a mandatory punishment for the offences listed, but he accepts that 'it remains the case that biblical law sees the death penalty as a potentially suitable response for some sexual relationships, at least in the case where there was sufficient evidence and the offended party wished to prosecute.' In his view, the severity of the penalty reflects the importance the Bible attaches to marital fidelity:

> ...marriage is explicitly called a covenant (*berit*) in the Hebrew Bible (e.g. Ezekiel 16:8) and the marriage covenant is the subject of divine interest (e.g. Malachi 2:14, Proverbs 2:16-17). It is also the picture of the relationship between God and Israel (Hosea 1-3). Against this background, sexual relationships that are opposed to marriage are viewed very seriously. The fact that we do not regard these offences as serious is probably because we do not see relationships as significant nor adultery as one of the worst breaches of trust and relational devotion. (pp.364-365)

Comparing biblical laws as set out in Leviticus 20 and contemporary law, Burnside notes that the *Sexual Offences Act 2003* is based on a view of equality. It regards both heterosexual and homosexual intercourse as equally permissible providing they take place between consenting adults. However it also makes a moral distinction between this and other acts such as necrophilia and voyeurism which are criminal offences. (pp.382-383)

Like this modern legislation, Biblical law also has a conception of equality that involves making moral distinctions. However the basis for these moral distinctions is different:

Many categories of sexual behavior, including homosexual relationships, are not treated on an equal basis to marital relationships. On the other hand, biblical law is similar to moral law in that homosexual offences are not treated any more severely than heterosexual offences, such as adultery. At the level of penalty there is no difference between adultery and homosexual intercourse in biblical law. As in modern law, distinctions are made between permitted and prohibited relationships, although in biblical law, these boundaries are intended to establish a positive understanding of relational order based on the following: (1) covenantal order, (2) species order, (3) gender order, (4) generational or 'descent' order, (5) kinship order. Consequently, biblical law, as with modern law, has a conception of equality; however, it is based on a different set of moral distinctions. (p.383)

Deuteronomy 23:17-18

Traditionalist scholars have not written a great deal about Deuteronomy 23:17-18, but as the following examples show, the work they have produced shows that they think these verses prohibit both cultic and non-cultic same-sex prostitution and that this prohibition contributes to our understanding of the general Old Testament view of homosexuality.

> **Jack Lundbom – Deuteronomy 23:17 probably refers to homosexuals associated with temple worship.**

In his commentary on Deuteronomy, [99] Dr Jack Lundbom writes that the *qadesh* referred to in 23:17 'is probably a sodomite...i.e. a practising homosexual associated directly or indirectly with temple worship.' He notes the statement by the Old Testament scholar Jeffey Tigay that a *qadesh* 'may be a male prostitute either heterosexual or homosexual'

---

[99] Jack Lundbom *Deuteronomy*, Grand Rapids/Cambridge: Eerdmans 2013.

and further notes that 'Male prostitutes associated with Canaanite worship in the time of Rehoboam (1 Kings 14:23-24) were severely censured by the Deuteronomic historian, who commended Asa for doing away with them (1 Kings 15:12) and Jehoshaphat the same for exterminating those who remained (1 Kings 22:46).' (p.650)

Lundbom notes on 23:18 that 'some think the prostitute here is homosexual' who performed 'using the stance of a dog' (which was why the name *keleb* or dog was used to refer to him). However, he does not elaborate further. (p.660)

Davidson and Gagnon offer more detailed accounts.

> **Richard Davidson - Deuteronomy 23:17-18 prohibit both cultic and non-cultic homosexual activity.**

In *Flame of Yahweh* Davidson holds that Deuteronomy 23:17 'specifically forbids an Israelite from becoming a temple prostitute.' He argues that:

> Although there is currently considerable debate over the exact function of these cultic 'holy ones,' the evidence is persuasive that they were indeed cultic personnel who (among other possible functions) engaged in ritual sexual intercourse at the high places. John Day summarizes crucial biblical lexical evidence for this position: 'That sacred prostitution was a feature of the religion is indicated by the parallelism of the word *zona*, 'prostitute,' with *qedesa*, lit. 'holy one,' in Deut 23:18-19 and Genesis 38:15, 22-23 and of *zonot*, 'prostitutes,' with *qedesot*, lit. 'holy ones,' in Hosea 4:14.' (p.103) [100]

Davidson also argues that the structure of the Book of Deuteronomy groups its material in a way which follows the sequence and content of the commandments of the Decalogue in Deuteronomy 5:6-21. The significance of this arrangement of material, he writes, is that

---

[100] The quotation is from John Day 'Canaan, Religion of' in *The Anchor Bible Dictionary*, Vol.1, New York: Doubleday, 1992, p.835.

Deuteronomy 23:17-18 comes in the section elaborating the prohibition of adultery:

> Therefore these instructions clearly have in view the sexual distortion involved in the functioning of the *qades* and *qedesa*. This structural placement, in addition to their usage in a clearly sexual content in Gen 38, forms strong evidence – to be supplemented with additional lines of evidence from the Prophets – that these 'holy ones' engaged in ritual sexual intercourse as part of the fertility cult practices of Israel's neighbors. Furthermore, the fact that this legislation prohibiting the *qades* and *qedesa* is placed in Deuteronomy as an expansion of the seventh commandment of the moral law (Decalogue) also gives evidence that cultic prostitution was objectionable not only because it was part of the pagan cult but because it was morally wrong in itself. (p.105)

According to Davidson, male cultic prostitution 'undoubtedly included male-male sexual intercourse.'(p.159). If these prostitutes serviced women this 'would presuppose a custom that cannot be documented elsewhere in the Ancient Near East.' In the Ancient Near East male cult prostitutes were usually castrated and engaged in passive same-sex activity. Also, if male cultic prostitutes serviced women this would contradict the care exercised by Israelites in guarding female sexual purity. In addition, the harsh language used to describe the *qedeshim* in I and 2 Kings and the use of the epithet 'dog' in Deuteronomy 23:18 suggests the sort of revulsion associated with same-sex activity in the Old Testament. (p.159 fn. 104)

In Davidson's view the parallel with the *zona* (or non-cultic female prostitute) means that the *keleb* referred to in Deuteronomy 23:18 was a non-cultic male prostitute. (p.159) This in turn means that Deuteronomy 23:17-18 prohibit 'all homosexual activity, both cultic and non-cultic' as a violation of the prohibition of the commandment against adultery in the Decalogue. (p.160)

236

> **Robert Gagnon – the qedeshim were viewed as abhorrent because they willingly took the role of women in sexual relations with other men. The abhorrence felt towards their activities helps us to understand better the condemnation of same-sex activity in Judges 19 and Genesis 19.**

Gagnon writes in his essay 'How seriously does Scripture treat the issue of homosexual practice?' that 'legal material from Deuteronomy and narrative material from the Deuteronomistic History (Joshua through 2 Kings) disparage the homoerotic associations of the *qedeshim*.' (p.167) He explains that this word literally means 'consecrated men', but that in context it refers:

> ... to male cultic figures who sometimes served as the passive receptive sexual partners for other men (i.e. homosexual cult prostitutes: Deuteronomy 23:17, 1 Kings 14:21-24, 15:12-14, 22:46, 2 Kings 23:7; cf. Job 36:14). Even Phyllis Bird...an OT scholar who writes on behalf of homosexual unions and has done extensive work on the *qedeshim*, concedes that the Deuteronomistic historian was especially repulsed by the consensual, receptive intercourse that these figures had with other men. The reference to such figures as 'dogs' (Deuteronomy 23:18) matches the slur made against parallel figures in Mesopotamia (the *assinnu*, *kurgarru*, and *kulu'u*), called 'dog-woman' and 'man-woman' because of their consensual attempts at erasing masculinity and being penetrated by other men (compare Revelation 22:15 'dogs' to Revelation 21:8 'the abominable'). (p.167)

He then addresses the issue of the relevance of these references to the *qedeshim* to the debate about the biblical attitude to same-sex relations. He argues that there are three reasons why they are relevant:

(1) The Deuteronomic and Deuteronomistic description of their behaviour as an 'abomination' (*toe'vah*, an abhorrent or detestable act) links these texts ideologically to Leviticus 18:22,

237

where the same tag is applied absolutely to all man-male intercourse and not limited to intercourse in a cultic context for pay.

(2) The disgust registered by these narrators for the qedeshim parallels the disgust registered in Mesopotamia for similar figures precisely on the grounds of their attempt to define themselves sexually as women in relation to men rather than as the men that they are.

(3) Despite the revulsion with which such figures were held in the ancient Near East, this was still one of the most accepted forms of homosexual practice (not the least), because it was believed that their androgynous demeanour was beyond their control (i.e. due to a goddess figure with androgynous traits). This has links to today's claim that homosexual attraction is beyond a person's control. (p.167)

His conclusion is that:

...although there is no exact one-to-one correspondence between qedeshim and homosexual persons today, Deuteronomistic abhorrence of the qedeshim was not confined to men who experienced no same sex attraction or who were affiliated with a foreign cult and received compensation. It was primarily focused on men who feminized themselves to attract male sex partners – which, incidentally, is also the focus of Paul's term malakoi ('soft men') in 1 Corinthians 6:9). (p.168)

Gagnon sees the attitude of the Deuteronomistic historian towards the qedeshim as important for our understanding of the stories of the Levite at Gibeah in Judges 19 and the judgement on Sodom in Genesis 19. This is because the fact that the qedeshim were men who engaged in consensual same-sex activity and their behaviour was nonetheless still condemned as an 'abomination' by the Deuteronomic historian indicates that for him all forms of male same-sex activity were seen as wrong. It follows, says Gagnon, that:

Since the Deuteronomistic Historian's attitude towards the qedeshim makes it clear that he would have been repulsed by a consensual act of man-male intercourse, it is evident that in telling the story of the Levite at Gibeah the Deuteronomistic historian was indicting man-male intercourse per se and not only coercive forms of man-male intercourse. Since too the story of a Levite at Gibeah in Judges 19:22-25 is in many respects a carbon copy of the Sodom narrative in Genesis 19:4-11 (there are even some verbatim agreements in the Hebrew), how the narrator of Judges 19:22-25 interpreted the attempt of the men of the city to have intercourse with a male visitor provides our earliest commentary of how the Yahwist would have interpreted the similar event at Sodom. In other words, the Yahwist is likely to have viewed the man-male dimension of the attempted act as a compounding factor in underscoring the depravity of the inhabitants. (p.168)

Romans 1:26-27

In their comments on Romans 1:26-27 traditionalist writers argue that in Romans 1 Paul refers in general terms to lesbian and gay sexual activity. What he says cannot be restricted to pederastic activity or sexual activity taking place in the context of idol worship in pagan temples. What is more, he is not talking about people who are naturally heterosexual, but who chose to engage in homosexual activity.

What Paul is talking about is homosexual activity in general being 'unnatural' in the sense of being a violation of God's creation of human beings as male and female and, as such, a sign of God's wrath against the way in which human beings have rejected the knowledge of God given to the through the created order. In addition, what Paul says about 'unclean' or 'impure' sexual behaviour in Romans 1 ties in with his warnings against sexual immorality in Romans 6:19 and 13:3-14 and in 1 Corinthians 5.

> **The National Council of Churches of Singapore – Romans 1:24-32 do not refer to pederasty or heterosexual people engaging in homosexual activity. They give a blanket condemnation of all homosexual acts.**

The report from the National Council of Churches of Singapore, *Homosexuality – Questions and Answers,* notes that 'many consider' Romans 1:24-32 to be 'the locus classicus of the NT teaching on homosexuality.' (p.16) After quoting the verses in question, the report goes on to criticise the interpretation of them offered by Robin Scroggs and John Boswell.

It rejects Scroggs' argument that Paul is referring to pederasty on the grounds that:

> While Paul's condemnation of homosexual practices in this passage includes pederasty, there is no basis to conclude that it only refers to this practice. Paul condemns sexual acts involving 'males with males' (v27), not 'men with boys.' In addition, the fact that Paul was concerned with homosexual acts in general terms is made clear by his reference to lesbianism: 'women who exchanged natural relations for unnatural ones.' v26. (p.19)

It rejects Boswell's argument that Paul is condemning those who are naturally heterosexual and yet choose to engage in homosexual activity on the basis that it wrongly assumes that 'Paul had an idea of sexual orientation, which he did not.' When Paul referred to what was 'natural:'

> ....he was not thinking about sexual orientation or preferences as such. He did not say that the people abandoned their natural sexual functioning, Rather, Paul was referring to the natural sexual functioning. What Paul called 'nature' and 'natural' has to do with God's creative intention. Thus, theologian Stanley Grenz is right when he says 'we ought to view Paul's concept of nature as a broad idea that refers to the world and human life as

intended by God, so that conversely everything that runs contrary to God's intention is 'unnatural.' (pp.20-21)[101]

The report's conclusion is that 'like the Holiness Code in Leviticus, Paul issues a blanket condemnation of all homosexual acts in this passage in Romans.' (p.21)

> **Gordon Kennedy, Jane McArthur, Andrew McGowan – in Romans 1:24-27 both gay and lesbian sexual activity is seen as the result of, and the punishment for, the corporate rebellion of humanity against God to which the grace of God in Christ is the solution.**

In their contribution to the Church of Scotland report Kennedy, McArthur and McGowan declare that 'dealing as it does with both male homosexual behaviour and lesbianism, Romans 1:24-27 is the most substantial and overt discussion on homosexual practice in the New Testament, if not in the Bible.' In this passage, they say, 'homosexual activity is shown to be (i) the result of sin, (ii) an indication of how far someone has strayed from God and (iii) a punishment from God.' (pp.1/112-113)

In their view, what Paul teaches in Romans 1 is that:

> Human beings are alienated from God as a result of their basic rebellion against him, which is demonstrated in their refusal to honour him. All other depravities and moral perversion grow out of this basic rebellion. In his wrath, God abandons the rebellious to their own devices. This is the import of the expression 'God gave them up' in verses 24, 26 and 28. (p.1/113)

This rebellion against God is not individual rebellion, but the corporate rebellion of humanity as a whole. This means that when Paul speaks of homosexuality as 'unnatural':

---

[101] The quotation is from Stanley Grenz, *Welcoming but not Affirming*, Louisville: Westmister John Knox Press, 1998, p.54.

....he means what he says. He is not getting into a discussion as to what might or not seem natural to any one individual, he is saying that homosexuality is against the creation order for all people. He is not discussing the question of orientation, a concept foreign to the New Testament. (p.1/113)

The point that Paul is making is that by his reference to homosexual activity is that:

The creation narrative points to male and female as normative, thus the practice of homosexuality is a rejection of [the] Creator God and creative order. He uses this illustration to demonstrate the growing power of sin in the life of the unbeliever or apostate as the antithesis of the power of the Holy Spirit in the life of the believer. Paul decries the unnatural desire of female for female or male for male as substituting truth for untruth. There is a progression here: first, a turning away from the truth and the believing of lies; second an intellectual confusion, in which fools think they are truly wise, then a collapse into idolatry. Following this, God gives them up and leaves them mired in sin. Homosexual acts are recognised to be part of this desperate, fallen condition from which men and women need to be redeemed. (p. 1/114)

However, there is an answer to this situation. As Paul reminds us in Romans 6:

...since Jesus lived, died and rose again, believers have been brought from death to life and are no longer in the grip of the results of the Fall. This shift from death to life described by Paul, the movement from 'slavery to sin' to 'slavery to righteousness' is a gift from God and a grace-enabled calling for every Christian. (p.1/114)

> **The Evangelical Alliance – Romans 1 refers to male and female sexual activity in general rather than culturally specific ways and it sees this activity as the result of our universal fallenness and God's judgement upon human society and culture.**

The Evangelical Alliance report also stresses the importance of Romans 1 for the debate about homosexuality. It states that 'Romans 1 is without doubt the most important biblical reference for the homosexuality debate as it provides by far the fullest theological reflection on same-sex sexual relations in the biblical canon and is almost certainly the only reference in Scripture to lesbian sexual activity.' (p.44)

The report begins its account of Romans 1 by declaring that:

> Paul describes a 'godlessness' (*asebeian*, v.18) which is demonstrated in both the *apathetic neglect* of God which fails to honour his purpose as revealed in the world and the more active idolatry which provides the key to interpretation of verses 26 and 27. In verse 23, Paul presents the first of three vital 'exchanges.' He states here that the wicked characteristically 'changed (*ellaxan*) the glory of the immortal God into images resembling a mortal human being or birds or four footed animals or reptiles.' This is broadened as 'they exchanged (*ellaxan*) the truth about God for a lie and worshipped and served the creature rather than the Creator' (v25, cf Exodus 20:1-3). The idolatrous exchange of creature and Creator in v25 is the lie (*to pseudei*) – the defining distortion of God's purpose for the world. From this defining distortion other distortions inevitably follow (cf Gen 3:5). So Paul casts homosexual practice against the backdrop not only of Mosaic law, but also of natural law, in relation to Genesis 1-3: humankind made 'male and female' in God's image and their complementarity as 'one flesh' (Gen 1:27, 2:24). (pp.44-45)

243

The misuse of the body described generically in verse 24 and in terms of same-sex relations in verses 26-37 are archetypes of the distortions that follow from the exchange of creature and Creator:

> Although these belong to a much broader catalogue of evils (cf v 29ff), within the structure of Paul's argument such bodily degradations are marked out for special attention because they constitute a particularly vivid paradigm of creation gone wrong. Although we may assume from v.24 that Paul is thinking of heterosexual as well as homosexual depravities, the third 'exchange' in vv.26-27 suggests Paul sees homoerotic activity as almost iconic of what he is condemning. Richard B Hays thus writes of engaging in homosexual behaviour as enacting 'an outward and visible sign of an inward and spiritual reality: the rejection of the Creator's design.' (p.45) [102]

In the report's view, the broad shape of Paul's argument in Romans 1 means that:

> Despite carrying other meanings in Scripture, sometimes culturally-specific (as in 1 Corinthians 11:14), and sometimes negative (Ephesians 2:3) the pervasiveness of Paul's wider argument from design here means that we cannot divorce *phusin* from the apostle's understanding of God's eternal intent for humans (cf.v20). Furthermore, the notion of homosexual practice as against or beyond nature (*para phusin*) and thus immoral is found in several contemporary Graeco-Roman sources, especially in that Hellenistic Jewish tradition with which Paul himself was associated. (p.46)

The idea of God 'giving up' people to the lusts of their hearts found in verses 24, 26 and 28 of Romans 1 means that:

---

[102] The quotation is from Richard Hays, *The Moral Vision of the New Testament*, Edinburgh: T&T Clark, 1986. p.386.

The sexual misconduct abhorred by Paul is thus the result of divine judgement – on fallen human society and culture, not specific individuals – rather than the cause of it. It is therefore as much to be regretted as castigated: it is a presenting symptom of a world estranged from its Maker. It is a mark of that universal fallenness in which we all share, and Paul correlates it with an idolatrous culture, suggesting that the more idolatrous a culture, the more it will distort the sexual norms and models that God has given us. Sexual misconduct therefore should not be singled out for particular scorn, even while it cannot be condoned. (p.46)

Going on to look in detail at verses 26-27, the report argues that few 'serious scholars' doubt that Paul has in mind 'sexual acts performed by men with men and women with women.' The clear 'rhetorical and grammatical parallels' between the two verses and the explicit reference to homosexual acts in verse 27 tells against alternative interpretations which see v26 as referring to certain forms of heterosexual activity by women. (p.47)

The report also rules out the idea that these verses are talking about 'a particular form of pagan temple prostitution' since the reference to the parties involved 'burning with lust' for one another does not fit 'the more dispassionate prostitution associated with religious ceremony and ritual.' Furthermore, it says, the linking together in these verses of lesbianism with male homosexuality makes it likely that Paul was talking in broad terms rather than referring specifically to pederasty, for which there was no female equivalent.

Finally, the report rejects the contention that Paul is only talking about naturally heterosexual people who engaged in homosexuality, quoting Richard Hays' comment that Paul is not 'presenting biographical sketches of individual pagans: he is offering an apocalyptic 'long view' which indicts fallen humanity as a whole.' (p.48) [103]

The report's conclusion is that 'the most authentic reading of Romans 1:26-27 remains therefore that which sees Paul prohibiting homosexual activity in the most general of terms, rather than in respect of more culturally and historically specific forms of such activity. '(p.48)

> **Ian Paul – same sex activity, which is against the visible natural purpose of the human body, is evidence that humanity is in rebellion against its creator and God has given human beings up to following their own futile thinking and desires.**

In *Same-Sex Unions* Paul declares that in Romans 1 the Apostle 'is strongly linking same-sex sexual relations with a failure to acknowledge God and worship him right.' He is not saying 'that same-sex activity is wrong *when* associated with idolatry; he is asserting that same-sex activity is wrong because it *manifests* an idolatrous world view.' (p.24)

The reason Paul chose homosexuality rather than some other vice to make his point is twofold. First, it is likely that he 'was influenced by other Jewish critiques of non-Jewish culture, in which same-sex activity featured strongly.' Secondly, same-sex activity:

> ...fits well with his argument from creation, in that he can appeal both to the Genesis [creation] texts and to the fact that male and female genitalia visibly fit one another, and in this sense same-sex activity is a rejection of the natural, visible intent of the body in a way that is analogous to the rejection of the natural, visible origins of the world. (p.24)

What all this means, he writes, is that when Paul talks about 'nature' he is not referring to the experiences of sexual attraction of particular

---

[103] The quotation is from, ibid, p.200.

individuals or their 'innate preferences.' Instead, what he is referring to is:

> ...the way the world was meant to be, as created by God; his categories are theological, not psychological and corporate rather than individual. It is 'the order intended by the creator, the order that is manifest in God's creation.' In the same way that Ps 106 tells the corporate story of the failure of God's people. Paul is telling here the cosmic story of the failure of humanity. And he is not simply referring to culture; he does appear to think (in 1 Corinthians 11:14) that women having long hair is the way that God intended it. Instead he is borrowing terms from existing ethical thinking (particularly in Stoicism) about what is 'natural (*kata phusin*) and what is unnatural (*para phusin*), which therefore rejects God's intention in creation. The language of 'impurity' or 'uncleanness' in verse 24 reinforces the connection with the Old Testament, but the surrounding language of 'sin,' 'wickedness,' and 'shame' shows these are equivalents. (p.25) [104]

Paul concludes by quoting the summary of Romans 1 offered by Richard Hays:

> The aim of Romans 1 is not to teach a code of sexual ethics; nor is the package a warning of God's judgment against those who are guilty of particular sins. Rather, Paul is offering a *diagnosis* of the disordered human condition: he adduces the fact of widespread homosexual behaviour as evidence that human beings are indeed in rebellion against their creator. Homosexual activity, then, is not a provocation of the wrath of God (Romans 1:18); rather it is a consequence of God's decision to 'give up'

---

[104] The quotation is from Joseph Fitzmeyer, *Romans*, New Haven: Yale University Press, 1993, pp.286-287.

rebellious creatures to follow their own futile thinking and desire. (p.25) [105]

> **Tom Wright - for St. Paul homosexual activity is a violation of the structure of the created order which shows that there is something wrong with humanity as a whole.**

Professor Tom Wright introduces his comments on Romans 1:24-27 in his commentary on Romans in his *Paul for Everyone* [106] series by noting that someone who has never come across a violin bow before will only be able to understand what it is for when someone picks up a violin and begins to play it. A violin and a bow are made for each other and 'only when they are together will either be complete.' While acknowledging the inadequacy of this illustration he says that it 'catches something of what Paul assumes as he begins to explain how human life has been distorted away from the creator's intentions.' (p.20)

In Wright's view, throughout Romans 1:24-27 Paul has in mind Genesis 1-3. He is concerned with how human have violated 'not simply a 'law' given at some point in human history, but the very structure of the created order itself.' Paul's assumption is that there is such a structure:

> Taking Genesis 1 as his starting point, he sees humans as created in God's image and given charge over the non-human creation. Humans are commanded to be fruitful: they are to celebrate, in their male-female complementarity, the abundant life-generating capacity of God's good world. And they are charged with bringing God's order to the world, acting as stewards of the garden and all that is in it. Males and females are very different, and they are designed to work together to make, with God, the music of creation. Something deep within the structure of the world responds to the coming together of like and unlike, something which cannot be reached by the mere joining together of like and like. (p.21)

---

[105] The quotation is from Hays op,cit. pp.387-388.
[106] Tom Wright, *Paul for Everyone – Romans Part 1*, London: SPCK, 2004.

Understanding this point, he says, helps to explain 'the otherwise baffling fact that the very first instance Paul gives of what he sees as the corruption of human life is the practice of homosexual relations.' According to Wright the point that Paul is making:

> ...is not simply 'we Jews don't approve of this,' or, 'relationships like this are always unequal or exploitative.' His point is, 'this is not what males and females were made for.' Nor is he suggesting that everyone who feels sexually attracted to members of their own sex, or everyone who engages in actual same-sex relations, has got to that point through committing specific acts of idolatry. Nor, again, does he suppose that all those who find themselves in that situation have arrived there by a specific choice to give up heterosexual possibilities. Reading the text like that reflects a modern individualism rather than Paul's larger, all-embracing perspective. Rather, he is talking about the human race as a whole. His point is not that 'there are some exceptionally wicked people out there who do these revolting things' but 'the fact that such clear distortions of the creator's male-plus-female intention occur in the world indicates that the human race as a whole is guilty of a character twisting idolatry.' He sees the practice of same-sex relations as a sign that the human world in general is out of joint. (pp.22-23)

This situation is the result 'of God allowing people to follow lust wherever it leads – once they have lost their grip on God's truth and, like Adam and Eve in the garden, listened to the voice of the creature rather than the voice of God.' (p.23)

> **Ben Witherington – for St. Paul homosexual activity is contrary to the way God originally created things to be and constitutes a refusal to acknowledge the manifestation of God in the created order.**

Professor Ben Witherington declares in his commentary on Romans[107] that Romans 1:26-27 are 'about as clear a condemnation of homosexual and lesbian behavior as exists in the NT.' What Paul is saying is 'that those who practice such behaviour have exchanged the natural function of intercourse for that which is against nature.' (p.69)

Witherintgton notes that there was a long history in both Jewish and Greco-Roman thought 'of seeing such behaviour as 'unnatural' or counter to the way God originally created and intended things to be (Plato, *Laws* 1.2, Ovid, *Metamorphoses* 9,578; Leviticus 18:22, 20:13; Philo, *Abraham* 26.135, *Special Laws* 2.14.50; Josephus, *Apion* 2.25, 199; 2 Enoch 10.4).' In line with this tradition of thought 'Paul certainly believes that there is a natural order of things that God put into creation which ought to be followed.' (p.69)

In v 27, Witherington writes, Paul writes about the corresponding penalty for such unnatural behaviour:

> 'The punishment not only fits the crime, but directly results from it as well.' Such behaviour is a constant means of putting God to the test. The just decree of God concerning all the listed vices is that those who do them deserve death – and yet God has sent his Son to call both Gentile and Jews to a better way, a way out of human darkness and fallenness. (p.69) [108]

Finally, Witherington explains that according to Paul, homosexual behaviour results from idolatry 'in that it is a rejection of the creation order that the Creator God set up in the first place. 'For him it is a way

---

[107] Ben Witherington, *Paul's Letter to the Romans*, Grand Rapids and Cambridge: Eerdmans, 2004.
[108] The quotation is from Tom Wright, 'Romans,' in *The New Interpreters Bible*, Vol. 10. Nashville; Abingdon Press, 2002, p.

in which human beings refuse to acknowledge the manifestation of God's activity in creation.' (p.69) [109]

> **Michael Brown – in Romans 1 St. Paul is not referring simply to homosexual acts linked to idolatrous pagan worship or to heterosexual people acting in a way that is contrary to their nature. Rather, he is denouncing all forms of male and female homosexual activity as sinful because they go against God's intended order for His creation.**

Brown writes in *Can you be Gay and Christian?* that in Romans 1:26-32 Paul is not referring simply 'to sins that people commit in the context of idol worship in a pagan temple.' Rather, what he is referring to are:

> ...the sins of the human race as a whole, which, he explains, are the result of our rejection of the one true God, who consequently gave us over to the sins of the flesh and the sins of the heart. Stop for a moment and reread the verses just cited. Is there any doubt that Paul was speaking of the universal nature of human sin? And is there anything on this list – from heterosexual promiscuity to homosexual acts (male and female) to 'evil, covetousness, malice' and 'envy, murder, strife, deceit, [and] maliciousness' to people being 'gossips, slanderers, haters of God, insolent, haughty, boastful, inventors of evil, disobedient to parents, foolish, faithless, heartless, ruthless' – is there anything listed here that is not sinful wherever it is found, whether in the context of idolatry or in the context of everyday life? Obviously not. (p.174)

This means, Brown contends, that:

> Paul was not specifically speaking about homosexual acts that took place in pagan temples as the people worshipped idols and engaged in sexual promiscuity. He was speaking generically about homosexual acts, both male and female, and denouncing

---

[109] The quotation is from Fitzmeyer, op.cit, p.

them as sinful in the strongest possible terms. This also means that he was not claiming that every person who engaged in these acts did so because they were inflamed with lust and depravity. Rather, he was explaining how these things become part of the human race. They are the result of God giving us over to our own ways, and our own ways are never the best ways. (p.174)

Brown then focuses on Romans 1:26-27, starting with verse 26. He quotes James Dunn's translation of the second half of this verse in his commentary on Romans 'for their females changed the natural function into what is contrary to nature' and notes that Dunn explains that 'Both θήλέιάι and άρσένές (v.27) 'females, males,' are used presumably because Paul has in mind particularly their sexual relationship, and indeed sexual complementarity (cf Mark10:6; Matthew 19:4; Genesis 1:27; Galatians 3:28).' (p.175) [110]

For Brown, the significance of this is that Paul is not saying that heterosexual women engaged in lesbian sex in a way that was contrary to their personal sexual nature. This is 'a concept that is not only contrary to Greek usage and the context...but is also based on contemporary conceptions about sexual orientation that would have been foreign to Paul.' Instead what the Greek is speaking about is:

> ...women abandoning the natural functions of their bodies – made for men rather than for women – a thought that Paul continues in the very next verse. As translated by Dunn, 'Likewise also the males gave up the natural function of the female' (Rom 1:27). Paul's point is quite clear! (p.175) [111]

What Paul is talking about, writes Brown, is:

> ...God's created order, about the natural functions of male and female, not about people individually doing what was

---

[110] The quotation is from James Dunn, *Romans 1-8*, Dallas: Word, 1998, p.64.
[111] The quotation is from ibid. p.64.

(allegedly) contrary to their normal sexual attractions, as some gay theologians argue. (Again, no one in recorded history ever came up with this far-fetched and utterly false idea until after the sexual revolution of the 1960s). (p.177)

Brown quotes the words of the New International Dictionary of New Testament Theology:

> ...*physis* [nature] stands further for the regular order of nature which determines the distinction between the sexes. God has given up the idolaters, so that they have exchanged natural (*physiken*) sexual intercourse between man and woman for unnatural (*para physin*, Romans 1:26). (p.178)[112]

He then comments:

> 'To say it once more: Paul is teaching that *females* 'exchanged natural relations for unnatural ones' – not heterosexuals exchanged natural relations for unnatural ones. In the same way,' he writes, 'the males abandoned natural relations with females.' (p.178)

Brown's final point is that in Romans 1:20 Paul points back to the creation and in verse 23 there is an undeniable verbal echo of the Septuagint version of Genesis 1:26. This reference back to the creation narrative in Genesis 1 continues with the use of *arsen* (male) and *thelus* (female) in Romans 1:26-27 echoing the language of the Greek version of Genesis 1:27. Brown sees these intertextual echoes as making it absolutely clear:

> ...that Paul is saying that homosexual acts (be they male or female) are contrary to God's natural, intended order for His creation – and that applies whether they are promiscuous or monogamous. They are wrong in God's sight either way, in every situation and setting.

---

[112] The quotation is from Colin Brown (ed), *New International Dictionary of New Testament Theology*, Vol.3 Grand Rapids: Zondervan, 1986, p. 660.

In the words of the (non-fundamentalist) German theologian Ernst Kasemann, 'Moral perversion is the result of God's wrath, not the reason for it.' Or, as expressed by another (non-fundamentalist) German theologian, Wolfhart Pannenberg: 'The biblical assessments of homosexual practice are unambiguous in their rejection.' And 'the entire biblical witness includes practising homosexuality without exception among the kinds of behaviour that give particularly striking expression to humanity's turning away from God. (p.179) [113]

> **William Loader – St. Paul sees all homosexual acts as the result of God's punishment of idolatry. He highlights this form of sin in order to lead his readers to see that all humans are under sin and in need of grace.**

In *The New Testament on Sexuality*[114] Professor William Loader surveys the various suggested interpretations of Romans 1 and then summarises his own view as follows:

> ...Paul assumes that people were created male and female with heterosexual orientation of their natural sexual emotions. Those who denied God's reality had perverted minds and engaged in perverted acts: they worshipped idols. As punishment God gave them over to perverted minds with perverted passions and desires whose intensity they followed by engaging in perverted acts, females with females, males with males, and for both their mind set and their actions they stand condemned. Paul does not differentiate between people of different sexual orientation, either to exempt homosexuals, or to make sure both are condemned. He may have known that some made such differentiation, but he would not have believed it. Nor does he

---

[113] The quotation from Ernst Kasemann is taken from Dunn op.cit. p.64 and the quotation from Wolfhart Pannenberg is from 'Should we support gay marriage? NO,' at http://tinyurl.com/lwbyrhv.
[114] William Loader, *The New Testament on Sexuality,* Grand Rapids and Cambridge: Eerdmans, 2012.

focus only on pederastic relations. Without differentiation he condemns all with such sexual attitudes and desires and all acts which give expression to them. He does so within the context of deliberately highlighting what he assumes his hearers will agree is outrageous sin, in order to bring them to see that in fact all are under sin and in need of grace, including those so willing to condemn. (p.326)

> **Robert Gagnon – the language St. Paul uses in Romans 1 is picked up later in Romans in a way that shows that he believes that the sexual sins he describes there are ones that Christians must judge as immoral and therefore avoid.**

Finally, in his essay 'How seriously does Scripture treat the issue of homosexual practice?' Gagnon focuses on Paul's use of the language of uncleanness and impurity in Romans 1.

Gagnon writes that in Romans 1:24 and 26-27 St.Paul:

> ...singles out homosexual practice as an especially reprehensible instance – along with idolatry (1:19-23, 25) – of humans suppressing the truth accessible in the material creation set in motion by the Creator. He refers to it as an act of sexual 'uncleanness' or 'impurity (*akatharsia*), an 'indecency' or 'shameful act' (*aschemosune*), a 'dishonoring (*atimazesthai*) of their bodies among themselves,' the product of 'dishonorable passions' (*pathe atimias*) and an act 'contrary to nature' (*he para phusin*) that, in part, was its own payback (*antimisthia*). (p.174)

He notes there are 'intertextual echoes' alluding back to 1:24-27 in Romans 6:19 and 13:13-14.

In 6:19 Paul tells his readers to no longer put themselves at the disposal:

...of the 'sexual impurity' (*akatharsia*) that had characterized their pre-Christian life, for to continue to engage in such behaviour was to engage in acts of which they should now be ashamed (echoing the shame language of 1:24-27) and which lead to the loss of eternal life (6:19-23; cf 1:32). (p.175)

In 13:13-14 Paul declares that Christians should 'lay aside works of darkness' such as 'immoral sexual activities (*koitai*) and licentious acts (*aselgeiai*) and thereby to 'make no provision to gratify the sinful desires of the flesh." The word *'koitai'* (which literally means 'lyings' or 'beds') 'links up with arsenokoitai, 'men lying with a male' in 1 Corinthians 6:9 as a particular example of an immoral 'lying." *Aselgeiai* refers to 'a lack of self-restraint with respect to refraining from prohibited sexual behaviours,' which obviously includes the kind of behaviour referred to in 1:24-27 and 6:19-22. (p.175)

For Gagnon the significance of these later passages in Romans is that they rule out the idea put forward by some interpreters that Paul's argument in Romans 2 means that Christians should refrain from judging the sins mentioned in 1:24-27.

> The subsequent allusions back 1:24-27 in 6:19 and 13:13 show that Paul is not telling his audience to stop passing judgment on sexually immoral acts in the community of believers. Indeed, a message to 'stop judging' could hardly be applied to [the] parallel case of idolatry in 1:19-23. Moreover, Paul positively insists in the case of the incestuous man in 1 Corinthians 5 that the community do its job precisely by passing Christ's judgment on the immoral person in their midst. (p.175)

1 Corinthians 6:9-11, 1 Timothy 1:10

In their comments on these passages traditionalist writers are agreed in arguing:

(a) that the terms *malakoi* and *arsenokitai* refer to the passive and active partners in male homosexual sex;

(b) that *arsenokoitai* is derived from the Septuagint version on Leviticus 18:22 and 20:13,

(c) the terms refer to male-male sexual activity in general (including consensual sex) and cannot be limited to pederasty, prostitution or exploitative sexual activity.

It follows that in both passages there is a general condemnation of male homosexual activity as a barrier to participation in the kingdom of God and as contrary to both the seventh commandment in the Decalogue and the prohibitions of homosexual activity in Leviticus.

1 Corinthians 6:9-11

> Roy Ciampa and Brian Rosner – the terms used in 1 Corinthians 6:9 refer to men who willingly engage in active and passive homosexual activity. Paul's opposition to such activity seems to be based on Leviticus 18:22 and 20:13.

Dr Roy Ciampa and Dr Brian Rosner write in their 2011 commentary on 1 Corinthians[115] that the terms used by Paul in 1 Corinthians 6:9 refer 'to homosexual behaviour of one form or another.' (p241) As they see it, rather than following *Today's New International Version* and referring to 'male prostitutes and practising homosexuals' we should see this verse as referring to:

> ...those who willingly play the passive and active roles in homosexual acts. Paul is not describing 'homosexuals' per se, but homosexual acts (commonly engaged in by Roman men who were also active in heterosexual relationships). (p.241)

---

[115] Roy E Ciampa and Brian Rosner, *The First Epistle to the Corinthians*, Leicester: Apollos, 2011,

They argue that the Roman world viewed willingly playing a passive homosexual role as shameful, but expected men of stature to penetrate others, both male and female, 'the Jewish and Christian perspective affirmed by Paul was quite different.' Paul opposed all homosexual behaviour (even if entered into willingly) and his opposition:

> ...seems to derive from Leviticus 18:22 and 20:13 which represent absolute bans. Paul's opposition to heterosexual acts was not because he had not thought about the subject or had simply taken over a conventional list of vices from Hellenistic authors whether Jewish or secular...Paul opposed homosexual behaviour on the basis of creation theology and because it is marked as a vice in the Torah and was stressed as a vice by Jews. (pp.241-242)

Tom Wright – In 1 Corinthians 6:9-11 St. Paul is referring to both passive and active male homosexual activity as unacceptable. Such behaviour, like other forms of sin, distorts and defaces God's image and therefore leads people away from God's kingdom. However, God has provided a way by which people can be delivered from it.

In his commentary on I Corinthians in his *Paul for Everyone*[116] series Tom Wright declares that in 1 Corinthians 6:9-11 St. Paul uses:

> ... two words which have been much debated, but which, experts have now established, clearly refer to the practice of male homosexuality. The two terms refer respectively to the passive or submissive partner and the active or aggressive one, and Paul places both roles in his list of unacceptable behaviour. (p.69)

He goes on to say that St. Paul is not suggesting:

---

[116] Tom Wright, *Paul for Everyone – 1 Corinthians*, London: SPCK, 2003.

...that sexual error is worse than any other kind – though the central place of sexuality within the human make-up indicates that we should not take it lightly. But the point he's making, with this as with other distorted ways of behaving, is that they take away from that full humanness which God longs to see come to flower in his creatures, and which will be completed in the final 'kingdom of God' (verse 10). It isn't, to repeat what we said before, that God has an arbitrary list of rules and if you break them you won't get in. It is, rather, that his kingdom will be peopled by humans who reflect his image completely; and behaviour in the present which distorts and defaces that image will lead in the opposite direction. The whole New Testament joins in warning of the real possibility of this happening.

But the whole New Testament also joins in announcing that it needn't – because God has himself provided the way in which people can leave their past, and indeed their present, behind, and move forward into his future. You can be washed clean, whatever has happened in the past. You can be made one of God's special people, whatever you are in the present. (pp.69-70)

> **Robert Gagnon – The language used by St Paul in 1 Corinthians 6:9 is derived from Leviticus 18:22 and 20:13. Malakoi refers to men who play the passive or 'female' role in same-sex activity whilst arsenokoitai refers to the active or penetrative role. He warns the Corinthians that participation in such behaviour endangers their inheritance in the kingdom of God.**

Gagnon looks in detail at the meaning of the words *malakoi* and *arsenokoitai* in 1 Corinthians 6:9 in the course of his debate with Dan Via in *Homosexuality and the Bible: Two Views*.

He begins his discussion by noting that in 1 Corinthians 6:9-11 Paul expands the vice list in 1 Corinthians 5:11 by naming three groups of offenders who fill out the meaning of *pornoi* (the sexually immoral). These are *moichoi* (adulterers) and *malakoi* and *arsenokoitai.* (p.82) He then lists five reasons for holding that *malakoi* means 'effeminate males who play the sexual role of females.' These are:

- The fact that it is placed in the midst of two other terms 'that refer to participants in illicit sexual intercourse.'
- The fact that it is placed immediately before *arsenokoitai*, a term which refers to 'the active *homosexual* partner.'
- The fact that being a *malakos* excludes someone from the kingdom of God 'suggests a form of effeminacy well beyond the stereotyped limp wrist.'
- The use of cognate terms by Philo of Alexandria 'to describe men who actively feminize themselves for the purpose of attracting other men.'
- The use of the 'comparable Latin term *molles* (soft men) in tandem with other terms that refer to effeminate males desirous of penetration by men.' These designations 'were not confined to adolescents or cult prostitutes, much less did they imply coercion.' (p.82)

Gagnon's conclusion is that when he used the term *malakoi*:

> ...Paul was thinking of the male described in Lev 18:22 and 20:13 who is lain with as though a woman. This background, plus Paul's choice of the term 'soft men,' indicates that one of the troubling aspects of male-male intercourse for Paul was that it blurred God-given, nature-imbedded gender differences. Issues of exploitation and orientation were beside the point. (p.83)

Turning to *arsenokoitai*, Gagnon states that the word is derived from the Septuagint translation of Leviticus 18:22 and 20:13. He holds that:

> In keeping with the fact that Lev 18:22 addresses the active or penetrating partner, the pairing of *arsenokoitai* and *malakoi* in 1 Cor 6:9 suggests that *arsenokoitai* refers to the active

homosexual partner, at least primarily. Ancient Christian literature limits the term to male-male intercourse but, commensurate with the meaning of *malakoi*, not to pederasts or clients of cult prostitutes. This inclusive sense is further confirmed by Rom 1:27, surely the best commentary on what *arsenokoitai* would have meant for Paul. There the contrast is between males who have sex with females and males who have sex with males – not between exploitative and non-exploitative forms of same-sex or opposite-sex intercourse. (p.83)

Gagnon further notes that Paul completes his vice list in verse 11 with a reminder to the Corinthians that they had been transformed:

Some of the Corinthians used to engage in incest, solicitation of prostitutes, adultery and male-male intercourse. Continuance in such practices would endanger their inheritance of the kingdom of God. Such was the case with the incestuous man in 1 Corinthians 5 whose temporary expulsion Paul was now recommending. Issues of 'sexual orientation' would have been irrelevant to Paul because the Spirit of Christ was present within to counteract the domination of any sinful impulses operating in the flesh. (pp. 83-84)

> **Michael Brown – as gay scholars have admitted, malakoi and arsenokoitai have sexual connotations and refer to the passive and active partners in homosexual intercourse. They are general terms and cannot be limited to pederasty or prostitution.**

In *Can you be Gay and Christian?* Brown also looks in detail at the meaning of *malakoi* and *arsenokoitai*. He writes that *malakoi* literally means 'soft' and that has the meaning in the Septuagint version of Proverbs 25:15 and Matthew 11:8. However, elsewhere in ancient Greek:

...the term is commonly used for the receptive partner in homosexual sex as well as for men who dressed and acted like women (hence the rendering 'effeminate' in the King James), but clearly not meaning a man who simply had some unintentional effeminate mannerisms. (p.166)

Arsenokoitai, he says:

> ...is composed of two Greek words meaning 'males who lie with males,' and is most likely derived from the Septuagint, the Greek translation of the Hebrew Scriptures (Old Testament) completed nearly two centuries before the time of Jesus. There the Greek translation of the Hebrew words for 'lying with a male' in Leviticus 18:22 and 20:13 include the words *arsen* (males) and *koites* (bed) leading to the compound word *arsenokoites*, a man who lies with a male. (p.166)

When these two words are used side by side, he argues, there are undeniable sexual connotations. That is why:

> ...there is virtually unanimous agreement in all major dictionaries and translations, despite some minor differences in the exact nuances of the words. And that's one of the reasons gay scholars like Professsor Brooten, cited previously, could say 'I see Paul as condemning all forms of homoeroticism.' For Brooten, the logical conclusion was to reject the authority of Paul for the church. (p.167) [117]

Brown cites the article on Paul in the online GLBTQ encyclopedia as another example of gay scholarship that supports the point that he is making.

On the term *malakoi* this article declares that the lexical evidence from both classical and post classical sources makes it clear that the term refers to 'males – boys, youth, or adults – who have consented, either

---

[117] The quotation is from Bernadette Brooten, *Love between Women: Early Christian Responses to Female Homoeroticism*, Chicago: Chicago University Press, 2003, page reference not given.

for money or for pleasure, for some perceived advantage or as an act of affectionate generosity, to be penetrated by men.'

On *arsenokoitai* it states that the term refers to ' 'men who lie with males,' and the Vulgate's mas*culorum concubitores* (when *masculorum* is objective genitive), render the Greek exactly to mean 'men who lie with males,' 'men who sleep with males,' men who have sex with males.' It further states that the 'dependence of Paul's *arsenonkoitai* on the Levitical *arsenos koitén* [from Leviticus 18:22] demonstrates unequivocally its source and confirms his intended meaning.' (p.167) [118]

Finally, Brown quotes the veteran New Testament scholar Anthony Thiselton as acknowledging that 'the translation of the Greek words *malakoi* and *arsenokoitai* has become notoriously controversial' but as then going on to say that:

> No amount of lexicographical manipulation over *malakoi* can avoid the clear meaning of *arsenokoitai* as the activity of males (*arsēn*) who have sexual relations, sleep with (*koitês*) other males.
>
> [Also], the view that one or both Greek words refer only to pederasty or to male prostitution for payment, as advocated by Kenneth Dover, Robin Scroggs and others, cannot withstand the battery of detailed linguistic arguments brought against by a number of historical and linguistic specialists. Moreover, it positively violates the contextual theme which has emerged of a general grasping beyond ordained boundaries in the face of what God assigns as the self's due which characterises every other habitual act in the list, culminating in Paul's rejection of

---

[118] The quotation is from Eugene Rice in GLBTQ, s.v. 'St Paul (d. ca 66 C.E.),' http://tinyurl.com/k22uspy.

the Corinthian slogan within the church 'I have the right to do anything' or 'all things are lawful.' (p.171) [119]

> Sam Allberry - the terms malakoi and arsenokoitai refer to the passive and active partners in homosexual sex. St. Paul holds that homosexual behaviour is incompatible with the new people the Corinthians have become.

Allberry explains in *Is God anti-gay?* that in 1 Corinthians 6:9-10:

> Paul is describing different kinds of people who (unless they repent) will be excluded from the kingdom of God. Four kinds relate to sexual sin, and two of those specifically to homosexual behaviour. The ESV takes the latter and puts them together as 'men who practice homosexuality' the NIV translates them as 'male prostitutes and homosexual offenders.'(p.34)

He goes on to say that because Paul 'is giving examples of people who will not be in heaven' we need to be clear exactly what it is he is talking about.[120]

The first of the two terms relating homosexuality, *malakoi*, literally means, he says:

> ...those who are soft. In classical literature it could be used as a pejorative term for men who were effeminate; for the younger, passive partner in a pederastic (man-boy) relationship; or to refer to male prostitutes (hence the NIV's translation). In 1 Corinthians 6 *malakoi* comes in a list describing general forms of sexual sin, and context suggests Paul is most likely using it in a broad way to refer to the passive partners in homosexual intercourse. (p.35)

The second term, *arsenokoitai*:

---

[119] The quotation is from Anthony Thiselton 'Can hermeneutics ease the deadlock?' in Timothy Bradshaw (eds) *The Way Forward? Christian Voices on Homosexuality and the Church*, Grand Rapids: Eerdmans, 2004, pp. 167-168.
[120] Ibid, p.35.

...is a compound of 'male' (*arsen*) and 'intercourse' (*koites*, literally 'bed'). These are the two words used in the Greek translation of Leviticus 18v22 and 20v13, suggesting Paul is referring back to these passages. (p.35)

This means that '*arsenokoitai*...is a general term for same-sex sex, and its pairing with *malakoi* indicates that Paul is addressing both the active and passive partners in homosexual sex.' (p.35)

According to Allberry the reason Paul thinks that the forms of behaviour he lists are not appropriate for the Christians in Corinth is because it is not who they now are:

> Some of them had clearly been active homosexuals. They did live in these ways. But no more. They have been washed, sanctified and justified, forgiven, cleansed from their sins, and set apart for God. They have a new standing and identity before him... That Paul is warning his readers not to revert to their former way of life suggests there is still some desire to. But in Christ we are no longer who we were. Those who have come out of an active gay lifestyle need to understand how to see themselves. What defined us then no longer defines us now. (p.37)

> **William Loader – the two terms refer to the passive and active partners in same-sex activity.**

In the New Testament on Sexuality, after examining the various suggestions that have been made about how to understand *malakoi* and *arsenokoitai*, Loader reaches a similar conclusion to the other writers that we have just looked at. He writes:

> On balance, then, Paul probably uses the two terms with reference to men who engage in same-sex behaviour, with the first referring to the willing passive partner, whether by private consent or as a male prostitute, 'those who submit to sexual penetration by other men,' and the second referring to 'those

who engage in sexual penetration of other men,' which would have a broader reference and include, but not be limited to, exploitation, also by force. (p.232)

> **The Evangelical Alliance – the term arsenokoites was most probably derived by St. Paul from the Septuagint version of Leviticus 18:22 and 20:13 and carries a homoerotic meaning. In 1 Corinthians 6 and 1 Timothy 1 homosexual practice is listed alongside a list of other sins that are incompatible with belonging the people of God.**

The Evangelical Alliance report looks at 1 Timothy 1:8-11 and 1 Corinthians 6:9 together. It declares:

> 1 Tim. 8-11 warns us against crude law-grace dichotomies. The need to integrate legal/doctrinal rectitude ('the law is good,' v.8) with 'love that comes from a pure heart, conscience, and sincere faith' (v.6) is central. One of Paul's concerns here is contraventions of 'sound doctrine.' As part of his list of those who commit such contraventions in verses 9-10 we encounter the word *arsenokoites* which appears in a similar Pauline list of vices at 1 Cor. 6.9-11. Most translations and commentaries associate *arsenokoites* in some way or other with practitioners of homoerotic acts. If, as G.W. Knight and others argue, the sins catalogued in 1 Tim. 1.9-10 are 'a deliberate echo of the second part of the Decalogue then Paul views those who undermine the seventh commandment as fornicators (*pornois*) and *arsenokoites*. Thus, both homosexual *and* heterosexual dimensions of sexual immorality are explicitly dealt with and both are seen as undermining the sanctity of marriage. (pp. 48-49) [121]

The report goes on to explain the meaning of *arsenokoites*. It argues that the word:

---

[121] The quotation is from George W Knight, *The Pastoral Epistles: A Commentary on the Greek Text*, Grand Rapids: Eerdmans 1992, p. 85.

...is...a compound of two terms which carried familiar sexual connotations: *arsēn* was a specific word for male, but was often used in connection with male sexuality, while *koitēs* usually meant 'bed,' but functioned as a widespread euphemism for sexual intercourse (cf.our term coitus). Paul's yoking of the two therefore points strongly to a homoerotic denotation. In fact, *arsenokoites* seems most probably to have been coined by Paul in response to the vocabulary of the Septuagint version of Lev. 18.22 and 20.13 where its constituent terms appear as a translation of the Hebrew *mishkav zakur* ('lying with a male'). (p. 49)

On the teaching of the two texts the report writes:

The context of Paul's remarks in both 1 Timothy and 1 Corinthians 6 is eligibility for God's kingdom in general, and for church membership in particular. Homoerotic sexual practice here belongs to a catalogue of sins, apparently no better, and no worse, than fornication, adultery, theft, greed, drunkenness, slander and robbery. In addition to disallowing the singling out of homosexual sin for special condemnation this also suggests that early church congregations contained what we would call homosexual people (cf 1 Corinthians 6:11) Although some of these may still have been sexually active, the clear teaching of Paul is that continuing attachment to this, as to the other sinful practices he mentions, is incompatible with authentic participation in the community of God's people. In this Paul is consistent with the witness of scripture as a whole. (p.49)

1 Timothy 1:10

> **Ben Witherington – arsenokoites refers to a man who has sex with other men.**

Ben Witherington states in his commentary on 1 Timothy[122] that *arsenokoites*:

> ..literally and graphically refers to a male copulator...a man who has sex with other men. In older commentaries this was sometimes translated 'sodomite' because it was assumed that this was the sin of Sodom in the story in Genesis 19. It is true that the term can refer to a pederast (an older man who has sex with a younger man or a youth), but the term is not a technical term for a pederast; rather it includes consenting adults who have sexual relationships in this manner, as well as any other form of male-with-male sexual intercourse. (p.198.)

> **George Montagu – arsenokoitai means those who practice homosexuality.**

Finally, in his commentary on First and Second Timothy[123] Professor George Montagu notes the range of English translations of *arsenokoitai*, but contends that the most exact translation would be 'those who practice homosexuality' since: 'anyone who engages in homosexual activity would be included, whatever their prevalent inclination may be.' There is, he argues, 'no reason to limit the meaning here to pederasty.' (p.40)

> **Robert Gagnon – the reference to 'the law in 1 Timothy 1:10 points to arsenokoitai being derived from Leviticus 18:22 and 20:13 and being an absolute ban on homosexual activity. The way that the vice list in 1 Timothy 1:10 corresponds to the order of the Decalogue indicates that arsenokoitai comes under the prohibition of adultery rather than theft and is therefore not a reference to those who have sex with those kidnapped for prostitution.**

---

[122] Ben Witherington III, *A Socio-Rhetorical Commentary on Titus, 1-2 Timothy and 1-3 John*, Leicester: Apollos, 2006.
[123] George T Monagu STM, *First and Second Timothy*, Grand Rapids: Baker, 2008.

Continuing his discussion of the meaning of *arsenokoitai* in his debate with Via, Gagnon observes that the occurrence of this term in 1 Timothy 1:10 'confirms that the term has in view Lev 18:22 and 20:13 since 'the law' referred to in 1:9-10 can only refer to the law of Moses.' Since the Levitical prohibitions are absolute 'the author of 1 Tim 1:10 (whether Paul or a later Paulinist) must have taken *arsenokoitai* absolutely.' (p.87)

Gagnon also criticises Scroggs' suggestion that the term should be taken with the following term *andrapodistai* (meaning those who kidnap young boys and girls for prostitution) and be understood to mean those who have sex with those kidnapped in this way. He argues that the last half of the vice list in 1 Timothy 1:9-10:

> ...corresponds to the order of the Decalogue:
>
> > Fifth commandment (honor one's parents) = 'killers of fathers and mothers'
> >
> > Sixth commandment (do not kill) = 'murderers'
> >
> > Seventh commandment (do not commit adultery) = *pornoi, arsenokoitai*
> >
> > Eighth commandment (do not steal) = *andropodistai* (man stealers)
> >
> > Ninth Commandment (do not bear false witness) = 'liars, perjurers.'

Parallel early Jewish and Christian vice lists and commentaries on the Decalogue establish that *pornoi* refers to 'sexually immoral persons' generally and *arsenokoitai* belongs with it under the rubric of the seventh commandment against adultery, while *andropodistai* finds its place under the distinct heading of the eighth commandment against stealing (*Pseudo-Phocylides* 3-8, Philo, *Special Laws* 3:1-82; 4:13-19, *Didache* 2:2-3; *Barnabas* 19:4). Accordingly, *arsenokoitai* should be understood in the broadest sense possible. Male-male intercourse is wrong not merely because it tends towards exploitation but because it contravenes the one valid union for sexual expression: a man-woman union. (pp.87-88)

> **Ian Paul – in I Timothy 1:10 the correlation with the Decalogue links arsenokoitai with sexual immorality rather than the abuse of power.**

Paul notes in a similar way in *Same-Sex Unions* that in 1 Timothy 9b-10 there are 'ten kinds of sinners' who are 'presented as four linked pair followed by six separate items.' In these verses, he states, there is:

> ...a broad correlation with the Decalogue, with more explicit correlation to five: the command to honour parents and the prohibitions on murder, adultery, stealing and bearing false witness. Some have linked *arsenokoitai* here with the following term, usually translated 'slave traders' (more literally 'man takers'), suggesting that *arsenokoitai* should then be interpreted as involving abuse of power. But the connection with the prohibition on stealing and the grammar argues against this; *arsenokoitai* is more naturally linked with preceding term *pornoi*, those involved in sexual immorality. (p.26)

> **Sam Allberry – in Timothy 1:9-10 arsenokoitai refers to homosexual practice in general as one of a number of forms of behaviour that do not conform to the new life Christians are meant to lead.**

Allberry writes in *Is God anti-gay?* that in 1 Timothy 1:9-10

> Paul again uses the term *arsenokoitai* (translated by the ESV as 'men who practice homosexuality' and by the NIV as 'perverts') as a catch all term for all forms of homosexual conduct. Also, in common with 1 Corinthians, same-sex sex is mentioned among other wide-ranging sins, non-sexual as well as sexual.

These forms of behaviour characterise those who are not 'just' and for whom the law was given, in order to bring conviction of sin and the need for mercy. All these practices contradict 'sound doctrine' and the gospel. They do not conform to the life Christians are now to lead. They go against the grain of the new identity they have in Christ. (pp.37-38)

Jude 7

Not many traditionalist writers have commented on Jude 7. All of those that have agree that Jude 7 refers to sexual activity by the men of Sodom and the neighbouring cities. However while Paul thinks the verse refers to the desire for sex with angels, other writers who comment on this verse think this is unlikely. They argue that the verse should be seen as referring to homosexual desire.

Ian Paul – Jude 7 could hint at sex with angels

Paul declares in *Same-Sex Unions* that the phrase 'went after strange ['or other'] flesh' is 'difficult to interpret; it would be an odd expression for homosexual activity, and perhaps hints at the strange idea of sex with angels.' (p.11)

Peter Davids – in line with other Jewish references to the Sodom story, Jude 7 probably refers to the men of Sodom seeking to engage in homosexual activity rather than seeking intercourse with angels.

Dr Peter Davids notes in his commentary on 2 Peter and Jude[124] that in Jude 7 the author links what he says about the judgement on Sodom and Gomorrah and the surrounding cities with the phrase 'in a similar way' thus indicating 'that the sin of the angels and the sin of these cities are similar.' (p.52)

---

[124] P H Davids, *The Letters of 2 Peter and Jude*, Grand Rapids/Nottingham: Apollos, 2006.

He goes on to explain that the charge against these cities is 'giving themselves up to sexual immorality and perversion.' The term used for sexual immorality (*ekporneuō*) is 'a general term indicating any type of sexual intercourse outside marriage' and is made more specific 'by the following phrase that, more literally translated, reads, 'departed after a different kind of flesh.' (p.52)

According to Davids:

> Virtually all commentators agree that this refers to the incident in Gen 19:4-11, and most believe that this means the attempt at homosexual relations, that is, as Neyrey puts it, a violation of the laws of purity, which prohibited the mixing of things, even between the sexes (Deut 22:5, 9-11). Thus seeking sexual intercourse with a person of the same sex would be seeking a different kind of flesh than that one was supposed to seek. (p.52)

Davids notes that Richard Bauckham takes a different view in his commentary on Jude, [125] arguing that when Jude 7 refers to seeking 'a different kind of flesh' this means that the men of Sodom sought intercourse with angels. On this interpretation the two incidents referred to in Jude 6 and 7 are the reverse of each other, with the fallen angels in verse 6 seeking intercourse with human women and the men of Sodom in verse 7 seeking intercourse with angels, but both incidents involve crossing a 'species' boundary. In support of this reading of Jude 7, Bauckham cites the Jewish apocryphal work *The Testament of Naphtali* (3:4-5) as making a comparison between the action of the fallen angels ('the Watchers') and the action of the men of Sodom:

> But you my children shall not be like that [the Gentiles who worship idols and follow wandering spirits): in the firmament, in the earth, and in the sea, in all products of his workmanship. Discern the Lord who made all things, so that you do not become like Sodom, which departed from the order of nature.

---

[125] Richard Bauckham, *Jude, 2 Peter*, Waco: Word, 1983.

Likewise the Watcher's departed from nature's order; the Lord pronounced a curse on them at the flood. On their account he ordered that the earth be without dweller or produce. (p.52)

Davids' view is that 'Bauckham is right in arguing that the comparison with the fallen angels has to do with crossing a 'species' boundary.' However, he says:

> ...even the evidence of *T. Naphtali* would be consistent with what Philo makes clear, that sexual intercourse with other males was viewed as crossing just such a boundary. In that none of the other references [to Sodom in Jewish writings] is at all concerned that the 'strangers' involved were angels, it is more likely that Jude too is thinking of homosexual activity as the 'different type of flesh' (different, not from themselves, but from the women they were supposed to desire). This would be in line with the general Jewish rejection of homosexual relations. (p.53)[126]

Dave Miller – the word heteros ('other') used in Jude 7 does not imply that the flesh desired by the men of Sodom was that of angels and the contextual indicators point the men of Sodom wanting to have sex with men.

The American writer Dr Dave Miller notes in his online article 'Homosexuality and 'Strange Flesh' '[127] that:

> Some defenders of homosexuality maintain that Jude condemned the men of Sodom—not for their homosexuality—but because they sought to have sexual relations with angels. They base this claim on the use of the expression "strange flesh": "as Sodom and Gomorrah, and the cities around them in a similar manner to these, having given themselves over to sexual

---

[126] The reference is to Philo *De Abrahamo,* 135-6.
[127] Dave Miller, ' Homosexuality and 'Strange Flesh'
http://www.apologeticspress.org/APContent.aspx?category=7&article=142

immorality and **gone after strange flesh**, are set forth as an example, suffering the vengeance of eternal fire" (Jude 7, emp. added). The reasoning is that the men of Sodom were guilty of desiring sexual relations with the angelic visitors (Genesis 19:1-5).

However, he argues that 'several problems are inherent in this interpretation.'

First, there is nothing in the Greek word *heteros* that implies that the flesh which the inhabitants of Sodom, Gomorrah and the surrounding cities went after was 'nonhuman or extra-terrestrial, i.e., angelic.' This is because, as lexicographers have pointed out, the word itself does not mean 'different,' but merely 'one other,' a second of two. Consequently:

> ....the notion of a different nature, form, or kind does not inhere in the word itself. Only contextual indicators can indicate, quite coincidentally, that the 'other' being referred to also is different in some additional quality.

Secondly, the contextual indicators exclude the idea that the sin of the men of Sodom was a desire for angelic flesh rather than homosexuality.

- Jude 7 refers not only to Sodom, but also to Gomorrah and the other two cities of the plain that were destroyed, Admah and Zeboin (Deuteronomy 29:23; Hosea 11:8). 'Do the advocates of homosexuality wish to hold the position that the populations of the four cities that were destroyed were all guilty of desiring sexual relations with angels?'

- Jude 7 indicates that the inhabitants of Sodom were already practising homosexuality and therefore under judgement prior to the arrival of the angels:

> That is precisely why the angels were sent to Sodom—to survey the moral landscape (Genesis 18:21) and urge Lot and his family to flee the city (Genesis 18:23; 19:12-13,15-16). The men

of Sodom were pronounced by God as 'exceedingly wicked and sinful against the Lord' back at the time Lot made the decision to move to Sodom (Genesis 13:13). Lenski called attention to the Aorist participles used in Jude 7 (i.e.,'having given themselves over' and 'going after') as further proof of this fact: 'An appeal to Gen. 19:4, etc., will not answer this question, for this occurred [i.e., the Sodomites descending on Lot's house— DM] when the cup of fornications was already full, when Jude's two aorist participles had already become facts, on the day before God's doom descended.'[128]

- Finally, there is nothing in Genesis 19 to indicate that the men of Sodom thought the visitors were angels:

They had the appearance of 'men' (Genesis 18:2,16,22; 19:1,5,8,10,12,16), whose feet could be washed (Genesis 19:2) and who could consume food (Genesis 19:3). The men of Sodom could not have been guilty of desiring to have sexual relations with angels, since they could not have known the men were angels.

> **Robert Gagnon - the history of the interpretation of the Sodom story, the teaching of Jude 8 and the interpretation of Jude 7 in 2 Peter 2:6 all point to a reading of Jude 7 in which the men of Sodom inadvertently sought sex with angels as a result of their desire to have sex with men.**

In his debate with Via, Gagnon declares that the meaning of Jude 7 is probably:

...that in their lust for sexual intercourse with other males, the men of Sodom inadvertently put themselves in the sacrilegious

---

128 The reference is to R.C.H Lenski, *The Interpretation of the Epistles of St. Peter, St. John, and St. Jude*, Minneaopolis: Augsburg, 1966, p.624.

position of pursuing sexual intercourse with angels (the 'other flesh'). (p.58)

He sees a reference to a desire to have sex with angels as unlikely for three reasons:

1. The history of interpretation of the Sodom episode assumes that the men of Sodom were unaware of the visitors' angelic status and intended to have sex with human males.

2. Jude 8 states that the false believers against whom Jude was writing 'likewise also defile (stain, pollute) (the/their) flesh, reject lordships, and slander the glorious ones' (i.e. angels). The false believers' lust for immoral sexual behavior had put them on a collision course with the angelic guardians of this world order, which subsequently led them to revile angels, not to lust after them (v.8). In a similar way, the immoral sexual desire of the Sodomites, in this case for male-male intercourse, led them to pursue sex with angels unknowingly.

3. This interpretation of Jude 7 fits best with Second Peter's own interpretation of Jude 7-8, referring as it does to the 'sexual licentiousness (*aslegeia*) of the conduct of the lawless' at Sodom (2:7) and to those following in their footsteps as 'going after (i.e. indulging) (the/their) flesh in (or: with its) defiling desire (2:7, 10).' The 'defiling desire' of the Sodomites can only be their desire to 'know' Lot's male visitors, whom they did not yet recognize as angels. (pp.58-59)

Gagnon's conclusion is that 'read with other Jewish texts of the period, the authors of Jude and 2 Peter undoubtedly understood a key offense of Sodom to be men desiring to have sex with males.' (p.59)

In his essay 'How seriously does Scripture treat the issue of Homosexual Practice?' Gagnon gives a further account of Jude 7.

He notes that:

> Some have argued that 'committed sexual immorality' in Jude 7 refers to sex with angels, not sex between men, because that is what the next phrase 'went after other flesh,' clearly refers to. (p.164)

This interpretation sees the verse as an example of parataxis: 'in parataxis one of the two clauses conjoined by 'and' is conceptually subordinated to the other; thus, 'they committed sexual immorality by going after other flesh.' ' However, he argues, in a Greek paratactic construction the first clause can just as easily be the subordinate one. In this case this would mean:

> ...by [or in the course of] committing sexual immorality they went after other flesh.' In other words, in the process of attempting the sexually immoral act of having intercourse with other men, the men of Sodom got more than they bargained for: committing an offence unknowingly against angels (note the echo in Hebrews 13:2: 'Do not neglect hospitality to strangers for, because of this, some have entertained angels without knowing it'). (p.164)

As Gagnon sees it, it appears that 2 Peter, the earliest 'commentator' on Jude 7, read Jude in this second way.

> For 2 Peter 2:6-7, 10 refers to the 'defiling desire/lust' of the men of Sodom. Since the men of Sodom did not know that the visitors were angels – so not only Genesis 19:4-11 but also all subsequent ancient interpreters – the reference cannot be to a lust for angels but rather be to a lust for men. (p.164)

> **Sam Allberry – the men of Sodom sought to have sex with men and Jude 7 reminds us that their destruction shows that God takes sexual sin very seriously.**

Allberry writes that Jude 7 'adds an important insight' into our understanding of the Sodom story. In this verse:

What happened at Sodom is clearly meant to be a cautionary tale. They are an example of facing God's judgment. Peter says much the same. Sodom and Gomorrah stand 'as an example of what is going to happen to the ungodly' (2 Peter 2:6). Jude makes it clear that their ungodliness involved sexual immorality. They were punished for sexual sin along with the other sins of which they were guilty. Their destruction serves as a warning: *God takes sexual sin very seriously.* (p.28)

In addition, Jude also highlights the perversity of the sexual desires of the men of Sodom:

> ...they pursued 'unnatural desire' (ESV) (literally, unnatural 'flesh'). Some have suggested that this relates to the fact that the visitors to the city were angelic, both Jude and Peter also reference angelic sin earlier in the letters. But these angels appeared as men, and the baying crowd outside Lot's house showed no evidence of knowing that they were angelic. Their desire was to have sex with the men staying with Lot. (p.28)

Chapter 8

Jesus' teaching and practice (II)

Traditionalist writers all make broadly the same points in relation to Jesus' teaching and practice:

(1) The fact that Jesus is not recorded as having commented specifically on the issue of homosexuality is not surprising given that this was not a topic of controversy in the Judaism of Jesus' day;

(2) All the evidence we have suggests that Jesus affirmed and indeed strengthened the sexual ethic laid down in the Old Testament law, that he saw God's creation of humanity as male and female as the foundation for sexual ethics and that his comments about *porneia* would have been understood as an implicit rejection on homosexual practice.

(3) Jesus' teaching about eunuchs in Matthew 19:10-12, rather than affirming gay relationships, declares that the alternative to marriage is celibacy and that there is no evidence that the story of Jesus' healing the centurion's servant involves Jesus' endorsement of a same-sex relationship.

(4) Jesus welcomed sinners on the understanding that this would involve repentance for sin. Jesus did not trade off compassion for sinners against the call to a holy lifestyle, but affirmed both.

> **The Evangelical Alliance – the argument from Jesus' silence is unconvincing. Jesus affirmed marriage between a man and a women and condemned porneia, a term which included homosexual practice.**

The Evangelical Alliance report notes that 'apologists for lesbian and gay sexual relationships point out that Jesus himself does not pronounce explicitly on homosexual practice.' However, it says, 'arguments from silence are notoriously suspect.' Jesus, it declares, 'hardly commented in direct terms on every ethical issue under the sun.

The gospels give us no explicit teaching from him on slavery or idolatry.'(p.43) Furthermore:

> ...not only did he affirm marriage between a man and a woman based on Genesis, his condemnation of porneia or sexual immorality in Matt 15:19 and Mark 7:21 would almost definitely have been meant and been understood, to include homoerotic sexual activity. As Michael Satlow has shown, such activity was typically condemned by the rabbis of the time whenever they considered it. (pp.43-44) [129]

Sam Allberry – Jesus' comments on porneia in Mark 7 included a reference to homosexual behaviour and he made it clear that the only legitimate alternative to marriage was celibacy.

Allberry likewise acknowledges in *Is God anti-gay?* that 'it is sometimes said that since Jesus never mentioned homosexuality directly he can't have been against it.' His response is that 'although Jesus does not directly mention homosexuality, in his teaching on sexual sin he does address it.' (pp.40-41) In support of this claim he quotes Mark 7:20-23 and comments that in these verses:

> Jesus says that there are things that make one spiritually unclean before God. In this list Jesus includes (among other things) examples of sexual sin: adultery, lewdness and sexual immorality. 'Sexual immorality translates a Greek word *porneia* (from which we get the word 'pornography'), something of a catch all term for any sexual activity outside marriage. This extends beyond intercourse to include any activity of a sexual nature. None of Jesus' hearers would have doubted that his reference to *porneia* included homosexual behaviour. (p. 41)

---

[129] The reference is to Michael Satlow, *Tasting the Dish, Rabbinic Rhetorics of Sexuality*, Atlanta: Scholars Press 1995.

Allberry further notes that that 'as well as condemning sexual sin outside marriage, Jesus indicated that the only godly alternative to marriage was celibacy.' He quotes Jesus' saying about eunuchs in Matthew 19:11-12 and explains:

> Eunuchs were the celibates of their day, and Jesus indicates that their celibacy might be the result of birth, or human intervention, or a voluntary decision to forego marriage. Whatever its cause, that Jesus goes there right after his disciples have baulked at the commitment and seriousness of marriage shows that Jesus regarded it as the only alternative. One marries, or remains single. There is no third possibility, whether of a homosexual partnership or a heterosexual unmarried partnership. As far as Jesus is concerned, the godly alternatives before us are (heterosexual) marriage or celibacy. (p.41)

Willard Swartley – there are eight elements of Jesus' teaching and practice which lead us to the conclusion that we are called to welcome those of homosexual orientation, while not approving of same-sexual activity or same-sex covenant unions.

Swartley begins his chapter on 'Jesus and the Gospels' in *Homosexuality: Biblical Teaching and Moral Discernment* by quoting the 'anecdotal quip' 'Did you see the book *Jesus and Homosexuality*?' 'No, what does it say?' 'Well, when you open it you only find blank pages!' However, he then proceeds to argue that this view of Jesus' teaching is mistaken. He puts forward eight elements of Jesus' teaching and practice recorded in the Gospels that he thinks 'have import for ethical discernment on homosexuality.' (p.39)

First there is 'Jesus' strong and unequivocal teaching against lust' (Matthew 5:26-28) together with his judgment against *porneia* (Matthew 5:32, 15:19, 19:9, Mark 7:21) which 'denotes all sexual genital relations outside heterosexual marriage.'

Secondly, there is Jesus' response to the question about divorce in Matthew 19 and Mark 10 in which Jesus appeals to God's original action in making human beings male and female and joining them together in marriage. 'It seems to me that this answer, so typical of Jesus who does not engage in casuistry, would also have been his answer had the question of same-sex covenant unions (unthinkable in Jewish culture) been posed to Jesus.'

Thirdly, there is Jesus' saying about 'eunuchs who have made themselves eunuchs for the sake of the kingdom of heaven' (Matthew 19:10-12). This refers to the possibility of celibacy as an act 'of freely choosing to be a eunuch in order to avoid violation of the divine will in sexual relationships.'

Fourthly, there is Jesus' teaching on adultery and his relations with those guilty of adultery and prostitution (Matthew 5:31-32; Luke 7, John 4, 8:1-12). 'When applying this teaching to the homosexuality issue, we should be quick to say that the Christian way is not to shun or ostracize those who are homosexual, but to provide a 'third way' (neither accepting their sin nor condemning them) that frees them from their social marginalization, offering transformed self-understanding through forgiveness of sins, as Jesus clearly did on both occasions' [Luke 7, John 4].

Fifthly, there is Jesus' association with outcasts, 'this clear and strong emphasis in the Gospel portrait of Jesus means that true followers of Jesus, regardless what position they take on homosexuality, must be welcoming and extending of hospitality to people of homosexual orientation and practice.'

Sixthly, there is Jesus' ethic of both compassion and holiness. 'In my judgment, it is a cheap deal to sacrifice holiness for compassion. Jesus' uniqueness lay precisely in his embodiment of both simultaneously.'

Seventhly, there is the constant emphasis in the Gospels, as well as the rest of the New Testament 'on judgment, especially on those who fail to heed the word of Jesus, by not responding in repentance and seeking forgiveness of sin.'

Eighthly, there is Jesus' call in Matthew 18:15-35 for the Church to exercise both discipline and mercy. This points us to the fact that 'on the one hand Jesus' followers are called to the ethic of perfection (or completeness in love), and on the other, to an unlimited bestowal of mercy and forgiveness towards those who sin against us' (Matthew 18:21-22). According to Swartley:

> These are important words for us as we seek to find our way on the issue of homosexuality. It seems to me that we as church have failed in carrying out direct address to those who offend, with the purpose of seeking restoration through love. How to do this in our present situation is not easy, since the debate often turns on whether any offense exists. But the motivation of mercy that forgives is the attitude that we should all have as we seek to find the way and live out our views on this subject. (pp.40-46)

Swartley finishes with 'three points of summary' building on these eight elements of Jesus' teaching and practice:

1. From a hermeneutical standpoint, it cannot be held that Jesus said nothing to guide us in the homosexuality debate. His citation of Genesis 1:27 and 2:24 to answer the trap-question of divorce is as pertinent for homosexuality as is the command to love the enemy for the issue of war, or the text in Mark 10:35-45 for slavery.
2. Jesus' teaching and example calls us to be welcoming and accepting of all people, including those of homosexual orientation, and even those practising, whether in covenant unions, or more promiscuously. It was precisely a promiscuous sinner in Luke 7 whom Jesus received and declared forgiven before God.

3. Our response in daily life is to accept all people, but not to approve of conduct that violates God's will as declared in Jesus and in Scripture more broadly. We need not trade holiness for compassion, nor compassion for holiness. It would be wrong to pit the first four emphases from Jesus against the last four. All eight are essential if we are to be Jesus-type people. (pp.46-47)

> **Ian Paul – Jesus' teaching about divorce and his references to sexual immorality indicate that he shared the characteristic Jewish rejection of same-sex relations. Jesus' association with sinners was about leading them to repentance and transformation. The arguments put forward in favour of Jesus's endorsing same-sex activity are unconvincing.**

Like Swartley, Paul also argues in *Same-Sex Unions* against the suggestion that Jesus' teaching has nothing to contribute to the discussion of same-sex unions. He contends that there are two sets of texts in the gospels that are relevant to this issue.

The first set consists of the sayings of Jesus about divorce in Mark 10:6 and Matthew 19:4. In these sayings:

> Jesus returns to the creation accounts. He emphasizes the gender binary of humanity by citing Gen. 1:27 first, before citing the explicit teaching on marriage in Genesis 2:24. Marriage is not to be dissolved trivially, since it represents the restoration of the original unity of humanity. (p.19)

The second consists of Jesus reference to sexual immorality in Matthew 15:19/Mark 7:21 'For out of the heart come evil thoughts, murder, adultery, sexual immorality, theft, false testimony, slander.' In this saying, writes Paul, it is:

> ...worth noting that 'sexual immorality' (*porneiai*) is in the plural, and is included as a separate item from 'adultery' (*moicheiai*). This term would include premarital sex before marriage, and sex with a prostitute, but would also refer to

illicit sexual union prohibited in Leviticus 18. Given Jesus' 'conservative' approach to sexual ethics generally (such as supporting the more restrictive of the approaches to divorce), it is difficult to imagine that he did not also share the characteristic Jewish rejection of same-sex relations. (p.19)

Paul acknowledges that Jesus association with 'tax-collectors and sinners' and his willingness to touch lepers and others who would have been considered unclean was clearly 'a significant aspect of Jesus' ministry.' However, he also notes:

- Had Jesus relaxed biblical teaching on sexual relations in any respect, it would have been the first thing used against him by his opponents. The silence here is very significant.
- Jesus explicitly reinforces his association with 'sinners' in his teaching about his mission and the kingdom of God: 'Truly I tell you, the tax-collectors and the prostitutes are going into the kingdom of heaven ahead of you.' (Matthew 21:31)
- Jesus' consistent teaching in relation to the kingdom is that it demands a response of 'repentance' (Mark 1.15). God's initiative in coming close to us must lead to a response of change, in our thinking, in our behaviour and in the direction of our life. (p.19)

The conclusion he draws from these points is that:

Jesus' association with 'sinners' was not simply a question of hanging around with undesirables, or even welcoming them, but being prepared take the risk of being with them in order to preach the good news of the transforming power of God's presence in his kingdom. If anything marked him out from the Pharisees, it was his belief that even these 'sinners' could change and be transformed. This is typified in the encounter with the woman caught in adultery in John 8. In this encounter, Jesus simultaneously confronts the hypocrisy of the accusers, pronounces forgiveness to the woman, and affirms the

285

possibility of change and transformation: 'Neither do I condemn you; go and sin no more' (John 8:11). (p.20)

Paul also addresses three other arguments the have been put forward to support the idea 'that Jesus' teaching should lead us to accept same-sex activity.'

First, he suggests that Via's appeal to Jesus' teaching in John 10:10 about his bringing 'life and life in all its fullness' in support of same-sex relationships fails to acknowledge Jesus' own singleness and the long Christian tradition of celibacy and also requires us to separate John 10:10 from Jesus' teaching in John 14:15 that fullness of life is linked to obedience to Jesus' commands. (p.21)

Secondly, he contends that the argument that Jesus set aside Old Testament laws relating to the Sabbath (Mark 2:27) and diet (Mark 7:14-19) 'on the basis of common sense and human need' fails to take into account that what Jesus is actually doing is 'restoring both Sabbath and food to their original creation purposes.' (p.21)

Thirdly, he declares that the suggestion the stories of the centurion's servant in Matthew 8:5-13 or the two men in a bed (Luke 17:34) are 'hidden affirmations' of same-sex relations involves 'imposing a sexualized reading for which there is no evidence in the text and no possibility historically.' (p. 21)

Paul also argues that the appeal to Acts 15 as a paradigm for the Church's acceptance of those with same-sex attraction ignores 'the nature and rationale of the fourfold prohibition in Acts 15.29, which correspond to the laws that apply to 'resident aliens' in Lev 17-18, including the prohibition on same-sex activity.' (p.21)

Michael Brown - Jesus addressed the issue of homosexual practice in the Sermon on the Mount, his teaching about what defiles people and his teaching about divorce. Neither his saying about eunuchs nor his healing of the centurion's servant can be rightly understood as endorsing same-sex practice.

Brown argues in *Can you be Gay and Christian?* that the argument from Jesus' supposed silence about homosexual practice overlooks that key fact that Jesus:

> ....was a first-century Jewish rabbi teaching His fellow Jews, and in first-century Jewish culture homosexual practice was explicitly prohibited and forbidden. In fact, ancient Jewish texts from the last centuries BC and the first centuries AD have some *very negative* things to say about homosexual practice and *not one single positive* thing to say. So, the fact that Jesus did not spend a lot of time teaching against homosexual practice shouldn't surprise us at all, nor does it prove anything....He didn't have to condemn it any more than He had to condemn sins like bestiality, since every God-fearing Jew in the nation knew these things were wrong according to God's Torah (teaching/law). (p.129)

However, according to Brown, this does not mean that Jesus did not address the issue of homosexual practice. In fact, he addressed it in three ways.

First, in the Sermon on the Mount, Jesus took:

> ...the moral laws of the Torah, which included statutes concerning marriage and sexual immorality, and took them to a deeper level – adultery including lust in the heart; murder including hatred in the heart – rather than doing away with them. And since homosexual practice was strictly prohibited in the Torah, not just for the people of Israel but for all nations...when Jesus said He was not abolishing the Law and the

287

Prophets but rather fulfilling them, He clearly intended that this prohibition would continue to stand as well. In fact, we could even argue that the prohibition is deepened, just as the prohibitions against adultery and murder were deepened. (p.131)

Secondly, in his discussion about what defiles people Jesus refers in Matthew 15:19 and Mark 7:21 to *porneia* ('sexual immoralities') as among the things that cause someone to be unclean before God. This term 'refers comprehensively to all sexual acts outside of marriage, which, as we know, consisted only of a union of a man and a woman in Jewish biblical law in Jesus' day.' This means, says Brown, Jesus taught:

> ...that all sexual acts outside marriage make us unclean. Yes, heterosexual fornication, homosexual acts, bestiality, incestuous acts – all of these are included by Jesus under the category of 'sexual immoralities' and all of them defile us and make us unclean. (p.132)

Thirdly, in his saying on divorce in Matthew 19:4-6 Jesus reiterated that God created human beings as male and female and established marriage as a union between one man and one woman. In the light of this:

> ....it is unconscionable to imagine that Jesus would sanction male-male or female-female unions, since, among other things, they fundamentally violate God's design and intent 'in the beginning.' Neither would Jesus agree with efforts devoted to 'eradicating gender or multiplying it exponentially,' nor would He sanction teaching concepts such as 'genderqueer' to children. And he would not agree that the 'gender binary' (meaning either male or female) is constricting. For Jesus, male-female distinctions expressed aspects of the image of God and were the foundation of God's order and the basis for marriage. (p.133)

Brown goes on to consider Jesus' teaching about eunuchs in Matthew 19:10-12 and contends that it is wrong for gay apologists to appeal to it as an endorsement of homosexual relationships by Jesus.

He notes that the reason that the issue of eunuchs came up was because:

> Jesus was talking to His disciples about never marrying - and therefore not having sex for life – and He was saying that not everyone can handle this. Some who are born without sexual capacity have no trouble with this; others, who have been castrated, have no trouble with this; still others, with God's gift of celibacy, can renounce marriage (and sex) for life by choice. (p.136)

Given that this was what Jesus was talking about, it follows that:

> To read anything into this teaching that somehow affirms homosexual practice or to argue that 'Christ's listeners had no doubt about what he was talking about, and understood by his comments that gay people are not meant to marry, but that they should be accepted for who they are' is to be guilty of the most gratuitous form of eisegesis imaginable. (p.136)

As Brown sees it, the argument that this text from Matthew says that people are born gay:

> ...is flatly contradicted by the context, which, to repeat, speaks of men who from birth had no sexual capacity – just as if they were castrated in later life – because of which they never married or had sexual relationships. What in the world does this have to do with gay men? Do they have no sexual capacity? Do they all agree that they cannot and should not marry?

> If fact, even if someone could prove that Jesus was including gay men in His teaching – which, to repeat once more – is incredibly far-fetched – He was affirming (if not taking for granted) that all

of them would practice lifelong celibacy, meaning no marriage and no sex. (p.138)

What this text actually points to therefore is the truth that there are two and, only two, paths, celibacy or heterosexual marriage. This means:

> ....as hard as this word may seem if you are a follower of Jesus who is same-sex attracted, you are called to put Him first and abstain from marriage and sexual activity unless you can find an opposite sex partner who will join you in marriage, even if your attractions don't change, or unless God changes your desires to heterosexual, which has happened for many.
>
> But here's the bottom line: it is no harder for a homosexually oriented person to follow Jesus than it is for a heterosexually oriented person to follow Him, since he requires everything from everyone who chooses to follow him as Lord. He said repeatedly, 'If anyone would come after me, let him deny himself and take up his cross daily and follow me' (Luke 9:23). (p.143)

Brown also considers the story of the healing of the centurion's servant in Matthew 8:5-13 and Luke 7:1-10. He argues that the idea that the centurion was in a sexual relationship with his servant which Jesus knew of and approved has no basis in either text.

First, the Greek word *pais* (servant) carries no sexual overtones:

> ...not one time in the entire Bible does *pais* refer to a servant with any sexual connotation, and it is used approximately ninety times in Septuagint and New Testament writings. That's why it never dawned on a single commentator or lexicographer in all of church history – meaning for almost two thousand years – that Jesus was enabling a Roman soldier to continue having sex with his younger male slave. (p.156)

Secondly, the Greek word *entimos* (Luke 7:2) means 'honoured or respected' (cf Luke 14:8, Philippians 2:29) rather than 'precious or valuable.' [130] 'He was an excellent servant, highly respected by his master rather than a hot sex toy.' (p.154)

Thirdly, the commendation of the Centurion by the local Jewish leaders as a good and God-fearing man is inconceivable if it had been known that he was regularly having homosexual sex with his slave. (p.154-55)

Fourthly, what is being proposed is that Jesus endorsed an exploitative sexual relationship involving homosexual rape since this is the form that master-slave homoeroticism generally took in the Roman world. (p.155)

> **Robert Gagnon - there are twelve reasons why we can be confident that Jesus was opposed to homosexual practice and the idea that the healing of the centurion's servant involved an affirmation of homosexual practice is unsustainable.**

Like Brown, in his essay 'How seriously does Scripture Gagnon gives an historical explanation as to why we have no explicit sayings of Jesus referring to homosexual practice:

> His ministry was to fellow Palestinian Jews, not to Gentiles in the Greco-Roman Mediterranean basin. Simply put, no Jew in first-century Palestine was advocating for homosexual practice, incest and bestiality, much less engaging in them. Running around first-century Palestine saying 'Stop lying with a male, or with your mother, or with an animal' would not have been the best use of Jesus' time since he would have been 'preaching to the choir.' The expansion of the discussion of sexual issues in Paul is a natural by-product of Jewish ministry primarily to a Gentile world. [131]

This having been said, Gagnon also holds that 'there are at least a dozen reasons why we can confidently conclude that Jesus was strongly

---

[130] The quotation is from I H Marshall, *The Gospel of Luke: A commentary on the Greek Text*, Grand Rapids: Eerdmans, 1978, p.279.
[131] Torrance and Stein (eds), op..cit. p.172.

opposed to homosexual practice of any sort.' These reasons are as follows:

(1) Jesus' adoption of a back to creation model for sex in which he predicated marital monogamy and indissolubility on the twoness of the sexes brought together in sexual union in Genesis 1-2 (Mark 10:2-12 par Matt 19:3-9).

(2) Jesus' retention of the Law of Moses even on relatively minor matters such as tithing (cf Matt 23:23 par Luke 11:42) to say nothing of a foundational law in sexual ethics; and his view of the Old Testament as Holy Scripture – Scripture that...was strongly and absolutely opposed to man-male intercourse.

(3) Jesus' further intensification of the Law's sex-ethic in matters involving adultery of the heart and divorce (Matt 5:27-32), suggesting a closing of loopholes in the Law's sex-ethic rather than a loosening and in his saying about cutting off body parts, warning that people could be thrown into hell precisely for not repenting of violations of God's sexual standards (5:29-30).

(4) The fact that the man who baptized Jesus, John the Baptist, was beheaded for defending Levitical sex laws in the case of the adult incestuous union between Herod Antipas and the ex-wife of his half-brother Philip, a woman who was also the a daughter of another half-brother (Mark 6:16-18).

(5) Early Judaism's univocal opposition to all homosexual practice.

(6) The early church's united opposition to all homosexual practice. This, combined with nos.2-5 above, completes the historical circle, underscoring the absurdity of positing a pro-homosex Jesus without analogue in his historical context: cut off from his scripture, cut off from the rest of early Judaism, cut off from the man who baptized him, and cut off from the church that emerged from his teachings.

(7) Jesus' saying about the defiling effect of desires for various forms of sexual immoralities (Mark 7:21-23), which distinguished matters of relative moral indifference such as food laws from matters of moral significance such as the sexual

commands in the Bible and connected Jesus to the general view of what constitutes the worst form of *porneia* in early Judaism (same sex intercourse, incest, bestiality, adultery).

(8) Jesus on the Decalogue prohibition of adultery (Mark 10:17-22) which presupposed a male-female prerequisite for valid sexual bonds both in its Decalogue context and in its subsequent interpretation in early Judaism as a rubric for the major sex laws of the Old Testament.

(9) Jesus' saying about Sodom which, understood in the light of Second Temple interpretations of Sodom (Matthew 10:14-15 par. Luke 10:10-12), included an indictment of Sodom for attempting to dishonour the integrity of the visitor's masculinity by treating them as if they were the sexual counterparts to males.

(10) Jesus' saying about not giving what is 'holy' to the 'dogs' (Matthew 7:6), an apparent allusion to both Deuteronomic law (Deuteronomy 23:17-18) and texts in 1-2 Kings that indict the *qedeshim*, self-designated 'holy ones' identified as 'dogs' for their attempt to erase their masculinity by serving as the passive-receptive partners in man-male intercourse.

(11) Jesus' comparison of 'eunuchs for the kingdom of heaven' with 'born eunuchs' (persons who are asexual and/or homosexual), a comparison that presumes that 'born eunuchs' are not permitted sexual relationships outside a man-woman bond (Matthew 19:10-12).

(12) The fact that Jesus developed a sex ethic that had distinctive features not shared by the love commandment (love for everyone does not translate into having sex with everyone), reached out to tax-collectors and sexual sinners while simultaneously intensifying God's ethical demand in these areas, insisted that the adulterous woman stop sinning lest something worse happen to her (i.e. loss of eternal life; cf John 8:3-11; 5:14), appropriated the context of the 'love your neighbour' command in Lev 19:17-18 by insisting on reproof as

part of a full-orbed view of love (Luke 17:3-4), and defined discipleship as taking up one's cross, denying oneself, and losing one's life (Mark 8:34-37; Matthew 10:38-39, Luke 14:27; 17:33, John 12:25). (pp.172-174)

Gagnon also looks at the suggestion that Jesus' healing of a centurion's 'boy' involved affirmation of a same-sex relationship. He argues that even if the centurion was having sex with his slave this does not mean that Jesus' approved of this: 'since it would make Jesus a supporter of one of the most exploitative forms of homosexual practice in the ancient world: a coercive relationship between a master and his young male slave.'[132] However, the assumption that there was a sexual relationship involved is unsustainable since:

> ...none of the earliest extant interpreters of the text understood it in this manner (John, Q, Matthew and Luke) and the earliest recoverable version of the story that stands behind John 4:46-53 and Matthew 8:5-13 (par. Luke 7:1-10) suggests a story about a Jewish official requesting a healing for his son. (p.174)

> **John Nolland – sexual ethics was a matter of profound concern to Jesus, his teaching about porneia involved a reference to homosexual practice and we have to understand his not making any explicit comments about homosexuality in the light of the continuity between his teaching and existing Jewish sexual ethics.**

Dr John Nolland notes in his article 'Sexual Ethics and the Jesus of the Gospels' [133]that the idea that sexual ethics was not a major element within Jesus' teaching is difficult to sustain in the light of a study of the frequency with which he referred to the topic.

---

[132] Ibid, p.174.
[133] John Nolland, 'Sexual Ethics and the Jesus of the Gospels,' *Anvil*, Vol.26, No.1, 2009.

Nolland compares Jesus' use of words relating to mutual love and concern for the poor with his use of words relating to adultery and sexual immorality in general. His conclusion is that:

> ...while Jesus commends the virtue of mutual love with fourteen uses of the *agap* word group and commends or models concern for the poor with about the same number of uses of *ptochos* and a few times in other ways, he speaks against adultery and other sexual immorality, explicitly or implicitly, with no less than twenty three uses of the key terms and somewhat indirectly another three times. (p.23)

He further notes that with the exception of John 7:53-8:11 it is Jesus rather than other people who initiates discussion about sexual matters, and that the importance that he attached to sexual morality is shown by his inclusion of the issue in the Matthean antitheses (Matthew 5:21-48), in his list of things that make people unclean before God (Matthew 5:19; Mark 7:21-22) and in his teaching about the Commandments in the story of the rich young ruler (Matthew 19:17-19, Mark 10:19, Luke 18:20). (pp.23-24)

Nolland's overall conclusion is that:

> In the light of these observations it seems hard to deny to the Gospel Jesus a profound concern for sexual ethics. Such a concern did not define his ministry, but to move sexual ethics to the sidelines is hardly in line with the values of the Jesus of the Gospels. (p.24)

On the specific issue of homosexuality Nolland argues that Jesus' references to *porneia* contain an indirect reference to homosexuality since on the basis of Leviticus 18 and 20 'in the Jewish context of Jesus' day, and in the Christian context that grew out of it, homosexual coitus would have been automatically embraced within the scope of *porneia*.' (p.25) He further contends that St. Paul's use of *porneia* provides additional support for this view, since Paul uses *porneia* to refer in general terms to the sexual offences forbidden under the Old Testament law while also using a range of other terms for sexual immorality as well in order to communicate Christian sexual morality in non-Jewish contexts. This use of additional terminology by St. Paul is because:

> By speaking of *porneia* in a Jewish context the Jesus of the Gospels would have been understood to have included incest, homosexual sex and sex with animals. But in the wider Greco-Roman world the same set of concerns begins to require explicit comment on this range as in this context – outside circles that had a significant Jewish influence – the spontaneous understanding of the range of *porneia* is likely to be narrower. (p.28)

On the question of the significance of the fact that Jesus does not say anything explicitly about homosexuality Nolland comments that:

> For any proper understanding of Jesus it is disastrous to ignore his context and the shared assumptions with his context that made Jesus intelligible and allowed him to communicate effectively. Jesus challenged those received patters he wanted to change. In sexual ethics, for example, he repudiated the double standard that allowed adultery to be viewed only as an offence against a husband and not an offence against a wife. But he also provided sufficient indicators of continuity with the sexual ethics of his Jewish tradition for it to be quite proper for us to fill in the details in relation to matters on which he remained silent on the basis of agreement and affirmation. (p.29)

> **Kevin Scott – Jesus applied the Old Testament law more strictly on matters such as murder, adultery and divorce. His teaching about porneia and aselgeia included a rejection of homosexual conduct and the accounts of his ministry in the gospels preclude the idea of people defining themselves in terms of their sexuality.**

In his book *At Variance*[134] Dr Kevin Scott comments on Mark 7:14-23 that while Jesus relaxed the food regulations of the Old Testament law he 'applies Old Testament law more strictly on matters such as murder, adultery and divorce.' (p.28) The reason for this heightening of moral standards, he says, has to do with Jesus's ministry of returning Israel from Exile:

> If the law prevailed when Israel was wandering far away, how much more will it apply now she has returned to God? If that great list of wrongs: evil thoughts, sexual immorality, theft, murder, adultery, coveting, wickedness, deceit, licentiousness, envy, slander, pride, foolishness, were forbidden to Israel when she was in Exile, how much more inappropriate are they to the new life which Jesus brings? Jesus came to save his people from their sins. It is not surprising that sins are ruled out in the Kingdom he establishes. (p.28)

Turning to the vocabulary used by Jesus in Mark 7, Scott writes that the word translated 'sexual immorality', *porneia* 'means any and all of the forbidden sexual activities of the Old Testament. It includes incest, rape, bestiality and homosexual conduct.' The word translated, 'licentiousness,' *aselgeia*, 'means open and shameless immorality.' The two words together suggest:

> ...that both secret or discreet acts of immorality and a brazenly open immoral lifestyle are equally forbidden. It is true that homosexual conduct is not mentioned specifically on this list

---

[134] Kevin Scott, *At Variance – The Church's Argument against Homosexual Conduct*, Edinburgh: Dunedin Academic Press, 2004.

but the only sound way to translate the words is to afford them the meaning which would come most naturally to the speaker and hearer in first-century Judaism. It is inconceivable that either speaker or hearer would ascribe anything but Old Testament sexual vices to these terms. Thus, homosexual conduct would most certainly be included in their meaning. The fact that porneia is not broken down into its constituent parts reminds us that no special pleading is possible for one manifestation of porneia over the rest. We cannot say that the homosexual conduct is admissible while incest is to be deplored. Conversely, if we want to exclude incest then homosexual conduct must go with it. (p.29)

Scott then goes on to observe that:

It is sometimes thought that the Old Testament is severe and the New Testament more relaxed on the question of moral standards. On careful examination of the texts the reverse is shown to be the case, but the thought persists because while the *demand* of the law is heightened in the New Testament the *punishments* are remitted. It is the sacrifice of Christ which does away with the latter, it is the reign of Christ which brings about the former. The Church of God is not governed by a regime of punishment (although it does stand under the judgment of God) but it is under the rule and command of Jesus the Son of God. There is no sign whatever that Jesus relaxed, by the slightest degree, the obligations of Old Testament law with respect to sexual conduct. (p.29)

Scott's final conclusion is that the Gospel accounts of the ministry of Jesus, and in particular the story of the new identity given to the paralyzed man at the pool of Bethesda in John 5:2-17, argue against:

...the tendency for practitioners of homosexuality to try to define themselves by their sexuality or sexual inclinations. As far as the Judaeo-Christian tradition is concerned, this is a form of idolatry. The only secure grounding for our identity as human beings lies I the fact that we have been created by God in his image and redeemed from our sins by his Son. Christians are taught to take their bearings from this point only. So strongly is this argued in the New Testament that even the age old distinction between Jew and Gentile collapses under its weight. We cannot define ourselves as gentile Christians, or Jewish Christians, far less as 'gay' Christians. We can only describe ourselves as Christians, followers of Jesus Christ. (pp.34-35)

Chapter 9

Examples of same sex relationships in Scripture? (II)

Traditionalist writers have argued that there is nothing in 1 and 2 Samuel or Ruth to support the idea that there was a homosexual relationship between David and Jonathan or Ruth and Naomi. Likewise, there is nothing in John's gospel to suggest that there was a homosexual relationship between Jesus and the Beloved Disciple or that Lazarus and his sisters were gay.

David and Jonathan

> **Gordon Kennedy, Jane McArthur, Andrew McGowan – nothing in the biblical text requires the idea of a homosexual relationship between David and Jonathan.**

Kennedy, McArthur and McGowan note in their contribution to the Church of Scotland report that the accounts of David and Jonathan in 1 Samuel 18-23 have been read by some as describing a homosexual relationship between them. However, they argue 'there is no necessary element of the text requiring this reading.' (p.1/106) They observe that there is 'always a danger of reading into a text what you want to take from it and without an explicit statement of homosexual activity between David and Jonathan it seems better to read these texts a celebrating the glory of non-sexual friendship between two men.' (p.1/106) They quote with approval the comment by Gagnon:

> Why were the narrators unconcerned about a hint of homosexual scandal? The answer is obvious, nothing in the stories raised any suspicion that David and Jonathan were homosexually involved with one another. Only in our day, removed as we are from ancient Near Eastern conventions, are these kind of connections made by people desperate to find the

slightest shred of support for homosexual practice in the Bible. (p.1/106)[135]

> Ian Paul – reading the account of David and Jonathan in 1 Samuel in terms of a homosexual relationship ignores the way that the text presents the two men as 'ideal men' in contrast to Saul.

In *Same-Sex Unions* Paul draws attention to the recent Grove booklet by Jonathan Rowe on the account of David and Jonathan in 1 Samuel. In this booklet, he says, Rowe notes that:

> ...a key concern of the story is the way that the characters measure up against the pattern of the 'ideal man,' who fathers children, shows concern as a husband, takes an interest in matters of worship and judgment in law, excels in intelligent speech and (most important of all) is a valiant warrior. (p.12)

In the account in 1 Samuel David and Jonathan match up well to this ideal, but Saul does not, particularly in the context of the challenge presented by Goliath.

Paul quotes Rowe as saying that the significance of this concern of the narrative in 1 Samuel is that in this narrative:

> Jonathan and David are portrayed as 'real men' in order that their narrative voices are credible to original readers. Homosexual acts were considered shameful – as evidenced by Leviticus – and it is virtually inconceivable that the portrayal of Jonathan and David as masculine heroes would have convinced should their liaison have been portrayed as erotic. They were, indeed, 'just good friends.' (p.12)[136]

---

[135] The quotation is from Gagnon, *The Bible and Homosexual Practice*.p.154.
[136] The quotation is from Jonathan Rowe, *David and Jonathan*, Cambridge: Grove Books, 2014, p.16

It follows, writes Paul, that in order to see a homoerotic element in the biblical account of David and Jonathan 'we would have to disregard both the historical and wider narrative context, and operate a 'hermeneutic of suspicion,' reading our own assumptions into the text.' (p.12)

> **Richard Davidson – a study of the key texts shows that the account of David and Jonathan is about the virtue of loving friendship rather than homosexuality.**

Davidson begins his critique in *Flame of Yahweh* of the idea that David and Jonathan were in a homosexual relationship by noting that:

> The many wives of David and his adulterous affair with Bathsheba indicate that David had heterosexual urges. Scripture also records that Jonathan was married and had children (1 Samuel 20:42; 2 Samuel 9). (p.166)

He therefore asks whether they could have been bisexual and concludes that the 'intertextual and contextual evidence suggests that they were not.'

First, the statement in 1 Samuel 18:1 'the soul of Jonathan was bound to the soul of David, and Jonathan loved him as his own soul' uses precisely the same Hebrew expression used in Genesis 44:30 to describe Jacob's paternal affection for Benjamin:

> In the case of Jacob and his son Benjamin, the phrase undoubtedly refers to a close, affectionate, but not homosexual attachment, and by using precisely the same phraseology regarding David and Jonathan, the narrator of the story also undoubtedly intended to describe a legitimate non-homosexual bond of affection between the two men. (p.166)

Secondly, the statements in 1 Samuel 18:1 and 3 and 20:17 that Jonathan loved David 'as his own soul/life' are illuminated by the warning in Deuteronomy 13:6 and 8 against being led into idolatry by 'your friend who is as your own soul.' This passage in Deuteronomy uses the same terminology used in 1 Samuel and 'in both cases, this is clearly not terminology for a homosexual relationship but for a close friendship (as is captured by the NLT translations 'closest friend' [...Deuteronomy 13:6] and 'best of friends' [1 Samuel 18:1]).' (p.166)

Thirdly, the verb 'loved' (*āhab*) used in 1 Samuel 18:1 is the same word used to describe the attachment of Israel and Judah for David in v16 and therefore does not carry any necessary sexual connotation. Similarly the verb 'delight in, take pleasure in' (*hāpēs*) used of Jonathan's feelings for David in 1 Samuel 19:1 is used of the regard that King Saul and his servants have for David in 18:22. Once again this indicates that the verb used carries no sexual connotation. (pp.166-167)

Fourthly, the fact that David and Jonathan kiss does necessarily indicate sexual attraction. In 1 and 2 Samuel there are numerous other examples of men kissing and none of them has sexual connotations (see 1 Samuel 10:1, 14:33, 2 Samuel 15:5, 19:39 and 20:9). (p.167)

Fifthly, while a covenant is established by David and Jonathan in 1 Samuel 18:3 this is 'not a covenant of sexual bonding.' He quotes the words of William Webb that rather than the establishment of a sexual union:

> ...the covenant between David and Jonathan was a covenant of loyalty and legal recognition set in the context of transferring throne rights to David and symbolized by Jonathan giving David his cloak and armour. (p.167)[137]

Davidson's conclusion is that the narrative in 1 Samuel is about the virtue of loving friendship:

> The whole setting of this narrative reveals that despite the political issues that should have interfered with their

---

[137] The quotation is from William Webb, *Slaves, Women and Homosexuals*, Downers Grove: Inter Varsity Press, 2001, p.102.

relationship (with Jonathan, by birth heir to the throne, realizing that David was chosen by God to rule instead), and amazingly close friendship developed between the two. Jonathan, the tender and faithful friend of David, shielded David's life at the peril of his own and gave eloquent witness to the existence and power of unselfish love. This is not a portrait of homosexual relationship but of friends who rose to the heights of self-abnegation. (p.167)

> **Michael Brown – nothing that is said in 1 and 2 Samuel points to the idea of homosexual relationship between David and Jonathan. David's lament for Jonathan in 2 Samuel 1 is about the depth of the bond of friendship between the two men.**

In *Can you be Gay and Christian?*, Brown makes a similar set of points to Davidson.

First, he notes that 'the Hebrew words 'the soul of x was knit to the soul of y are never once used in the Old Testament for a sexual or romantic relationship.' (p.98)

Secondly, Jonathan's covenant with David and his transfer of his royal robe and weapons to David are about his willingness to transfer his position as heir apparent to David. This is confirmed by the covenant Jonathan makes with the 'house of David' (David's future dynasty) in the Hebrew text of 1 Samuel 20:16. (pp.98-99)

Thirdly, in 1 Samuel 16-18 the way in which a range of people love David is a key theme (16:21, 18:1, 3, 16, 20, 22, 28) and 'to read something sexual and romantic into the 'love' expressed here is ridiculous, except in the case of Michal, who actually becomes David's wife.' (p.99)

Fourthly, there is no evidence that Saul's anger with Jonathan expressed in 1 Samuel 20:30-31 in terms of Jonathan choosing 'the son of Jesse to your own shame, and the shame of your mother's nakedness' was because David and Jonathan were in a homosexual relationship.

Rather the issue was that 'Jonathan's friendship with David was perceived to be a direct betrayal of his family line, thereby shaming his mother.' (p.101)

Fifthly, the fact that David and Jonathan kiss is irrelevant since 'in the biblical world the act of kissing (as distinguished from 'making out') was a common way of saying hello or good-bye as it is in many cultures today.' Examples of non-sexual kissing include Genesis 27:26, 45:15, Exodus 4:27, 1 Samuel 10:1 and 2 Samuel 19:39. (pp 103-104)

Brown's conclusion in the light of these points is that:

> ....since there is not a single erotic term used with regard to David and Jonathan's relationship, since the terms 'love' and 'kiss' are used all over the Bible in nonsexual ways, since both of them were eventually married to women and David got into trouble because of his heterosexual lust, and since everything we know about the ancient Hebrew culture indicates that a homosexual relationship would not have been tolerated let alone celebrated – remember David *loved* the very Torah that calls man-male sex an abomination – it is completely unconscionable to make David and Jonathan into gay lovers. (p.104)

His interpretation of David's lament for Jonathan in 2 Samuel 1:25-26 is therefore:

> I have been involved with a number of women, sexually and romantically, but the love we had between us, the covenantal bond that existed between us, the depth of loyalty and friendship, was more extraordinary than anything I've enjoyed with a woman. (p.104)

Ruth and Naomi

Gordon Kennedy, Jane McArthur, Andrew McGowan - there is no evidence to support a lesbian reading of Ruth.

In their contribution to the Church of Scotland report Kennedy, McArthur and McGowan see no merit in a lesbian interpretation of the Book of Ruth. They write:

> Ruth is clearly a harvest tale and appropriate for that setting. We regard as baseless the claim that Ruth and Naomi were involved in a lesbian relationship. Similarly, we are not persuaded by those who argue that, in chapter 3, Ruth enticed Boaz into pre-marital sexual relationship, since there is no compelling evidence that the relevant phrase in 3:2,7 'then go and uncover his feet and lie down,' has any sexual connotations. (p. 1/106)

Michael Brown – the idea of a lesbian relationship between Ruth and Mary is a total fabrication as are the attempts to find homosexual elements in the stories of other Old Testament characters.

Brown is similarly dismissive of a lesbian interpretation. In *Can you be Gay and Christian?* He notes that the best argument that gay theologians have to offer for this interpretation is the fact that the words of Ruth in in 1:16-17 are often used in wedding ceremonies:

> So, because a heterosexual daughter-in-law whose husband has died feels closely joined to her mother-in-law whose husband has also died (she also feels close to her mother-in law's faith; Naomi was an Israelite; Ruth had come from a pagan background), and because three thousand years later some Christians use her words in a marriage ceremony, then Ruth and her mother-in-law must have been lesbians! (And to repeat; after Ruth accompanies Naomi back to Israel, she marries a man named Boaz and they have kids together.)

To make them into lesbians is not simply a matter of special pleading. It is a matter of complete fabrication, creating something out of nothing, thereby providing another example of just how much the Bible is a heterosexual book, to the point that alleged lesbian relationships like this have to be created out of whole cloth since the Bible never once says a single word about a lesbian relationship except to condemn lesbian acts as a violation of God's intended order. (pp.92-93)

Brown is similarly critical of attempts to find homosexual elements in the stories of Elijah, Jehu, Ehud and the chief Babylonian eunuch which in his view simply show 'just how much the biblical text must be radically re-written in order to 'find' alleged positive examples of homosexual unions or homosexual activity in the Scriptures.' (pp.91& 93) [138]

> **Richard Davidson – The story of Ruth is about her radical faith in the God of Israel and the search for a husband for her. The homosexual interpretation is something read into the text.**

Davidson is less rhetorical than Brown, but equally strong in his rejection of a lesbian reading of the text.

He notes that Ruth's statement of her loyalty to Naomi 'is not one of homosexual intimacy but of radical faith (like Abraham's) to throw in her lot with the covenant community of Israel and its God, leaving behind her ties with Moab.' (p.164)

Furthermore, he writes, the focus of the lives of Ruth and Naomi is not a lesbian relationship but the search for a husband for Ruth:

---

[138] Brown is referring to referring to Ken Stone (ed), *Queer Commentary and the Hebrew Bible*, Cleveland: Pilgrim Press, 2001, pp.176-179 and Daniel Helminiak *What the Bible Really Says About Homosexuality*, New Mexico: Alamo Square Press, p.127.

Heterosexual, married love, not a lesbian relationship was the experience for both of them before the death of their husbands and remains the goal of both throughout Ruth. 'Naomi functions as something of a matchmaker for Ruth and Boaz, and Ruth's marriage to Boaz at the end of the book 'fills up' the empty and bitter Naomi. The intimacy between the two women seems fully accounted for in the 'mother and daughter' model that the story presents.' (pp.164-165) [139]

Davidson cites with approval the work of Ronald Springett as showing that the aim of the author of Ruth 'was to portray the idyllic scene of a God-fearing pastoral community.' Springett, he says, summarises the main points made by the book 'praise of Ruth as a model of virtue, the commendable piety of marriage within kin, and Ruth's inclusion in the ancestry of David' and concludes that 'the last thing the author would want to do here is to introduce a foreign person whose character could be questioned in any way in the light of Jewish morality.'(p.165) [140]

According to Davidson, Springett is 'on the mark' when he declares that 'the homosexual interpretation appears to be a speculation read into the text rather than an interpretation arising from or even suggested by the text and context of the book itself.' (p.165) [141]

Jesus and the Beloved Disciple

> **Robert Gagnon - there are seven reasons for rejecting the idea of a sexual relationship between Jesus and the beloved disciple.**

---

[139] The quotation is from Webb, op.cit.p. 103.
[140] The quotations are from Ronald Springett, *Homosexuality in History and the Scripture*, Washington D.C. Biblical Research Institute, 1988, p.79.
[141] The quotation is from ibid, p.79.

Gagnon presents a detailed critique of the idea that that there was a sexual relationship between Jesus and the beloved disciple. He gives seven reasons for rejecting this idea.[142]

First, references to 'the disciple whom Jesus loved' are limited to five stories in the last half of the fourth Gospel. He is mentioned as being:

> ....at the Last Supper (13:23-25); at the foot of the cross alongside the three Mary's (19:25-27); at the empty tomb with Peter (20:2-10); in the boat with the other disciples on the Sea of Galilee after Jesus' death (21:7); and following behind Peter and the resurrected Jesus at the shore of the Sea of Galilee (21:20-23). This same disciple is then identified as "the disciple who testifies concerning these things and the one who wrote these things, and we know that his testimony is true" (21:24)

In none of these passages is there 'any reference to sexual activity between Jesus and the beloved disciple.'

Secondly, the verbs that are used to describe the love between Jesus and the beloved disciple are *agapaō* and *phileō* and their cognates, which do not have a sexual connotation 'If the Fourth Evangelist had wanted his readers to know that Jesus was in a sexual relationship with this disciple he would have chosen the appropriate words for sexual love between males.'

Thirdly, according to John's Gospel, the reason for the love that Jesus has for the beloved disciple is his faith and his love for his fellow believers, not his sexual attractiveness:

> The usage of *agapaō* and *phileō* throughout John's Gospel explain *why* the beloved disciple was specially "loved" by Jesus and *what* that love consisted of. For the references above show that those whom Jesus loves and who "abide" in his love are

---

142 Robert Gagnon 'Was Jesus in a sexual relationship with the Beloved Disciple?' http://www.robgagnon.net/articles/HomosexBelovedDisciple.pdf

those who (a) believe in Jesus specifically as the man from heaven who becomes human in order to atone for human sin and (b) obey his commandments, especially the commandment to love one another. This is confirmed by the portrayal of the beloved disciple as (a) the one who is the first to have insight into the miracle behind the empty tomb ("believed" 20:8) and the first to recognize the resurrected Lord on the shore of the Sea of Galilee (21:7), as well as (b) the one who, unlike Peter, does not need to be told, "If you love me, feed my sheep" (21:15-23). There is no hint anywhere in the Gospel of John that Jesus is sexually attracted to the beauty of the beloved disciple, as is often the case in Greco-Roman discussions, even philosophical discussions, of man-male love. The beloved disciple is specially loved because he is a model of the kind of disciple that Jesus loves. There is nothing sexual about this. It is the love of a friend for a friend, as Jesus' words in 15:14-15 make clear: "You are my friends (*philoi*) if you do what I am commanding you (to do). No longer do I call you slaves, for the slave does not know what his master [or: lord] is doing. But you I have called friends because all the things that I have heard from my Father I have made known to you."

Fourthly, the fact that the beloved disciple 'was lying close to the breast of Jesus' at the Last Supper (John 13:23) has no sexual overtones:

In ancient banqueting practice there was nothing necessarily erotic about reclining on a couch slightly to the side of, in front of, and parallel to the host such that conversation required leaning the head back on the host's chest. The parable of the rich man and poor Lazarus has Lazarus reclining after death on Abraham's chest without any sexual connotation (Luke 16:22-23). A text in Pliny's *Epistles* refers to a senator named Veiento who "was reclining [or: leaning back] on the chest" of the emperor Nerva, again without any sexual connotation (4.22.4).

310

The beloved disciple occupies a position of intimacy for the asexual reasons specified above.

Fifthly, the historical context makes a sexual relationship between Jesus and the beloved disciple an impossibility. 'In the context of early Judaism, where homosexual practice of any sort would incur a capital sentence, how likely is it that Jesus would have had sexual intercourse with a male disciple and have done so *without apparently raising an eyebrow among any of his other disciples?*'

Sixthly, everything else that we know about Jesus shows that he was opposed to homosexual practice. To support this argument Gagnon refers to the twelve points already listed in the previous chapter of this survey.

Seventhly, the purpose of the references to the beloved disciple in the fourth gospel is to give support to the Johannine community's claim to bear the preeminent witness to Jesus and this would have been undermined by any hint of a sexual relationship between Jesus and the beloved disciple.

> The scenes where the beloved disciple outruns Peter (literally and figuratively) are probably symbolic, at least in part, of friendly tension in the author's day with dominant Petrine Christianity. The Johannine Jesus is a more thoroughgoing fusion of the historical Jesus and risen Christ than one finds already at work in the "Petrine" trajectory of Mark and Matthew. The image of the beloved disciple's closeness to Jesus is designed to convey the deeper existential truth of the Johannine community's more spiritualized portrait of Jesus. Had the community out of which the Gospel of John arose wanted to present a sexual relationship between Jesus and their own patron disciple, it would have succeeded only in making themselves outcasts in relation to the rest of Christendom.

Gagnon's conclusion from all these points is that:

...there is no credible historical or literary basis for contending that Jesus and the beloved disciple were entwined in some homosexual relationship. Attempts to convert the relationship to such only underscore the desperation on the part of some to find something, anything, remotely helpful in Scripture to support a homosexualist agenda.

Mary, Martha and Lazarus

> **Michael Brown – there is nothing in John 11 to suggest that Lazarus and his sisters were gay.**

Brown is equally critical of the idea that the living arrangements of Mary, Martha and Lazarus referred to in John 11 and elsewhere means that they were gay 'since they were all unmarried adults living in the same house, whereas one would have expected them to be married based on Jewish practice of the day' (p.94), an idea that opens the way to Dale Martin's suggestion of a *menage a quatre* between the three of them and Jesus. He notes;

(1) There is no evidence from the first-century Jewish world that all young men and women would automatically be married just as Jesus never married (and Paul might never have been married), and no special attention is given to this.
(2) It is possible that one or more of the siblings was already widowed or divorced.
(3) The biblical text does not say explicitly that Lazarus was not married.
(4) There might have been a family situation that called for them to delay marriage or live together after one or more was widowed or divorced. (pp.94-95)

'All in all,' he says, 'no big deal and nothing in the least bit exceptional.' Furthermore, given the Jewish antipathy to homosexuality as a Gentile vice 'it is completely ludicrous to think that the Gospel authors writing in this first century Jewish context, just casually painted a picture of this lovely gay trio.' (p.95)

Part 3
Evaluation

Chapter 10

An evaluation of the biblical material in the light of these studies

In the Introduction to this report it was noted that the claim made in the Pilling Report that in the face of conflicting scholarship and conflicting belief the Church should be 'cautious about attempting to pronounce definitively on the implications of Scripture for homosexual people' raised the question of which of three possible scenarios was correct.

- Scripture itself is inherently unclear about the issue of homosexuality.
- The scholarly debate about the teaching of Scripture in relation to homosexuality remains inconclusive.
- The teaching of Scripture is clear and the conflict is due to the fact that the people on one side of the conflict have simply failed to interpret Scripture properly.

If the first two scenarios are correct then the Church would be justified in speaking with caution. However, if the third scenario is correct then such caution would not be justified.

In order to answer the question of which of these scenarios is correct, this report has looked at material from both sides of the current debate in the Church about same-sex relationships produced since 2003 with the aim of seeing (a) whether a survey of this material still allows us to say that Scripture gives us clear teaching about homosexuality and (b) what this teaching is. The report has focussed on the interpretation of specific biblical texts, but before looking at these it began by drawing on material from both sides of the debate on the prior issue of the nature of the Bible and its proper use in the debate about sexuality.

The aim of this final chapter of the report is to evaluate the material surveyed by the report to see what conclusions we can reach about the nature of the Bible and its proper use in the debate about sexuality and about the teaching of Scripture in relation to homosexuality.

The nature of the Bible and its use in the debate about human sexuality

If we begin by looking at the revisionist approaches to this issue the first point is whether it is legitimate to distinguish between Jesus as the Word and the word of God in Scripture and to give authority to the former over the latter in the way that Rowland and Thatcher propose.

It is true that there is a distinction in Scripture between Jesus as the Word as referred to in the prologue to John's gospel and the word of God in Scripture. One is God present in a person and the other is the revelation of God given through written words. However, it is incorrect to suggest that the former has more authority than the latter. This is because as John Wenham points out, if we look at what Jesus the Word actually taught what we find is that 'to him, what Scripture said, God said' and that this something that can be seen to apply to both the Old and New Testaments.[143] Because what Scripture says is what God says it follows that we cannot contrast the authority of God the Word and the word of God. Both are God speaking to us.

Furthermore, because this is so, we have to draw a 'firm line' between Scripture and tradition contrary to what Thatcher suggests. This is because all human tradition, however venerable, is human and therefore subject to error, whereas Scripture, as God's inspired Word, is not.

Secondly, while Maggi Dawn is undoubtedly right to say that there is no method that will 'unerringly elicit 'right answers' from the Scriptures' and we have to be aware constantly that our interpretation of Scripture may be wrong this does not mean that we have to permanently suspend

---

[143] John Wenham, *Christ and the Bible,* Leicester: IVP, 1972, pp. 37 and 123.

judgement and simply learn to live with conflicting interpretations. There are times and there are issues when decisions have to be made and at that point the Church has to come off the fence and make a decision one way or another using best scholarly tools available and praying for the guidance of the Spirit.

Thirdly, because Scripture is God's word we cannot say, as Via does, that it is only authoritative 'in those parts that are existentially engaging and compelling.' Scripture has authority in and of itself, if we don't find it compelling or convincing then the problem lies with us and not with Scripture. Also, because all of Scripture is God's words we cannot say that 'some texts are simply disqualified by the whole meaning of the gospel.'

This is because, as Oliver O'Donovan says

> Unless we can think that Scripture is readable as a whole, that it communicates a unified outlook and perspective, we cannot attribute doctrinal authority to it, but only to some part of it at the cost of some other part. The authority of Scripture, then, presupposes the possibility of a harmonious reading; correspondingly, a church which presumes to offer an unharmonious or diversifying reading may be supposed to have in mind an indirect challenge to the authority of Scripture itself.[144]

Fourthly, because Scripture is God's word it is not right to follow Haller and to give experience 'a limiting function even over the fundamental authority of Scripture.' If Scripture's authority is truly fundamental then nothing, including experience, can limit it. What Haller really means is that we should be prepared to correct Scripture, including its moral teaching, on the basis of our experience, which effectively means making our interpretation of our experience, rather than Scripture, the norm for theology.

---

[144] O M T O'Donovan *On the Thirty Nine Articles* Exeter: Paternoster Press 1993, pp.56-57.

Fifthly, because Scripture is God's word, it is not legitimate to do as Good, Jenkins, Kitteridge and Rogers suggest, and read the Bible in ways that 'challenge the perspective of the biblical authors.' If what Scripture says, God says, to challenge the perspective of the biblical authors is to challenge the perspective of God himself, something that as creatures we cannot rightly do.

Sixthly, while the fact that tradition can be wrong means that we have to be aware that traditions of interpretation can distort our reading of Scripture, Lings' suggestion that biblical interpretation of the post-biblical era was all based on misplaced asceticism and misogyny and can therefore be simply set aside fails to take seriously C S Lewis' point that we should be wary of thinking that we are the first people to understand the meaning of a text and that we need to allow the witness of the past to challenge our current preconceptions.[145]

Finally, we need to not only have proper guidelines for reading Scripture, but also apply them properly. Thus Rogers' seven guidelines for reading Scripture are all excellent, but he arguably applies them badly.

For example, his second guideline is 'Let the focus be on the plain text of Scripture, to the grammatical and historical context, rather than to allegory or subjective fantasy.' This is very helpful. However, his application of it is to say that reading the Bible in this way leads him to ask:

> ...whether biblical statements that condemn idolatrous and immoral sexual activity can appropriately be applied to the sexual relationships of contemporary Christian gay and lesbian people who are neither idolatrous nor immoral. Is it right to take verses that condemn the worship of other gods and use

---

[145] See C S Lewis, 'On the reading of old books' at
http://www.theelliots.org/Soapbox2008/OntheReadingofOldBooks.pdf

them against Christian people who are worshipping the one true God who Jesus called us to worship?[146]

As we shall see below, this interpretation of the biblical passages prohibiting same-sex relationships is not in fact a reading of the plain text of Scripture, but a reading into the text of Scripture what is not there.

A better approach to understanding the nature of the Bible and its use in the debate about human sexuality is provided by the traditionalist writers we have looked at.

First of all, they remind us that for the Christian the Bible is the norm given to us by God for making or evaluating ethical decisions. In the words of Thomas Cranmer in his homily 'A fruitful exhortation to the reading and knowledge of Holy Scripture,' 'As many as be desirous to enter into the right and perfect way unto God, must apply their minds to know Holy Scripture, without the which they can neither sufficiently know God and his will, neither their office and duty.'[147]

Secondly, this is because, as Torrance argues, Scripture in all is parts not only contains but *is* God's word, called into being by God through the Spirit (2 Timothy 3:16, 2 Peter 1:21) and given to us for our instruction. Because of this Scripture is a unity with a single overall coherent message.

Thirdly, because Scripture is inspired by the Spirit this means, as Kennedy, McArthur and McGowan remind us, both that we need to seek the mind of the Spirit when interpreting the Bible and also that 'the Spirit will never contradict what is given to us in Scripture.

Fourthly, as Goldingay, Marquand, Sumner and Westberg write, the aim of biblical interpretation is to 'try to achieve an objective understanding of the text according to its own presuppositions and concerns.' As they

---

[146] Ibid, p.57.
[147] Ian Robinson (ed), *The Homilies*, Bishopstone, Brynmill/Preservation Press, 2006, p.4.

318

go on to say, this will involve reading the Scriptures as a whole and in the company of the Church as whole.

Fifthly, as they remind us, and as Richardson also maintains, we need to take seriously the continuing validity of the Old Testament law in the life of the Church. The law cannot save us and aspects of the law such as the food laws or the laws regarding sacrifice have been fulfilled in the coming of Christ and therefore do not apply directly to the Church. Nevertheless, the witness of the New Testament is that the moral laws contained in the Old Testament, including its laws relating to sexual ethics, do still apply to Christians today.

Sixthly, we need to take seriously Brown's point that 'the Bible is a heterosexual book.' Obviously, the use of the term 'heterosexual' is an anachronism given that that concept of heterosexuality was not invented until the nineteenth century. However, the point that Brown is making by his use of the term is a valid one. From Genesis to Revelation the Bible assumes that the norm for sexual activity is sex between a man and women in marriage. That is the norm from which everything else is a deviation. This feeds into Gagnon's point that accepting the authority of the Bible means accepting its core values and an approach to sexual activity that limits it to marital sex between a man and a woman is among these.

Finally, as Goldingay points out, the Church has changed its mind over the interpretation of Scripture because it has been driven back to ask fresh questions about the biblical text and come back with a fresh way of reading it. As he says 'one way of formulating our dilemma over same-sex relationships' is to see it as a debate over whether the same conclusion applies:

> The universal Christian tradition and its interpretation of scripture see scripture as viewing same-sex relationships as irregular and morally inappropriate. The question is whether human insight, particularly in the Western world, is opening our eyes to other possibilities within scripture.

319

This is the challenge this report is seeking to explore.

Bearing all these points in mind, we shall now go on to evaluate the ways in which revisionist and traditionalist writers have interpreted the biblical texts.

Genesis 1-3

If we begin by looking at the narratives of the creation and the Fall in Genesis 1-3 the first thing we find is that there is nothing in the creation stories in Genesis 1-2 to suggest that humans were originally androgynous or should be viewed as androgynous today.

Genesis 1:27 is constructed in terms of Hebrew parallelism with the second half of the verse explaining the meaning of the first half. Thus the meaning of the statement in the first half of the verse that God created humanity (the meaning of the word *adam* here) is made clear when it is said in the second half of the verse that God created human beings as male and female.

That this is the correct reading of the verse is shown by the explicit statement in Genesis 5:1-2

> When God created man, he made him in the likeness of God. Male and female he created them, and he blessed them and named them man when they were created.

This is a clear recapitulation of what is said in Genesis 1:27 and it makes clear that 'man' is the generic term for human beings, who have been created by God in two sexes, male and female.

It is also shown by the command to the first humans to be fruitful and multiply in Genesis 1:28, a command which, as Davidson observes, can only be fulfilled by a pair of sexually differentiated human beings.

It is further shown by the second creation account in Genesis 2:4-25, which in terms of the structure of the book of Genesis is intended as a narrative expansion of what has already been said in Genesis 1:26-28. This second account can be read in two ways. It can be read in terms of an originally sexually undifferentiated human being becoming divided into two sexes by God's action in verses 21 and 22, or it can be read in terms of God creating a female complement to an existing male human being. Given that there is no hint of any change taking place in the makeup of the 'man' (*adam*) as the result of the creation of the first woman, the latter reading seems a better one, and it has support from 1 Corinthians 11:8 and 1 Timothy 2:13. However, even if the first reading is adopted, it delivers the same end result, the creative action of God has resulted in the fact that human beings exist in two sexes, male and female and that they are to fulfil their God given vocation within this context.

The existence of people with intersex conditions does not fundamentally challenge the biblical picture. The fact that some people are congenitally blind or deaf does not mean that human beings were not created by God to be creatures who see and hear. Similarly, the fact that there is a small minority of people whose sex is biologically ambiguous does not mean that humanity was not created to be male and female. It means that in a fallen world this basic binary sexuality does not always find clear biological expression.

Secondly, in Genesis 1 the image of God is something that human beings bear as individual male and female human beings. It is not simply, as Kraus suggests, a spiritual quality that belongs to the community of God's people collectively. However, this does not mean that human beings have to be married to a member of the opposite sex in order to be in the image of God. The Bible recognizes that some human beings will be unmarried (Matthew 19:10-12), but it never suggests that this makes them less than human.

As Gagnon suggests, what does mar the image of God is a failure to live as male and female human beings by having sex with someone of one's own sex. As Genesis 2 explains, to live rightly as God's image bearer is to live in obedience to God's commands and not transgress the limits that God has laid down (see 2:15-17) and later biblical material makes it clear that sex with a member of one's own sex (along with any other form of sexual activity outside marriage) is such a transgression.

Thirdly, Genesis 1 and 2 describe human beings as not only similar, but also different. The point in both Genesis 1 and 2 is that both men and women are human, but that they are human in different ways and human beings are called to fulfil their vocation as God's image bearers in the light of this unity in difference. Contrary to what Haller seems to suggest, Genesis does not talk about humanity as being like a pair of scissors with two identical blades (as would have been the case if God had created another male human being to be Adam's helper). Instead they are like a pair of scissors with blades that are alike, but not identical - as with a pair of scissors where one blade is flat and the other is serrated. It is this unity in difference that is meant by the language of male-female 'complementarity' and this does seem to be what Genesis teaches.

It is true that Genesis 1 and 2 does not spell out in any detail what this complementarity involves, but it clearly involves a sexual complementarity that will enable human beings to fulfil the vocation given in Genesis 1:28 to be fruitful and multiply.

Fourthly, we learn from Genesis 2:24 that marriage is intended to give expression to this complementarity. The 'therefore' at the beginning of verse 24 indicates that it is because God has created human beings as male and female that men and women come together in marriage. Marriage is thus built on the foundation of the complementarity between men and women.

It is not the case, as both Mein and Johnson suggest, that the Genesis account gives room for a parallel form of marriage for those who feel a companion of the same sex is more appropriate. In Genesis 2 it is not because he delights in her that Eve is the appropriate companion for Adam. Rather, he delights in her because she is the appropriate, God given, complement to him as a male human being. In Genesis it is God who decides who is the appropriate companion for male and female human beings in marriage and his decision is that it is a member of the opposite sex.

It is true, as Brownson argues, that according to Genesis 2:24 marriage creates a new kinship group, but it is a kinship group with a very specific foundation. It is a new social unit based on the coming together of the two parts of humanity, male and female, in an exclusive sexual union. This is what is emphasized in Genesis 2:24. Warner's idea that the text is about the transgression of the normal Israelite rules about who people can marry reads more into 'a man leaves his father and his mother' than the text itself contains. There is nothing in the context in Genesis to suggest that this is how we are meant to read this verse.

There is no specific reference to procreation in Genesis 2:24, but in the wider context of Genesis the coming together of men and women in the way that this verse describes is what enables them to fulfil the mandate to reproduce given in Genesis 1:28. We can see this because, having been brought together by God in the prototype for all later marriages, Adam and Eve go on to fulfil the reproductive mandate in Genesis 4:1-2.

Fifthly, contrary to Guest's reading there is nothing in Genesis 3:16 to suggest that women might 'justifiably' walk away from having sexual relations with men. The text acknowledges that after the Fall the relationship between men and women will be distorted by sin, and that part of this distortion will be that the male-female relationship will be marked by domination rather than equality, but there is nothing in the Genesis text that suggests that this means that people are free to walk away from what God has established in Genesis 1 and 2.

The biblical message is not that human beings are free to escape the consequences of sin by establishing their own versions of reality, but that they have to face up to the challenge of living in obedience to the way that God has created them in a context that makes this much more difficult than it would have been had humanity not fallen.

Genesis 19 and Judges 19

The first thing to note about the story in Genesis 19 is that, contrary to what is suggested by Lings, it does involve a sexual element. There are four pieces of internal and external evidence that make this clear.

- The use of *yada*, 'know,' in an unambiguously sexual sense in Genesis 19:8 and the fact that Lot offers his daughters to the crowd indicates that 'know' in Genesis 19:5 also has to be understood in a sexual way. In the literary context of Genesis 19 it does not make sense to read Genesis 19:5 any other way.
- As James DeYoung has pointed out, following Robert Alter, Genesis 19 fits into a wider section of Genesis running from Genesis 18-20 which consists of a series of stories to do with sexual sin and its punishment. A sexual reading of the Sodom story fits best into this structure.
- The literary similarities between Genesis 19 and Judges 19 show that the latter is clearly intended to echo the story of Sodom and Judges 19 is unambiguously concerned with sexual wrongdoing. The earliest biblical commentary on Genesis 19 thus understands it as having to do with sex.
- Ezekiel 16:49-50 in the Old Testament and Jude 7 and 2 Peter 1:6-8 interpret the story in sexual terms.

The suggestion that Genesis 19 is simply about the punishment of inhospitality thus fails to do justice to the biblical evidence.

Secondly, there is nothing in the text to support the idea that the men of Sodom knew that Lot's visitors were angels. Verse 5 tells us that the men of Sodom referred to them as 'men.' The reader of Genesis knows that the visitors are angels. The men of Sodom do not.

Schuh is therefore incorrect to suggest that the story in Genesis 19 is about sex with angels. It is not. It is about men wanting to have sex with other men. This is also true in Judges 19 where angels are never an issue.

Thirdly, the ideas that the men of Sodom were motivated by xenophobia, or homophobia, or that they were intent upon rape are all read into the text. As Hamilton has pointed out, Hebrew has a vocabulary to describe rape and it is not used in this text. All that Genesis 19:5 tells us, therefore, is that the men of Sodom wanted to have sexual relations with Lot's visitors. It does not limit what the men of Sodom were contemplating to rape even if the context suggests that this may have been what the crowd had in mind.

The fact that the text leaves it at that and that it says nothing about the motivation of the crowd, or about whether they were homosexual or bisexual, is theologically significant. In order to make it clear that Sodom was a gravely sinful place all the text has to say is that its inhabitants wanted to have sex with men. That in itself constitutes a wicked act (Genesis 19:6) which illustrates the more general wickedness for which Sodom, Gomorrah, and two neighboring cities are going to be destroyed.

In Genesis 19, and in Judges 19, the desire for homosexual sex is in itself evidence of the wider sinfulness of a society that has turned from God. This is the same point that is made on an even wider canvas by Paul in Romans 1:26-27.

Fourthly, it is a mistake to read the texts as if the behavior of Lot and the old man in Gibeah were meant to provide an example for the readers of these texts to emulate. This is what Thatcher and others seem to assume, but there is nothing in the text to suggest that we are not meant to be appalled by their actions.

Part of the point of story in Genesis is that despite the fact that Lot is a righteous man (2 Peter 2:7-8) he and his family are as deeply flawed as anyone else and are only saved by the unmerited grace of God, and like many characters in Genesis they go wrong when they seek their own solutions to the problems they are facing (see, for example, how Abraham does this in Genesis 16:1-6 and 19:30-38). In Judges, the story in chapters 19 and 20 is meant to illustrate that because 'every man did what was right in his own eyes' (Judges 21:25) Israelite society in its entirety has reached the same level of corruption that brought the judgment of God on the previous inhabitants of the land of Canaan such as the men of Sodom. The action of the old man, just like the homosexual desires of those outside his house, are a sign of a society that has reverted to paganism.

The behavior of Lot and the old man do not therefore provide examples to emulate, but are instead a warning to us about the endemic and multi-faceted nature of the fallenness of human beings (which is again similar to the point that Paul makes in Romans 1).

Leviticus 18:22 and 20:13

The first point that needs to be made about these two texts is that the language used is, as Davidson notes, untechnical in character and involves a permanent negative prohibition. What these texts say is simply that men should not have sex with a man instead of a woman. Furthermore, the fact that both parties deserve punishment in 20:13 indicates that even consensual homosexual sex is forbidden.

There is nothing in these texts to suggest that what is forbidden can be limited to anal penetration as Greenberg and Michaelson suggest. What is forbidden would clearly include anal penetration, but it is not limited to it any more than the various forms of incest listed in Leviticus 18:6-18, or the prohibition of adultery in Exodus 20:14, are limited to vaginal penetration. In both instances general terms for sexual activity are used. It is true that later Rabbinnic commentary on Leviticus 18:22, seeking to be as legally precise as possible, focused on anal sex, but that is not something that that can be derived from the text itself.

Furthermore, there is nothing to suggest either that what is forbidden is male-on-male incest as Stewart argues. In both Leviticus 18 and 20 where incest is forbidden the degree of relationship that is prohibited is what is specified (see 18:6-18 and 20:11-12 and 14), whereas in 18:22 and 20:13 it is the sex of the people concerned rather than their relationship that is specified.

Secondly, the prohibition cannot be limited to the people of Israel or to the land of Israel as Milgrom suggests. As Brown points out, Leviticus 18:3 sees the offences listed in the chapter as actions that are wrong wherever they are committed, whether in Egypt or in Canaan, and 18:26 makes it clear that they are also binding on the 'stranger (i.e. non-Israelite) who sojourns among you.' Furthermore, the New Testament sees them as applicable to Gentile Christians living outside the land of Israel.

Thirdly, there is nothing in the text to suggest that there is a limited reason for the prohibition, such as a concern with the importance of procreation, or a belief in the superiority of men over women, or an association between homosexuality and pagan idolatry.

To take the first of these suggestions, the fact that the prohibition on male-to-male sex in Leviticus 18 and 20 sits alongside offences of incest and adultery which have procreative potential, but are nonetheless prohibited, suggests that the absence of procreative potential in homosexual sex is not the underlying issue. The existence of a range of offences, which includes offering children to Moloch and bestiality, also suggests that male superiority, and hence a prohibition on treating a man like a woman, is likewise not the issue at stake, since the issue of male superiority does not apply in relation to the other offences mentioned.

The idea that the prohibition of homosexuality is linked to idol worship or the practices of the Canaanites is again ruled out by the range of offences prohibited in these chapters, since it is hard to think that every case of incest or adultery was somehow linked to a pagan cult and by the fact that the word *toevah* ('abomination') used in 18:22 and 20:13 is used elsewhere in the Old Testament to apply to serious moral offences and not just to ritual transgressions or actions that are culturally unacceptable.

As Davidson notes, the reason that a reference to sacrificing children to Molech is included in 18:21 is because it was regarded as an offence

327

against the sanctity of family life and thus a sexual offence. This means that the fact that the prohibition on homosexuality comes next cannot be used as an argument that homosexuality was prohibited because of a link to idolatry.

Fourthly, if we ask what the motivation behind the prohibition of all male-to-male sexual activity was, Burnside's careful analysis of the structure of Leviticus 20 suggests that it was forbidden, like all the other sexual offences prohibited there, because it came under the overall category of adultery. That is to say, the starting point for the thinking about sexual morality in the Torah is a marriage between one man and one woman in line with the way that God created the human race. All the prohibited sexual offences are offences because in various ways they involve sex outside this context, sex before marriage, sex with someone other than your wife, sex with someone of the same sex, or sex with another species. The issue is therefore the way that God has created the world and the calling of human beings to behave in a way that corresponds to that.

Lesbianism would seem to fit into this list of prohibitions just as well as male homosexual activity and this raises the question of why it is not mentioned in Leviticus. Davidson may well be right in his suggestions that a prohibition of lesbianism may be implicit in the general prohibition in Leviticus 18:3 against following the practices of the Egyptians and the Canaanites, as the Rabbis thought, or that the prohibitions in the masculine singular may have been seen as applying generically to both men and women. Certainly Paul sees lesbianism as forbidden alongside male homosexuality in Romans 1:26, and this would seem to indicate that he understood the Levitical prohibitions inclusively.

Fifthly, Thatcher's claim that a consistent attitude towards the continuing validity of the laws in Leviticus would involve wanting to apply the death penalty to homosexual activity today fails to take note of the point noted by Allberry and others that what the text may in fact be saying is that homosexual practice is worthy of death rather than that the death penalty should be applied, and the fact that from a New Testament the death penalty for sin has already been paid by Christ (see 1 Peter 2:24) and that the proper response of the Church to sexual offences is church discipline, not the death penalty (1 Corinthians 5:1-13).

Deuteronomy 23:17-18

There is continuing debate amongst Old Testament scholars about the existence and nature of cultic prostitution in Old Testament times. However, as noted by Davidson and Gagnon, there does seem to be evidence that the *qedeshism* (cult prostitutes of the sons of Israel') mentioned in Deuteronomy 23:17 were male homosexual cult prostitutes and that the *keleb* ('dog') mentioned in 23:18 was a non-cultic male prostitute.

This material in Deuteronomy reinforces the Old Testament's witness against all forms of homosexual activity as 'abomination' (Deuteronomy 23:18) and may possibly underlie the references to 'dogs' in Revelation 22:15.

What is unlikely, for the reasons explained above, is Schuh's argument that the sort of cultic prostitution mentioned in Deuteronomy is what is specifically forbidden in Leviticus. For reasons explained below it is also unlikely that this is what Paul is referring to in Romans 1:26-27 either.

Romans 1:26-27

The first point to note in relation to Romans 1:26-27 is that Lings' argument that Romans 1:18-32 are the words of a Jewish opponent of Paul in Rome rather than the views of St. Paul himself builds on an idiosyncratic suggestion by Douglas Campbell that has not been accepted by any other major commentator on Romans. There is a debate about whether Romans 15 and 16 were originally part of Romans,[148] but not about the Pauline character of Romans 1:18-32.

This is for two reasons:

- There is nothing in the vocabulary or theology of these verses that suggests that they could not have come from Paul.

- They form an integral part of Paul's argument in Romans.

  As the 'for' (*gar*) at the beginning of verse 18 indicates they connect back to what Paul says in Romans 1:16-17 because they begin to illustrate why the 'righteousness of God is revealed through faith for faith.' The universal sinfulness of human beings which 18-32 begins to describe, illustrates why human beings cannot become righteous on any other basis than faith in what God has done for them in Christ.[149]

  They also link to what Paul says in Romans 2:1 ff as the word *dio* ('therefore') at the beginning of 2:1 shows. It is because what is said in 18-32 is true of humanity in general that the Jewish objector addressed in chapter 2 has no basis for claiming moral superiority.[150] If Paul does not agree with what is said in Romans 1:18-32 then what he says in chapter 2 makes no sense.

Secondly, there is also general agreement amongst commentators that, contrary to the arguments of Haller, Schuh and others, 1:26 does refer to lesbianism rather to some form of non-coital heterosexual activity. There are four reasons for this consensus

- The linguistic parallels between the wording in verses 26 and 27 and the fact that Paul uses the word 'likewise' (*homoios*) to link them indicates that he is describing the same sort of activity in both verses. As verse 26 is explicitly about same-sex

[148] See Charles Cranfield, *Romans*, vol. 1, Edinburgh: T & T Clark, 1975, pp.5-12.
[149] For this interpretation of Romans 1:18 see ibid,p.108.
[150] Ibid, pp.140-142.

activity between men this therefore indicates that the previous verse is about same-sex activity between women.

- The idea that same-sex relations were 'unnatural' (*kata phusin*) was a standard critique of such relations among both Jewish and Greco-Roman writers and therefore the description in verse 26 of women abandoning natural for unnatural relations reads most naturally as a reference to lesbianism.
- If what is described is a deviant form of heterosexual activity it is hard to see why women alone are singled out for mention in verse 26. Heterosexual sex has to involve men as well!
- If what Paul is describing is a very specific and unusual form of heterosexual activity in the context of cultic activity, as Schuh suggests, it is not clear that his intended readers in Rome would know what he was referring to. Simply talking about 'unnatural relations' would be a very oblique and obscure way of referring to this.

It is true that Clement of Alexandria, Athanasius and Augustine interpret 1:26 in terms of non-coital heterosexual activity, but their comments have to be weighed against the evidence of the text itself and other early interpreters of the verse, such as the fourth century commentator known as Ambrosiaster, and St John Chrysostom, do see the verse as being about lesbianism.

If verse 26 is about lesbianism then this means that the argument put forward by Ruden that what St. Paul is attacking in verses 26-27 is pederasty falls away. This is because pederasty was an exclusively male form of same-sex activity and therefore by bracketing together both male and female same-sex activity Paul shows that pederasty is not the focus of his criticism. A specific reference to pederasty is also ruled out because of the general nature of the language used. The vocabulary used to describe pederastic relations is not employed here.

Thirdly, it is unlikely that St. Paul is only talking about same-sex activity in the context of cultic activity. It is true that Paul sees same-sex activity as one of the results of a world in which idolatry is rampant, but he nowhere makes a specific link between the sins he describes in verses 24-32 and cultic activity in pagan temples. No one would argue, for example, that there was a link between disobedience to parents (v30) and pagan worship and there is no reason to make this link in verses 26-27 either. In addition, as the Evangelical Alliance report points out, the language of men being 'consumed with passion for one another' seems hard to apply to the impersonal relationships of temple prostitution.

Fourthly, there is also no reason to think that Paul objects to same-sex relations in Romans 1 because they break social conventions about gender roles, because they are non-procreative, or because they involve an excess of passion. These ideas all have to be read into the text. There is nothing in the vocabulary used in verses 26-27, or the overall argument of Romans 1, or what St. Paul writes about sexual ethics elsewhere, which supports them.

Fifthly, as the majority of commentators of Romans hold, what Paul is criticizing is a violation of the order of creation. Both the fact that Paul's whole argument in Romans 1:18ff is about how human beings have turned away from the evidence for God and his will presented by the created order and the numerous intertextual echoes of Genesis 1 and 2 in these verses indicate that Paul has the creation accounts in mind. Furthermore, as has already been noted, the standard Jewish and Greco-Roman critique of same-sex relations was that they went against the created order and were therefore 'unnatural' (which is what Paul says in Romans 1:26-27). [151]

These two converging pieces of evidence point to the fact that what Paul thinks is wrong with both female and male same-sex activity is

---

[151] Against the argument of Scroggs and others this also means that the 'exchange' in Romans 1:26-27 is not about men and women who are heterosexual by nature engaging in homosexual acts, as if this mean that some people are not created to be heterosexual. Paul's point is that all human beings were created to be heterosexual in the sense of being intended to have sex only with a member of the opposite sex and is *for this reason* that the fact that some people have homosexual desires is a problem.

that it is a violation of the created order laid down by God as witnessed to by Genesis 1 and 2 and that it involves a refusal to accept the witness of creation in that it entails human beings ignoring the obvious fact that male and female human beings are so designed physically as to be sexually complementary. It is this latter point, alongside the strong Jewish dislike of homosexual relations as a distinctively Gentile form of vice, which explains why Paul chooses to use them as his prime example of the result of human beings turning away from God.

Thatcher's contention that the whole basis of Paul's critique is flawed because we no longer accept the 'mythological structure' underlying Paul's argument is unpersuasive because there is still a good case for the view that monotheism was in fact prior to polytheism[152] and because even if it could be shown that all human cultures were originally polytheistic this would not undermine Paul's argument that the witness of the created order shows that this ought not to have been the case and was the result of some universal and primordial turning away from God.

This brings us to the sixth and final point which is that, while same-sex relations are not the only forms of sin highlighted by St. Paul in Romans 1, and while it is true that they are the result of the outworking of God's universal judgment on the human race as whole, nevertheless, as Gagnon emphasizes, the vocabulary that Paul uses indicates that they are a grievous form of sin and his use of similar vocabulary in Romans 6:19 and 13:13-14 makes it clear that they are a form of sexual immorality incompatible with Christian discipleship.

This point addresses the suggestion that Paul's argument does not address the case of contemporary Christian same-sex couples who have not turned away from God, but are seeking to live lives of faithful discipleship. According to the argument of Romans the fact that they are engaging in sexually immoral behavior indicates that, in this area of

---

[152] See chapter IV of G K Chesterton, *The Everlasting Man*, San Francisco: Ignatius Press, 1993, for what is still a persuasive argument on this point.

their lives at least, they are not living out their discipleship as faithfully as they should be.

1 Corinthians 6:6-11, I Timothy 1:10

The first point that needs to be noted in relation to these verses is that David Wright's argument[153] that *arsenokoitai* was a word coined either by St. Paul himself, or by some preceding Hellenistic Jewish writer, on the basis of the Septuagint version of Leviticus 18:22 and 20:13 and that it is a general term for men who sleep (i.e. have sex) with other men, is one that has stood the test of time. No one has yet successfully refuted it.

The term *malakoi* that precedes it in 1 Corinthians 6:9 is a term that can simply mean 'soft' in the sense of 'effeminate,' but in this context, when it is paired together with *arsenokoitai* as part of a list of sexual offences, by far the most likely interpretation is that it means the passive partner in male same-sex sexual intercourse with *arsenokoitai* referring to the active partner.

In 1 Timothy 1:10, where it stands on its own, *arsenokoitai* has to be read less specifically as referring to same-sex activity in general.

Secondly, what Paul is doing by his use of these terms is describing same-sex activity in general. He is not addressing specific forms of such activity. There is nothing in either of the passages involved to suggest that Paul has in mind pederastic or exploitative same-sex activity or that he has in mind only same-sex activity involving adultery or incest or that takes place in the context of pagan idol worship.

The language of pederastic activity is not used in either passage and the attempt by Brownson, Rogers and Martin, to link together *arsenokoitai* and kidnappers in 1 Timothy 1:10 (with the latter being those who kidnap boys for sex and the former being those who have sex with such boys) fails to observe two points:

---

[153] D F Wright 'Homosexuals or Prostitutes? The Meaning of ἀρσενοκοῖται (1 Cor. 6:9, 1 Tim. 1:10),' Vigilae Christianae. Vol 38, No.2 (June 1984) pp.125-153.

(1) That kidnapping was not solely for the purposes of prostitution and that this therefore cannot be assumed to be the meaning here.

(2) That I Timothy 1:10 is based on the Decalogue and that in this framework *arsenokoitai* belongs with 'immoral persons' as terms for those who violate the seventh commandment against adultery (understood in terms of extra-marital sexual activity in general) in heterosexual and homosexual ways, while kidnappers are those who are guilty of a separate offence against the prohibition of stealing in the eighth commandment (in this case the stealing of people).

In 1 Corinthians 6:9 adultery and the activities of *malakoi* and *arsenokoitai* are clearly distinguished as two separate offences and there is nothing that links either to the incest referred to in 1 Corinthians 5:1 as Cadwallader suggests. In Leviticus the offences of incest and homosexual sex are clearly distinguished so the argument that Paul is conflating the two here does not make any sense.

There is also nothing to be said for Schuh's suggestion that idolatry is the controlling offence in the vice list in 1 Corinthians. What we have in this list is a series of separate vices, which cannot all be plausibly linked to pagan cultic activity. No one would argue, for example, that adultery or theft have any necessary connection with pagan cults so why should this be so in the case of *malakoi* and *arsenokoitai*?

Thirdly, in both passages Paul makes it clear that the Old Testament prohibitions against same-sex relationships are still in force (and apply to Gentiles as well as Jews) and that such relationships are to be repudiated by Christians as contrary to the new status they have in Christ (1 Corinthians) and as contrary to the 'gospel' and 'sound doctrine' (1 Timothy).

Jude 7

There is general agreement that Jude is referring to the story of the destruction of Sodom and the surrounding cities in Genesis 19. The common view among revisionist writers, which is supported by Richard Bauckham in his commentary on Jude, is that both Jude 6 and 7 are concerned with the topic of sex with angels:

The revisionist view is that 'just as' at the start of Jude 7 means that just as the angels in verse 6 sinned by lusting after mortal women as recorded Genesis 6:1-4 so in a parallel manner the inhabitants of Sodom sinned by lusting after the angels who were staying with Lot.

This interpretation notes that the literal wording of the second half of verse 7 is that the inhabitants of Sodom and Gomorrah and the neighbouring cities were 'going after other flesh (*sarkos heteras*)' and it claims that this reference to other flesh cannot mean homosexual desire.

On the other hand, there are five points that can be made on the other side:

1. There is nothing in the Genesis story itself that suggests that Sodom, Gomorrah and the surrounding cities were judged for desiring to have sex with angels. First of all, as Miller correctly notes, they were not judged simply on the basis of what happened to the visitors to Lot. What happened on that occasion was simply the presenting example of a wider pattern of sinfulness, including sexual sin, most of which had nothing to do with angels. Furthermore the story in Genesis 19:4-11 indicates that the men of Sodom did not know the visitors were angels and so could not have desired to have sex with them on the basis that they were. All this would have been as obvious to Jude as to any other reader of Genesis.

2. Subsequent Jewish interpretations of the Sodom story both in the Bible and in other Jewish sources say nothing about a desire for sex with angels. Bauckham suggests that this idea can be found in the *Testament of Naphtali*, but, as Davids points out, it is not necessary to read this text in that way.

336

3. The term 'other flesh' does not itself carry any implication of sex with angels. What 'other' means is determined by the context and, as Davids says, it could perfectly well mean 'other' in the sense of 'different, not from themselves, but from the women they were supposed to desire.'

4. It is possible that the comparison between the two stories is not about the sexual component, but about the fact that both acts of sin resulted in acts of divine judgment.

5. 2 Peter, which draws on Jude, and as such constitutes the earliest commentary on its meaning, also refers to the Sodom story, talking about the 'licentiousness' and (v7) and 'lust of defiling passion' (10) which were characteristics of the inhabitants of Sodom and Gomorrah, but saying nothing about sex with angels.

These five points mean that there is no necessity to read Jude 7 in terms of wanting sex with angels, rather than more straightforward homosexual lust, and good reasons for not reading in that way.

The most likely readings are either Davids' suggestion that 'going after other flesh' means 'desiring homosexual sex' or Gagnon's grammatically possible suggestion that it means that 'in the course of committing sexual immorality they inadvertently lusted after angels.' In both cases homosexual desire is seen as a reason for God's judgment.

The teaching and practice of Jesus

As Tom Wright argues in detail in his book *Jesus and the Victory of God*,[154] when undertaking serious study of the historical Jesus it is vital to explain how the proposed picture of his teaching and practice makes sense both in terms of the teaching and practice of the Judaism of his day and in terms of the subsequent teaching and practice of the Early Church. An account of Jesus that isolates him from both is necessarily historically implausible.

---

[154] Tom Wright, *Jesus and the Victory of God*, London: SPCK, 1996.

This is the key point in mind when considering the idea that the Gospels can be read in terms of Jesus being sympathetic to, or accepting of, homosexual practice.

If this was the case then the first thing that has to be explained is why there is no trace of this in the gospels.

As traditionalist writers have pointed out, the fact that there are no recorded sayings of Jesus specifically relating to the issue of homosexuality can be perfectly satisfactorily explained because this was a non-issue in the Palestinian Judaism of Jesus' day. Same-sex activity was seen by Palestinian Jews as contrary to creation, forbidden by the Torah and a characteristic vice of idolatrous Gentiles. There was therefore no need for Jesus to remind people that is was wrong. As Gagnon observes, he would have been 'preaching to the choir.'

However, if Jesus had supported same-sex relationships, then this would have caused enormous controversy for the reasons just given and there would be a record of this in the Gospels, just as there is a record of the ways in which he challenged the thinking of his contemporaries on other matters.

Furthermore, if Jesus did take this revolutionary approach, then there is a further question about why this apparently had no effect whatsoever on the Early Church which, as far the evidence goes, seems to have remained universally opposed to same-sex practice. When the Church moved out into the wider Greco-Roman world it simply said, as we have seen above, that homosexuality was wrong, just as Judaism had always done. We can see how the Early Church followed the teaching and practice of Jesus on a whole host of other matters[155] so why they did they not follow him on this issue? The most plausible explanation was that there was nothing to follow.

---

[155] See for example, David Wenham, *Paul: Follower of Jesus or Founder of Christianity?*, Grand Rapids, Eerdmans, 1999 and *Did St Paul Get Jesus Right?*, Oxford: Lion Books, 2010.

The 'argument from silence' over homosexuality thus points strongly in the direction of Jesus taking the same negative attitude to homosexual practice as Palestinian Judaism and the Early Church.

However, we are not left simply with the argument from silence. We also know:

- That Jesus founded his sexual ethic on the fact that God created human beings as male and female and joined them together in marriage as recorded in Genesis 1 and 2 (Matthew 19:1-9, Mark 10:2-12).
- That Jesus did not reject the teaching of the Torah on sexual ethics, but rather intensified it by including desire as well as action and by taking a stricter line on divorce (Matthew 5:27-32).
- That the Gospels tell us that Jesus included *porneia* as one of those things that renders an individual unclean in the sight of God (Matthew 5:19, Mark 7:21). In spite of the arguments of Haller to the contrary, the lexical evidence still suggests that *porneia* was a catch all term that included not only adultery, but also incest, homosexuality and bestiality. Obviously, Jesus himself probably did not use the actual term *porneia* because he would normally have spoken in Aramaic rather than Greek, but by using this term Matthew and Mark are testifying that Jesus regarded homosexuality as something that made people unclean before God.

These three known facts together do not seem to leave any space for Jesus to have approved homosexuality.

Furthermore, Gagnon's points that in a first century Jewish context Jesus' references to the judgment of Sodom (Matthew 10:14-15, Luke 10:10-12) would have been taken to include the fact that it was judged by God for homosexual vice and that Jesus's saying about not giving that which is holy to dogs (Matthew 7:6) may include an intertextual echo of Deuteronomy 23:17-18 seem to be well made and provide additional evidence that Jesus accepted what the Old Testament had to say about God's judgment on homosexual practice.

It is true, as Browne says, that Jesus' primary call was to follow him and it is also true, as numerous revisionist writers have pointed out, that Jesus welcomed the outsider and the outcast, including those rejected by contemporary society because of their sexual misbehaviour. However, it is also true that we cannot separate Jesus' call to follow him and his welcoming of sinners from a call to repentance and discipleship (see Matthew 16:24-25, Mark 1:15, Luke 5:32, 19:1-10) and if we ask what repentance and discipleship involved according to Jesus then we are led back to Jesus' rigorous sexual ethic as set out above.

As Allberry, Brown and others have pointed out, it is also illegitimate to appeal to Jesus' saying about eunuchs (Mathew 19:10-12) or the story of his healing of centurion's servant (Matthew 8:5-13, Luke 7:1-10) as indicating that Jesus approved of same-sex relationships. What Jesus is saying about eunuchs tells us is that he saw the only alternative to (heterosexual) marriage as celibacy and in the case of the story of the centurion's servant: (a) there is nothing in the language used in the story to indicate a sexual relationship, (b) the Jewish authorities would not have regarded the centurion as a 'righteous man' had he been in such a relationship, (c) Jesus' endorsement of such a relationship would have meant endorsement of a exploitative relationship involving pederasty and probably rape.

It is also illegitimate to appeal to John 10:10 in support of same-sex relationships as Via does, since, as Gagnon points out in his response to Via, the abundant life Jesus offers involves living in obedience to Jesus' command which in turn means either living a faithful married life or a faithful celibate one.

Finally, what about the ideas of the 'Queer Jesus' and the 'queer disciples' on the road to Emmaus?

On the first, it is perfectly acceptable to say that Jesus can be identified with all those who suffer, whether because of homophobic violence or for any other reason. Jesus' identification with the human race in his incarnation, death and resurrection means that he identified with everyone. However, Jesus identified with sinners not in order to endorse their sinful lifestyle, but in order to enable them to break free from it. As Paul puts it in 2 Corinthians 5:14-15, 'we are convinced that one has died for all; therefore all have died. And he died for all, that those who live might live no longer for themselves but for him who for their sake died and was raised.'

On the second, there is nothing in Luke's story of the disciples on the road to Emmaus (Luke 24:13-35) that gives any support at all to Goss' notion of people experiencing Jesus' resurrection through 'embodied erotic experiences.' On the contrary, the message of the Bible is (a) as the Emmaus road story itself reminds us, the risen Christ makes himself known to us through word and sacrament and (b) that in so far as the erotic experiences to which Goss refers involve same-sex activity the power of the resurrection is encountered when people are given the ability to forsake such experiences and live a new life that is free of them (see Romans 6:1-14).

Examples of same-sex relationships in Scripture

David and Jonathan

The arguments of Greenberg, Thatcher and Jennings that there was a homosexual relationship between David and Jonathan are called into question even by revisionist scholars such as Michaelson, Stone and Harding and fall away completely in the face of the detailed examination of the relevant evidence by Rowe, Brown and Davidson. What the narrative in 1 Samuel 18-20 is about in its canonical context is not a homosexual relationship, but Jonathan's steadfast loyalty to David as God's chosen successor to Saul as king of Israel. Jonathan acts as a foil to Saul by showing loyalty to the Lord's anointed while Saul seeks to kill him.

This narrative also tells us about the importance of loving friendships between those of the same sex within the company of God's people (an idea that is also present in the story of Ruth and Naomi), though Harding steps outside the biblical witness when he suggests that it might be legitimate for such friendships to be sexual in nature.

Jennings' argument that there was a homosexual love triangle involving Saul, David and Jonathan, that this taught David how to love, and that he in turn then taught God how to love through a homoerotic relationship between them has no grounding in the biblical text.

As has already been noted, there is no evidence for a two way relationship between David and Jonathan, let alone a love triangle. God is never depicted in Scripture as being in a homoerotic relationship with anyone (the biblical picture of the relationship between God and his people is that of heterosexual marriage). The idea that God ceases to inflict judgment and becomes loving in the course of his relationship with David falls foul of the biblical affirmation of the changelessness of God (Numbers 23:19, Malachi 3:6, James 1:17) and the biblical witness that both God's love and his willingness to perform acts of judgment remain constant before, during and after David's time.

Ruth and Naomi

Brown and Davidson also demolish the argument that the relationship between Ruth and Naomi is depicted as a lesbian relationship. The book is about how God brings about the birth of David (and therefore in wider biblical terms the birth of Christ) through a heterosexual marriage and through familial loyalty between Ruth and Naomi that is rooted in heterosexual marriage in the sense that it is because of heterosexual marriage that they are related to each other in the first place.

To use modern phraseology what the book teaches is a 'heteronormative' view of both marriage and family life. This means that the attempts by Jennings, Mathieson and West to invoke this story as providing 'survival strategies' for queer people and their

342

relationships in a heteronormative world goes completely against the grain of the text.

In addition, Mathieson's argument that because Ruth is a member of an 'excluded minority' her actions provide 'a biblical precedent for modern day minorities to participate in the reinterpretation of biblical laws which may currently exclude them from the church and prohibit them marrying' ignores the fact that the point of story is that Ruth the Moabitess has renounced her status as part of an excluded minority. She has by her own choice renounced being a member of the people of Moab and become a member of the people of Israel and subject to Israel's God and his laws.

A genuine modern day parallel to the Ruth story would be Rosaria Butterfield renouncing her status as a lesbian and tenured professor in women's studies to become a Christian and live according to the disciplines of the Reformed Presbyterian Church. [156]

The Beloved Disciple

Gagnon explains in detail the reasons why the suggestion by Jennings, Goss and Sharpe that Jesus and the beloved disciple were lovers is untenable. Put simply, he points out that (a) the evidence is not there, (b) the existence of such a relationship is impossible to conceive given what else we know about Jesus' teaching and practice and (c) the existence of such a relationship does not make historical sense in a first century Jewish context.

Jennings' interpretation of Mark 14:51-52 quoted by Thatcher is similarly improbable. The entire evidence that there is any homoerotic element to the story rests on the fact that the person was concerned was young and nude. The fact that he was young is irrelevant (young does not equal 'in a pederastic relationship') and the fact that he was nude was not because of any involvement in gay sex but because he lost

---

[156] See Rosaria Champagne Buttterfield, *Secret Thoughts of a Reluctant Convert*, Pittsburgh: Crown and Covenant, 2012.

his garment by accident when escaping arrest. Moreover, any appeal to the conventions of 'Hellenistic pederastic culture' ignore the fact that this is a story involving Jewish people in a Jewish setting for whom pederasty was religiously and culturally unacceptable.

The most plausible explanation of the story is that it is Mark's modest signature to his gospel, saying 'I was there' and most plausible explanations for his only having one garment are either that he had come from his house to warn Jesus of his impending arrest or, as John Wenham suggested, because the garden belonged to his family and he was sleeping out there to alleviate overcrowding at home over the Passover period.[157]

Thatcher's comment that 'Jesus we may speculate was just the sort of company with whom a sexually exploited young man could relax and feel accepted' rests on the assumption that the young man was sexually exploited and also ignores the evidence outlined above that in so far as he was engaged in homosexual activity Jesus would have made clear to him that he must repent of it.

Secret Mark remains a much debated text, but even if it even if it is genuine rather than a forgery it seems probable that it represents an expansion of the canonical gospels in the interest of Gnostic theology rather than a genuinely independent source of information about the historical Jesus.[158] It would thus be unwise to use it as a basis for sexual ethics.

Finally, Martin's homoerotic reading of the gospels is based on a consistent misreading of the gospel texts. Thus, as Brown points out, there is nothing in John 11 to suggest that Lazarus and his sisters were gay, when we are told that Jesus 'loved' the rich young ruler (Mark 10:21) there is nothing in the text that suggests that Mark has erotic

---

[157] See John Wenham, *Easter Enigma,* Exeter: Paternoster Press, 1984, pp. 47-49.

[158] See the discussion in R H Gundry, *Mark: A Commentary on His Apology for the Cross*, Grand Rapids: Eerdmans, 1993, pp.603-623.

love in mind, the account of the washing of the disciples feet in John 13 says nothing about a 'special seduction' of Peter and the *'nolli me tangere'* in John 20:17 has to do with Jesus' coming ascension and not with his dislike of physical contact with a woman.

Conclusion

The conclusion that emerges from the evaluation in this chapter, is that the work of revisionist writers since 2003 has failed to successfully challenge Brown's contention that 'the Bible is a heterosexual book.' There is no instance covered in this report in which it can be shown that a revisionist reading of the biblical material makes more sense than a traditionalist one.

Of the three scenarios sketched out at the beginning of this report it is the last one that is accurate.

Nothing we have looked at suggests that the Bible is unclear in its teaching about homosexual conduct.

Nothing we have looked at points to the conclusion that the debate about the matter must be judged inconclusive. Although writers about the issue continue to disagree the traditionalist position has not been successfully called into question.

This means that the continuing conflict about the teaching of Scripture has to be judged to be the result of the revisionist side failing to interpret Scripture properly in accordance with the principles for biblical interpretation discussed at the beginning of this chapter.

This being so, the existence of conflict is not a legitimate reason for the Church of England to be 'cautious about attempting to pronounce definitively on the implications of Scripture for homosexual people.' Such caution would constitute a failure by the Church of England to follow St. Paul's example by teaching clearly the 'whole counsel of God' (Acts 20:27).

Those on the traditionalist side are still entitled to say that a proper, detailed, and informed study of the biblical material supports the traditional belief of the Church of England:

- That God created human beings in his image and likeness as male and female
- That marriage involves a sexual union between one man and one women and that marriage should be open to the procreation of children
- That sexual relations are intended by God to take place solely in this context and that the only alternative to this is either temporary or permanent celibacy
- That all forms of same-sex sexual activity, both gay and lesbian, are a result of humanity's having turned away from God and are themselves sinful. In the Old Testament such activity is therefore prohibited by God's law, is seen as deserving of death, and provokes God's judgment. In the New Testament, it is seen as defiling people in God's sight, it is incompatible with the new life believers have been given in Christ and is a barrier to people inheriting the kingdom of God.

However much we may rightly be concerned about homophobia and homophobic violence, however much we may sympathize with the struggles faced by those who have same-sex attraction, and however much we may feel that the Church's teaching makes mission more difficult in our current context, the fact remains that if the Church of England is to remain loyal to Scripture these four points need to remain the basis of its teaching and practice.

Bibliography

Church of England reports

Report of the House of Bishops Working Group on Human Sexuality, London: CHP, 2013.

Some Issues in Human Sexuality, London: CHP, 2003.

Revisionist approaches

James Brownson, *Bible, Gender, Sexuality*, Grand Rapids/Cambridge: Eerdmans 2013.

Arnold Browne, *'The Call of Christ: Reading the New Testament'*, in Duncan Dormer and Jeremy Morris (eds), *An acceptable sacrifice? Homosexuality and the Church*, London: SPCK, 2007, pp. 33-45.

Michael Carden, *Sodomy – A History of a Christian Biblical Myth*, London: Equinox, 2004.

Nicholas Coulton (ed), *The Bible, the Church and Homosexuality*, London: DLT, 2005.

William Countryman, *Dirt, Greed and Sex: Sexual ethics in the New Testament and their implications for today*, Philadelphia: Fortress Press, 1988.

Maggi Dawn, *'Whose text is it anyway?'* in Duncan Dormer and Jeremy Morris (eds), *An acceptable sacrifice? Homosexuality and the Church*, London: SPCK, 2007, pp.10-21.

Lewis R Donelson, *1 and 2 Peter and Jude*, Louisville: Westminster John Knox Press, 2010.

Robert Geiss, *Same-Sex in Scripture*, Lanham: University Press of America, 2009.

Stephen Greenberg, *Wrestling with God and Men*, Madison: University of Wisconsin Press, 2004.

Deryn Guest, *When Deborah met Jael*, London: SCM, 2005.

Deryn Guest, Robert E Goss, Mona West, Thomas Bodache (eds), *The Queer Bible Commentary*, London: SCM, 2006.

Deidre J Good, Willis J Jenkins, Cynthia B Kitteridge and Eugene F Rogers, *A Theology of Marriage including Same-Sex Couples: A view from the Liberals*, Anglican Theological Review, Vol 93, No 1, Winter, 2011.

Tobias Haller, *Reasonable and Holy*, New York: Seabury Books, 2009.

James Harding, *The Love of David and Jonathan – Ideology, Text, Reception*, Sheffield: Equinox Press, 2013.

James Harding, '*Opposite sex marriage a biblical ideal? The case of David and Jonathan*', in Alan H Cadwallader (ed), *Pieces of Ease and Grace*, Adelaide: ATF Theology, 2013, pp. 35-52.

Arland J Hultgren, *Paul's Letter to the Romans*, Grand Rapids: Eerdmans, 2011.

Theodore Jennings, *The Man Jesus Loved: Homoerotic Narratives from the New Testament*, Cleveland: Pilgrim Press, 2003.

Theodore Jennings, *Jacob's Wound- homoerotic narrative in the literature of Ancient Israel*, New York & London, Continuum, 2005.

William Stacy Johnson, '*A Time to Embrace – Same-Gender Relationships in Religion, Law and Politics*', Grand Rapids/Cambridge: Eerdmans, 2006.

C Norman Kraus, *On being human - sexual orientation and the image of God*, Eugene Oregon: Cascade Books, 2011.

Michael Kelly, *The Erotic Contemplative*, Vol 6, Video Talk, Oakland: Ero Spirit, 1994.

K Renato Lings, *Love Lost in Translation*, Trafford Publishing, 2013.

Dale Martin, *Sex and Single Savior*, Louisville: Westminster John Knox Press, 2006.

D B Martin '*Arsenokoites and Malakos: Meanings and Consequences*' in R L Bawley (eds), *Biblical Ethics and Homosexuality*, Louisville: Westminster John Knox Press, 1996.

Ruth Mathieson, '*Ruth and Naomi*' in Alan H Cadwallader (ed), *Pieces of Ease and Grace*, Adelaide: ATF Theology, 2013, pp.17-33.

Andrew Mein, *'Threat and promise, the Old Testament on Sexuality'* in Duncan Dormer and Jeremy Morris (eds), *An acceptable sacrifice? Homosexuality and the Church*, London: SPCK, 2007, pp.22-32.

Jay Michaelson, *God vs. Gay?*, Boston: Beacon Press, 2011.

Jacob Milgrom, *Leviticus*, Minneapolis: Fortress Press, 2004.

Gareth Moore, *A Question of Truth*, New York: Continuum, 2003.

Jack Rogers, *Jesus, the Bible and Homosexuality*, Louisville: Westminster John Knox Press, 2ed, 2009.

Sarah Ruden, *Paul Among the People*, New York: Image Books, 2010.

Steve Schuh, *'Challenging conventional wisdom – How a conservative reading of the biblical references to homosexuality fails to support their traditional interpretation'* at http://www.anglicancommunion.org/listening/book_resources/docs/Challenging_Conventional_Wisdom-Schuh.pdf

Robin Scroggs, *The New Testament and Homosexuality*, Philadelphia, Fortress Press, 1983.

Keith Sharpe, *The Gay Gospels*, Winchester and Washington: O Books, 2011.

Peta Sherlock, *'Reading Romans as Anglicans – Romans 1:26-27'* in Nigel Wright (ed), *Five Uneasy Pieces – Essays on Scripture and Sexuality*, Adelaide, ATF Press, 2012, pp.31-45.

Adrian Thatcher, *The Savage Text*, Chichester: Wiley Blackwell, 2008.

Matthew Vines, *God and the Gay Christian*, New York, Convergent Books, 2014.

Meg Warner, *'Were the Sodomites Really Sodomites? Homosexuality in Genesis 19'* in Nigel Wright (ed), *Five Uneasy Pieces – Essays on Scripture and Sexuality*, Adelaide, ATF Press, 2012, pp. 1-11.

Meg Warner, *'Set in tradition and history: Genesis 2:24 and the marriage debate'* in Alan H Cadwallader (ed), *Pieces of Ease and Grace*, Adelaide: ATF Theology, 2013, pp.1-15.

Traditionalist approaches

Sam Allberry, *Is God anti-gay?* The Good Book Company 2013.

Bill T Arnold, *Genesis,* Cambridge: CUP, 2009.

Michael Brown, *Can you be Gay and Christian*? Lake Mary: Front line, 2014.

Jonathan Burnside, *God, Justice and Society*, Oxford: OUP, 2011.

Roy E Ciampa and Brian Rosner, *The First Epistle to the Corinthians*, Leicester: Apollos, 2010.

Gerald Coleman, *Homosexuality: Catholic Teaching and Pastoral Practice,* Mahwah: Paulist Press, 1995.

Peter H Davids, *The Letters of 2 Peter and Jude*, Grand Rapids/Nottingham: Apollos, 2006.

Richard Davidson, *Flame of Yahweh*, Peabody: Hendrickson, 2007.

Robert Gagnon, *The Bible and Homosexual Practice*, Nashville: Abingdon Press, 2001.

Robert Gagnon, *'Was Jesus in a sexual relationship with the Beloved Disciple?* http://www.robgagnon.net/articles/HomosexBelovedDisciple.pdf

Robert Gagnon, *'How seriously does the Bible treat the issue of Homosexual Practice?'* in David Torrance and Jock Stein (eds) *Embracing Truth – Homosexuality and the Word of God*, Haddington: Handsel Press, 2012, pp. 151-178.

Andrew Goddard and Don Horrocks (eds), *Biblical and Pastoral Responses to Homosexuality*. London: Evangelical Alliance, 2012.

John Goldingay, *Key Questions about Christian Faith*, Grand Rapids: Baker Academic, 2010.

John Goldingay, Grant Le Marquand, George R Sumner, Daniel L Westberg, *'Same-Sex Marriage and Anglican Theology: A view from the Traditionalists,'* Anglican Theological Review, Vol 93, No 1, Winter 2011.

Richard Hays, *The Moral Vision of the New Testament*, Edinburgh: T&T Clark, 1996.

Walter Kaiser, *What does the Lord Require?*, Grand Rapids: Baker Academic, 2009.

Jack Lundbom, *Deuteronomy*, Grand Rapids/Cambridge: Eerdmans 2013.

Dave Miller, *'Homosexuality and 'Strange Flesh'*
http://www.apologeticspress.org/APContent.aspx?category=7&article =142

George T Monagu STM, *First and Second Timothy*, Grand Rapids: Baker, 2008.

National Council of Churches of Singapore, *Homosexuality – Questions and Answers*, Singapore: Genesis, 2014.

John Nolland, *'Sexual Ethics and the Jesus of the Gospels,'* Anvil, Vol.26, No.1, 2009.

Ian Paul, *Same Sex Unions – The Key Biblical Texts*, Cambridge: 2014.

John Richardson, *What God Has Made Clean*, The Good Book Company, 2ed, 2012.

Jonathan Rowe, *Jonathan and David; An Unexpected Love*, Cambridge: Grove Books, 2013.

Kevin Scott, *At Variance – The Church's Argument against Homosexual Conduct*, Edinburgh: Dunedin Academic Press, 2004.

Jay Sklar, *Leviticus*, Downers Grove/Nottingham: IVP, 2014

Willard Swartley, *Homosexuality – Biblical Interpretation and Moral Discernment*, Scottsdale: Herald Press, 2003.

David Torrance *'The Authority of Scripture; is the Bible the Word of God or does it only contain the Word of God?'* in David Torrance and Jock Stein (eds) *Embracing Truth – Homosexuality and the Word of God*, Haddington: Handsel Press, 2012, pp. 57-66.

Ben Witherington, *Paul's Letter to the Romans*, Grand Rapids and Cambridge: Eerdmans, 2004.

Ben Witherington *A Socio-Rhetorical Commentary on Titus, 1-2 Timothy and 1-3 John*, Leicester: Apollos, 2006.

Donald Wold, *Out of Order*, Grand Rapids: Baker Books, 1998.

Tom Wright, *Paul for Everyone – Romans Part 1*, London: SPCK, 2004.

Tom Wright, *Paul for Everyone – 1 Corinthians*, London: SPCK, 2003.

Writings with material from both sides
The Church of Scotland's Theological Commission on Same-Sex Relationships and the Ministry, APS Group Scotland, 2013.

Wiliam Loader, *The New Testament on Sexuality*, Grand Rapids and Cambridge: Eerdmans, 2012.

Dan O Via and Robert Gagnon, *Homosexuality and the Bible – Two Views*, Minneapolis: Fortress Press, 2003.

Other works cited.
Karl Barth, *Church Dogmatics III/2*, New York and London: T&T Clark, 2004.

Douglas Campbell, *The Deliverance of God: An Apocalyptic Re-reading of Justification in Paul*, Grand Rapids Eerdmans, 2009.

Rosaria Champagne Buttterfield, *Secret Thoughts of a Reluctant Convert*, Pittsburgh: Crown and Covenant, 2012.

G K Chesterton, *The Everlasting Man*, San Francisco: Ignatius Press, 1993,

Brevard Childs, *Old Testament Theology in a Canonical Context*, Philadelphia: Fortress Press, 1985.

Charles Cranfield, *Romans, vol. 1*, Edinburgh: T & T Clark, 1975.

James DeYoung, *Homosexuality: Contemporary claims examined in the Light of the Bible and other Ancient Literature and Law*, Grand Rapids: Kregel, 2000.

Robert Gagnon, *The Bible and Homosexual Practice*, Nashville: Abingdon, 2001.

Victor Hamilton, *The Book of Genesis Chapters 18-50*, Grand Rapids, Eerdmans, 1995.

Sakae Kubo, *Theology and the Ethics of Sex*, Washington, Review and Herald, 1980.

C S Lewis, *'On the reading of old books'* at http://www.theelliots.org/Soapbox2008/OntheReadingofOldBooks.pdf

O M T O'Donovan *On the Thirty Nine Articles* Exeter: Paternoster Press 1993.

Ian Robinson (ed), *The Homilies*, Bishopstone, Brynmill/Preservation Press, 2006.

Michael Satlow, *Tasting the Dish, Rabbinic Rhetorics of Sexuality*, Atlanta: Scholars Press 1995.

Ronald Springett, Perspectives on Homosexuality, Washington D.C.: Biblical research Institute, 1988.

William Webb, *Slaves, Women and Homosexuals*, Downers Grove: Inter Varsity, 2001.

David Wenham, *Paul: Follower of Jesus or Founder of Christianity?* Grand Rapids, Eerdmans, 1999.

David Wenham, *Did St Paul Get Jesus Right?* Oxford: Lion Books, 2010.

John Wenham, *Christ and the Bible*, Leicester: IVP, 1972.

John Wenham, *Easter Enigma,* Exeter: Paternoster Press, 1984

D F Wright *'Homosexuals or Prostitutes? The Meaning of ἀρσενοκοῖται (1 Cor. 6:9, 1 Tim. 1:10),'* Vigilae Christianae. Vol 38, No.2 (June 1984)

Tom Wright, *Jesus and the Victory of God*, London: SPCK, 1996.

SUBJECT INDEX

Note: author names follow the form found most frequently in the text with respect to capitalization and placement of particles such as 'von'. (The practice varies from name to name.)

INDEX OF BIBLICAL REFERENCES

Old Testament

Genesis
1 40-3, 181-2,
195, 197, 248-9,
332-3
1-2 29-50, 199-
200, 218, 292, 320,
339
1-3 34-52, 180-
200, 320-3
1:21 321
1:22 321
1:26 180, 253
1:26-27 34-7, 44,
186, 195, 199
1:26-28 186-7,
320
1:27 40, 41, 181,
185, 191-2, 229-
30, 243, 252, 253,
283, 320
1:27-28 183, 214,
215, 229-30
1:28 180, 181,
184, 187, 199, 320,
322, 323
2 40-5, 47-8, 180,
182-3, 187-90,
195-6, 197-8, 332-
3
2:4-25 189, 320-1
2:7-8 182
2:15-16 182
2:15-17 321-2
2:18 37, 48-9, 187
2:18-20 37, 182
2:18-24 183
2:18-25 199
2:20 43, 187, 189
2:20-25 181, 184
2:21 37

2:21-22 37
2:21-24 192, 194
2:22-23 182-3
2:22-24 214, 215
2:23 40, 43, 48
2:23-24 36
2:24 38-9, 47, 147,
183, 184, 185, 188,
191, 229-30, 243,
283, 322-3
3 50-2, 196
3:5 243
3:16 51-2, 196,
200, 323
4:1 205
4:1-2 323
4:17 205
4:25 204, 205
5:1-2 320
5:2 181
5:3 186
6 112
6:2 114
6:6 114
9:1-15 184
9:18-29 17
9:21-22 65
13 203
13:13 275
15:1-21 184
16:1-6 325
18-19 208
18-20 324
18:2 62, 275
18:16 275
18:21 274-5
18:22 275
18:23 274
19 52-62, 110-11,
200-13, 324-6
19:1 62, 275
19:1-5 274

19:3 275
19:4 275
19:4-11 239, 272
19:5 60, 201, 204,
205, 208, 275, 324,
325
19:6 325
19:6-7 205
19:8 202, 205,
208, 275, 324
19:9-11 206
19:10 275
19:12-13 274-5
19:12-14 212
19:12 275
19:15-16 274-5
19:16 205, 275
19:30-38 275
20 208
24:16 205
26:10 214
27:26 305
34:2 209
35:22 214
38:15 235
38:22-23 235
43:42 214-15, 218
44:30 302
45:15 305
46:34 218

Exodus
4:27 305
20:1-3 243
20:3-14 232
20:14 326

Leviticus
5:1-5 118-19
11:12 77
13-14 119

365

367